Radical Reform
IN Yeltsin's Russia

Also from M. E. Sharpe

PROPERTY TO THE PEOPLE
The Struggle for Radical
Economic Reform in Russia
Lynn D. Nelson and Irina Y. Kuzes

THE FORMER SOVIET UNION IN TRANSITION
Edited by Richard F. Kaufman and John P. Hardt
for the Joint Economic Committee, Congress of the United States

HARD TIMES: IMPOVERISHMENT AND PROTEST
IN THE PERESTROIKA YEARS
The Soviet Union 1985–1991
William Moskoff

THE GREAT MARKET DEBATE IN SOVIET ECONOMICS
Edited by Anthony Jones and William Moskoff

Radical Reform
IN Yeltsin's Russia

POLITICAL,
ECONOMIC,
AND SOCIAL
DIMENSIONS

Lynn D. Nelson
Irina Y. Kuzes

M.E. Sharpe
Armonk, New York
London, England

Library of Congress Cataloging-in-Publication Data

Radical reform in Yeltsin's Russia : political, economic, and social
dimensions / by Lynn D. Nelson and Irina Y. Kuzes.
p.   cm.
Includes bibliographical references and index.
ISBN 1-56324-479-9 (alk. paper). — ISBN 1-56324-480-2 (pbk. : alk. paper)
1. Russia (Federation)—Economic policy—1991–
2. Privatization—Russia (Federation)
3. Russia (Federation)—Economic conditions—1991–
4. Russia (Federation)—Politics and government—1991–
I. Nelson, Lynn D., 1943–   II. Kuzes, Irina Y.
HC340.12.R33   1995
338.947—dc20   94-41114
CIP

Printed in the United States of America

The paper used in this publication meets the minimum requirements of
American National Standard for Information Sciences—
Permanence of Paper for Printed Library Materials,
ANSI Z 39.48-1984.

∞

BM (c)   10   9   8   7   6   5   4   3   2   1
BM (p)   10   9   8   7   6   5   4   3   2   1

To Grigorii Kaganov

Contents

Introduction

This study examines political, institutional, and organizational factors that shaped Russian economic reforms from late 1991 until mid-1994, and further inquires into the implications of the reforms for both economic and noneconomic institutions in Russia. This work continues the stream of research on which our earlier volume, *Property to the People* (1994), was based. That book title was inspired by Boris Yeltsin's proclamation, as voucher privatization was about to begin, that Russia needed "millions of owners" rather than "a few millionaires."[1] The interviews for that study (which numbered more than 5,700) were conducted in mid-1992. Our positive initial judgment about the direction of Russia's reforms is reflected in the title of that book. But our findings forced us to modify our point of view, if not the work's title, during the course of the project.

Our research for this book included interview data that were collected in mid-1993 in Moscow, Ekaterinburg, Voronezh, and Smolensk, as well as primary and secondary material from a variety of sources. The 5,019 respondents included political and opinion leaders at the federal and local levels, directors and other administrators of privatized and privatizing enterprises, privatization administrators, and general population subsamples in each of the four cities. (Details are provided in Appendix A.) At various points in the book we also introduce interview data collected during 1992.[2]

Our earlier work had made us skeptical about the course the reformers had set. In this continuation project, however, we pointedly attempted to search as widely as possible for critical data related to the study's themes—whatever conclusions those data might support—and to utilize as fully as we could these varied materials in developing our interpretations. Our claim is not to unquestionable comprehensiveness and objectivity, certainly, but rather to have engaged in inquiry more than advocacy in the study.

Our analysis combines elements of both what has been termed the "state-centered" approach, which tends to emphasize the causal influence of the political sphere, and "society-centered" analysis, which focuses more on the dependence of political outcomes on changes in other spheres of society, including the economy.[3] Our overarching perspective is consistent with Robert Gilpin's emphasis on "a unified methodology or theory of political economy" that strives for "a general comprehension of the process of social change, including the ways in which the social, economic, and political aspects of society interact."[4] When the subject is radical change, Theda Skocpol's conclusion is persuasive: "In future revolutions, as in those of the past, the realm of the state is likely to be central."[5] Yet, as Rueschemeyer, Stephens, and Stephens observe, the relative degree of state autonomy is variable in societies. Further, they suggest, a comprehensive study of influences on modern states should include an examination of both internal and external factors, since each state "must be seen as part of a system of states."[6] Throughout this study, we attend closely to the significance of Western perspectives about preferred economic reform strategies for Russia. These influences have come from a variety of sources. Western advisers were active proponents of a perspective on economic reform that we identify as the "Western approach," and international financial institutions as well as leaders of Western governments, especially in the United States, were also prominent players on the Russian political stage as reforms were being planned and implemented.

Russia diverges sharply from the familiar Western pattern in the influence that economic actors command over political decision making. Rueschemeyer and his coauthors speak of "a special dependence on the interests of capital owners and managers" in capitalist countries, which, they argue, is "the basic dependence constraining state autonomy" in these nations.[7] In Russia, however, institutions for autonomous political control over economic decisions that developed under Bolshevik rule have proven to be tenacious, and today Russia's private sector has as yet neither the institutional support nor the economic power to exert commanding influence over political decision making. If the prevailing business climate is often "decisive for the success of state policies" in the

West,[8] the Russian example highlights a very different aspect of the relationship between politics and the economy—"the fundamentally opposed logic of the market and that of the state."[9] In this context it is also important to consider, however, the significance of economic failure in promoting political transformation in the Soviet Union and Eastern Europe.[10]

Russia's political terrain is further distinguishable from characteristic Western arrangements in the absence of a robust civil society tradition that could provide institutional supports for citizen action. Post-Gorbachev Russia shows few signs of moving away from highly centralized elite domination through the development of pluralistic structures. Political parties are weak and unappealing to most of the electorate, and Russia's current executive leadership has strongly resisted the sharing of power with other branches. Efforts among Russian lawmakers and quasi-organized citizen groups to prevent the resurgence of centralized decision making, in the aftermath of the democratic experiment that was initiated under Gorbachev, illustrate Rueschemeyer and Evans's observation that state apparatuses, "in the real life of a society, will inevitably become arenas of social conflict."[11]

In chapter one, we review aspects of Russia's historical experience that prepared the ground for reform developments from 1991 onward, and we describe important features of the approach to reform that has characterized the Yeltsin years through late 1994. Because the demise of the Soviet Union is integrally tied to Yeltsin's consolidation of power in Russia, on the one hand, and Russian reform challenges, on the other, we highlight features of this development that underscore the book's principal themes.

Chapters two through four consider different but related aspects of the Western approach to Russian economic reform, a strategy that was strongly urged on Russia by prominent Western advisers, Western policy makers, and representatives of international financial organizations such as the International Monetary Fund (IMF) and the World Bank. We suggest in chapter two that fundamental requirements for constituency building were neglected by the reform planners in favor of an attempt to coopt interest groups in the hope of buying time for the reforms to be made irreversible. In chapter three, we argue that the reformers failed to adequately take into account the necessity for economic arrangements of a nation to be articulated with its social and cultural sphere. Our discussion in chapter four focuses on the fit of the

"Western approach" with requirements for effective reform that were presented by specific features of the Russian economy. We conclude that by neglecting critical considerations in all of these areas, the Western approach both recast and magnified distortions that had long characterized the Soviet economy, while impeding progress toward the realization of a normal market economy.

Voucher privatization was the centerpiece of the Russian privatization program during 1993, and in chapters five and six we discuss achievements and failures of the program, as well as coordination issues that have been central to this approach to enterprise restructuring.

In the final chapter, we discuss prospects for the future, in light of the public opinion context of reforms through late 1994 and the inadequacies of the path that was followed through the completion of the voucher privatization period. We suggest that the reform course was ineffective both in promoting economic improvement and in facilitating democratic institution building. Russia's dominating reform task, in the wake of voucher privatization, had become to work toward overcoming the negative effects of earlier reforms.

Our data collection procedures are described in Appendix A, and the tables cited in the narrative have been placed in Appendix B.

Chapters five and six are revisions of previously published articles: "Coordinating the Russian Privatization Program" (*RFE/RL Research Report* 3 [20 May 1994], 15–27); and "Evaluating the Russian Voucher Privatization Program" (*Comparative Economic Studies* 36 [Spring 1994], 55–67). We appreciate the permission of the publishers to use these materials in the book.

We are indebted to the respondents in our 1993 project, who gave willingly of their time and knowledge, and to the staff of more than one hundred interviewers and data processors who worked energetically through the summer to make the study possible. We are especially grateful to our colleagues who served as field work directors: Olga Klimashevskaia in Moscow; Sergei Khaikin, who supervised data collection in Voronezh and Ekaterinburg; and Svetlana Petrushina in Smolensk. Our research benefited in numerous ways from the participation of officials, opinion leaders, and business people in each of our research cities who provided valuable suggestions, steered us past obstacles of various kinds, and repeatedly offered encouragement and support.

Many other colleagues in Russia also provided valuable help and advice. We want particularly to thank Aleksei Levinson, Leonid Sedov, and Inna Shpileva of the Russian Center for Public Opinion Research (VTsIOM); Vyacheslav Nikonov of the International Fund for Economic and Social Reforms and currently a member of the State Duma; Aleksandr Kryshtanovskii of the Institute of Sociology in Moscow; Viktor Kuvaldin and Aleksandr Likhotal of the Gorbachev Foundation; Dmitrii Furman of the Institute of Europe; Mikhail Maliutin of the Association of Political Experts and Consultants; and Yan Rachinskii of the Memorial Society. Our many discussions with Julia Wishnevsky of the RFE/RL Research Institute contributed immeasurably to the development and refinement of a number of ideas in the book. The many individuals we name in the book who provided perspectives on our research problem are due special thanks. Grigorii Kaganov, to whom this book is dedicated, has helped and participated in innumerable ways, for which we are deeply grateful.

In the United States, Vladimir Toumanoff, president of the National Council for Soviet and East European Research, was an exemplary contract administrator. Eugene Trani, president of Virginia Commonwealth University, has supported this extended project consistently from its inception and provided critical seed money during its initial phase in 1991. Ella Kagan and Pavel Ilyin gave personal and professional support. Patricia Kolb, our editor at M.E. Sharpe, has seen our research through two books now and has consistently provided generous encouragement and insightful critiques.

The work leading to this book was supported from funds provided by the National Council for Soviet and East European Research, which, however, is not responsible for the contents or findings of the study.

We have generally followed the Library of Congress transliteration system, but we began proper names with *Ya* and *Yu* rather than *Ia* and *Iu*. We sometimes changed *ii* and *ia* endings to *y* and *ya* to match customary spellings in English-language material.

Radical Reform
IN Yeltsin's Russia

1

The Twentieth-Century Russian Dialectic

In six months we will have built socialism.
> —V.I. Lenin (early 1918)[1]

A one-time changeover to market prices is a difficult and forced measure, but a necessary one. For approximately six months things will be worse for everyone, but then prices will fall, the consumer market will be filled with goods, and by the autumn of 1992 there will be economic stabilization and a gradual improvement in people's lives.
> —Boris N. Yeltsin (October 28, 1991)[2]

In January 1992, for the second time in this century, a new Russian government that was determined to radically restructure the economy launched a program of reforms based on an economic vision imported from the West. In both cases, Russia hoped to establish a robust economic system through plans developed and administered by an elite cadre of planners who worked to insulate themselves from close public scrutiny. In the 1990s, as well as after the October Revolution, hasty improvisations were required to implement directives whose theoretical assumptions did not mesh well with prevailing social and economic conditions in Russia. Again, as in the seventeenth century and beyond, the rising tide of Western influences in Russia, and the resulting social dislocations, were seen as both welcome and intrusive—both promising and alarming.[3] As under Lenin, early results fell notably short of expectations, which threatened to fundamentally reorient the reforms.

On the one hand, we do not want to force parallels here. On the other, however, historical comparison of the course of social change in different time periods within a country can provide valuable insights into larger, enduring cultural features that influence both policy formation and policy outcomes. We think it is worthy of note, for example, that when Russia's Provisional Government leaders embraced a radical shift to democracy in 1917 they "carried it to excess," as historian Robert Daniels characterizes this initiative. They "extended it to areas," Daniels observes, "where liberal regimes of the West did not dare to venture." Factory committees and military committes were created to bring democracy into areas where it had not been before. Such actions, and the turmoil they created, helped quickly to turn the "democratic dictatorship of the proletariat and the peasantry" under Lenin into a mere dictatorship.[4]

The initial path of radical economic reform under Yeltsin was in some ways similar—thrusting enterprises and their management into an economic environment for which they were not prepared either organizationally or individually, and arguably pursuing macroeconomic stabilization policies with considerably more tenacity than would their Western counterparts under conditions of rapid economic deterioration and the alarming undermining of core institutions that Russia saw from 1991 onward.

In Russian reforms, a pronounced cultural tendency to embrace radical reversals was reinforced by a Western perspective on how reform should be carried out in developing countries that emphasized the money economy above all else—taking little notice of the "human capital" basis of economic relations. If educational, scientific, and other cultural institutions are not highly developed in a country, the larger implications of such neglect are not likely to be as pronounced as in a nation such as Russia with an impressive scientific and technological base. And in Russia, institutional arrangements outside the purely economic sphere had also become severely distorted under Soviet rule—resulting in a scientific establishment, for example, that was abundantly staffed but, in recent years, showed worrisome signs of slippage.[5] In such a context, reforms that were too narrowly focused on macroeconomic stabilization and rapid privatization, as Russia's were, threatened to weaken the human capital base on which Russian economic improvement depended. Markets are not so difficult to create. Filling those markets with useful and valued commodities is another matter, however, as is creating political conditions conducive to the protection of these new markets. We will develop these themes throughout this book.

Tsarist Beginnings

If Peter the Great was not the first of Russia's monarchs to reach out for Western ideas, the urgency of his mission to open a window to the West was unmatched until the twentieth century.[6] "Peter taught us," Alexander Herzen wrote, "to make seven-mile steps—to step from the first month of pregnancy right into the ninth one."[7] Peter's eighteenth-century drive to Westernize Russia produced conflicts and dislocations that would be repeated with fierce intensity under Lenin and Yeltsin. James Billington characterizes the seventeenth and early eighteenth centuries as "a period of continuous violence, of increasing borrowing from, yet rebelling against, the West."[8]

More than a century after Peter's death, the "great reforms" of Tsar Alexander II, which included the emancipation of serfs in 1861, also triggered massive social and economic changes that tied Russia to the West more profoundly than ever before—a trend that continued during the reactionary period that followed. Under Alexander III, who ascended the throne after the assassination of his father in 1881, the government began exerting sharply increased control over the direction and pace of economic development. As the gentry's hold on power and privilege was irreversibly undermined, a series of finance ministers orchestrated widespread reforms that after 1893 produced a surge of industrial development intended to establish Russia as an equal with the West's economic leaders.[9]

But it did not. In spite of having imported a large amount of Western technology—so much that a number of Russian enterprises boasted more advanced equipment than the Western plants they had copied— Russia knew uneven economic progress on the eve of World War I. Russia remained, in the tsardom's twilight years, the least economically developed power in Europe, with a per capita GNP in 1913 that was only 24 percent of that enjoyed by the United States.[10] And in spite of impressive gains in industrial production, the slower rate of increase in agriculture meant that Russia's real income per capita was *relatively* higher in comparison with the United States and Japan in 1860, before Alexander II's "great reforms" began, than in 1913.[11]

Rapid Restructuring Under Lenin

Lenin believed that Marx's analysis offered usable guidelines for rapid social and economic transformation in Russia, although the conditions that most Marxists considered to be prerequisites for overthrowing capitalism were not present there. Thus, five weeks after coming to power, on December 15, 1917 (new calendar), the fledgling Soviet government created the Supreme Economic Council (VSNKh) to completely reorganize the national economy. The nationalization of enterprises soon began, and responding to the spread of unauthorized nationalization brought about by local authorities, in January 1918 the VSNKh decreed that no nationalization should be carried out without its explicit approval. By May, thirty-eight provincial and sixty-nine district regional councils had been set up to administer the economy under VSNKh's supervision. By September 1919, VSNKh had acquired control of 1,300 enterprises employing about 1.3 million people. A year later, 80 percent of large-scale industry had been nationalized. Thousands of small enterprises were also nationalized during this period. According to an August 1920 industrial census, ownership had been transferred in more than 37,000 enterprises by that time.[12]

The Yeltsin Offensive

Seventy-four years after Lenin found power "lying in the streets" of Petrograd, Boris Yeltsin capitalized on another power vacuum, which appeared in the wake of the August 1991 coup. Two months later, on October 28, he announced a new plan for Russian radical reform, this time one that was intended to supplant the socialism that Lenin had set out to establish. To replace central planning, market relations would be promoted through "a one-time changeover to market prices."[13] The system for central economic planning and control that had been quickly organized after Lenin took power would just as swiftly be abolished by Yeltsin.

Yeltsin's overall political agenda both gave direction to Russian economic reforms and restricted the policy alternatives that were available to the reformers at the end of 1991. Below, we highlight critical features of this larger picture, which had profound effects on Russia's economic reform course from late 1991 onward.

From Marx to the Market

On October 18, just ten days before he announced his intention to pursue "shock therapy" for Russia, Yeltsin signed the Treaty on an Economic Community of Sovereign States, in which he pledged "to carry out a *coordinated economic policy* [with the other participating republics] and common measures to get out of the crisis," including "a *coordinated policy* of changing over to free price formation." Further, the signatories "mutually pledge[d] not to permit unilateral, uncoordinated actions with respect to the division of property that they recognize[d] as joint property."[14] But on October 28, Yeltsin proclaimed, "The Russian Federation will have to conduct an independent policy." Then he announced price liberalization, which would be implemented by Russia alone.[15]

Eighteen days later, with Gorbachev still in office as the Soviet Union's president, Yeltsin signed a package of ten decrees and resolutions that were designed to set Russia on the independent economic course that he advocated, a course that would severely hobble the Union government in addition to introducing grave economic complications to the economies of the Union republics. With these decrees, Yeltsin delivered what Sergei Razin termed a "crushing knockout . . . to the Union structures."[16] Russia would now take control of the USSR State Repository for Precious Metals and the USSR Chief Administration for the Production of State Bank Notes, Coins and Medals. The USSR Ministry of Finance was no more, and its functions were to be transferred to the jurisdiction of Egor Gaidar, Russia's new deputy prime minister. Further, Yeltsin decreed that day the elimination of almost all Union ministries and departments, in addition to taking control of all financial agencies of the USSR that were on Russian soil. "Thus, at a single stroke," Razin observed, "Yeltsin has taken full economic power into his own hands."[17] The World Bank country study *Russian Economic Reform*, published in 1992, underscores this judgment, noting that after the August putsch, "the Russian republic continued its policy of bankrupting the Union Government." And Yeltsin's November actions, the study continues, "complete[d] the process of extending Russian government control over Union government functions."[18]

The Dissolution of the USSR

On December 8, in further violation of the Treaty on an Economic Community that he had signed in October,[19] Yeltsin and the heads of the two other Slavic republics, Ukraine and Belarus, agreed in a secret meeting near Minsk to disband the Soviet Union entirely, in favor of a vaguely specified Commonwealth of Independent States. They did not even hold a press conference to announce their act. Yeltsin quickly took a plane to Moscow, leaving it for a reporter to announce the event on the 9:00 P.M. news program "Vremia."[20]

Reflecting later on the circumstances surrounding the signing of the Minsk Accord, Pavel Voshchanov, Yeltsin's press secretary at the time, stated, "If people could ever see how it happened, they would never forgive those people [Yeltsin, Ukraine's Leonid Kravchuk, and Stanislav Shushkevich of Belarus]. You could forgive them for the sake of a big idea, but there weren't any ideas there."[21] (Kravchuk and Shushkevich both ran for reelection in 1994, and both were defeated.)[22]

Within a few days, the Supreme Soviets of the three Slavic republics approved the Minsk Accord, and on December 21, eleven of the USSR's fifteen republics agreed to the creation of a Commonwealth of Independent States (CIS).[23]

In retrospect, a number of analysts have characterized these developments as a "collapse" of the Soviet Union. But the events surrounding the signing of the Minsk Accord bear more the stamp of an assault than a collapse. On December 18 Yeltsin decreed that the USSR Ministry of Foreign Affairs was abolished and that its property and functions were to be in the hands of a newly established Ministry of Foreign Affairs of the Russian Federation. The next day he decreed, "An RSFSR Ministry of Security and Internal Affairs shall be formed . . . in place of the USSR Ministry of Internal Affairs, the RSFSR Ministry of Internal Affairs, the Interrepublic Security Service and the RSFSR Federal Security Agency, which are being disbanded."[24] Without a pause, he then took over the Moscow Kremlin and a large number of USSR cultural institutions, including the Bolshoi Theater, Moscow State University, and the Hermitage Museum. On December 17, the Russian parliament claimed the property of the USSR Supreme Soviet, and attempts by USSR lawmakers to consider the agreements on the CIS, which spelled doom for the Soviet Union, were thwarted when the deputies from the Russian SFSR walked out, thus rendering it impossible to obtain a quorum. Gorbachev resigned eight days later, and Yeltsin quickly claimed his Kremlin office.

The "December coup" was made possible by the shifting mood of the country at the time, especially in the wake of the failed August putsch. It is clear that many people in a number of republics wanted swift and decisive change—that, for them, the Union center and much of what it represented had been thoroughly discredited. But the enormous implications of the Minsk Accord were not thoughtfully discussed by either the people or the Supreme Soviets of the affected republics,[25] although this was an action that would profoundly affect every aspect of public and private life among millions. It would quadruple the number of sovereign governments on the territory of the former Soviet Union (FSU), within whose borders nuclear weapons were located—with unknown consequences for the international political order. Several republics would now become locked into continuing authoritarian rule. The Soviet Union's dissolution would threaten to accelerate other separatist initiatives, with uncertain and potentially disastrous consequences for the entire region. Several republics would soon become embroiled in internal and interregional armed conflict.

The Yeltsin team's late 1991 actions against the USSR closed economic as well as political doors. Until that time, a carefully coordinated and more gradual reform program might have been feasible. But after the events of November and early December, the Russian economy was in too much turmoil to permit the luxury of cautious planning. The unilateral political actions of Yeltsin and his close circle had severely restricted the economic alternatives available to Russia. Sergei Vasil'ev, a member of the Gaidar team who was the director of the Russian government's Center for Economic Reform, underscored this point in April 1992, stating, "The program for disbanding the Union and creating the CIS was worked out by Gaidar. Egor Gaidar is not experiencing any political remorse. And now it is necessary, using Yeltsin's charisma, to provide an economic mechanism for Yeltsin's political program."[26]

Gaidar later tried to account for the Russian government's decision to take an independent economic course. The economies of the republics "were so tightly bound together," he began, "that any attempt to surgically cut these connections was certain to cause pain." That is why, he suggested, treaty negotiations among the republics had proceeded in the fall of 1991. "Effective coordination of economic reforms would have been optimal," he continued, but "unfortunately these wonderful dreams had very little in common with actual relations among the republics following the failure of the August putsch. . . . Life in the country could not be stopped while the republics engaged in excruciating discussions to coordinate reform strategy. In this situation, Russia's government had no choice left. It had to act as an initiator—starting the transformation."[27]

Vasil'ev interpreted this pivotal action in similar terms, with a perceptible shift in emphasis. "After the putsch, it became clear what a burden the Union had become," he stated in April 1992. "The [traditional] idea, 'Let's be friends,' had lost its meaning. Why should we consult with Kravchuk about stabilization of the ruble? Why should we coordinate [our activity] with Middle Asia, which is half-feudal and half-Communistic?"[28]

Later, before the December 1993 elections, Gorbachev underscored Vasil'ev's interpretation. Explaining why he did not intend to vote for Gaidar's Russia's Choice bloc, Gorbachev said, "If you just look at the list of their candidates, you will see people there who put huge pressure on Yeltsin in August 1991 to prevent him from signing the new Union treaty. Those people today are on the Russia's Choice list—people who directly participated in preparing papers for Belovezhskaia pushcha [the Minsk Accord], such as Burbulis, or voted for the Belovezhskaia decision in the Supreme Soviet. These decisions destroyed the country and, to a great degree, created the immense difficulties that we are experiencing now."[29]

Not only was Gaidar's contribution pivotal, as Vasil'ev saw it, to the dissolution of the USSR, but his action was implicated in a stream of historical inevitability. "Empires are fated to collapse," Vasil'ev continued. This "inevitability" notion is, for Vasil'ev, adequate justification for the Belovezhskaia pushcha decision. "There are some problems which cannot be decided democratically," he insisted.[30]

Gennadii Burbulis, one of Yeltsin's closest strategists during this period, underscored this inevitability claim in a June 1992 interview. "No one 'invented' the Belovezhskaia pushcha, the CIS. It was an objective historical act. It needed to find its performers."[31] Economist Grigorii Yavlinskii's response to the reasoning of Burbulis and Vasil'ev was unequivocal. " 'Empires fall apart inevitably, unavoidably,' " Yavlinskii agreed. "But because a person must eventually die, 'inevitably, unavoidably,' must he, then, be killed?"[32]

The republics of the beleaguered USSR were already undertaking to reorganize themselves, collectively and in some cases individually, at that time—a process that had been signaled originally by Lithuania and that accelerated after the August coup. Earlier in the year, on March

17, an overwhelming 76 percent of voters in participating USSR republics (minus the Baltics, Armenia, Georgia, and Moldavia) had indicated their desire to preserve the Union in a special referendum. Eighty percent of qualified citizens in those republics had voted. But the August putsch dramatically reoriented public and legislative opinion.

Lithuania had declared independence back in March 1990, and Georgia had moved conspicuously in that direction later in the year.[33] During the August putsch, Estonia and Latvia followed their Baltic neighbor, and Ukraine declared itself independent a few days later. Before the end of August, Moldavia, Azerbaijan, Belorussia, and Uzbekistan followed suit, to be followed in September and October by Kirgizia, Tajikistan, Armenia, and Turkmenia. Thus, by the time Yeltsin, Kravchuk, and Shushkevich signed the Minsk Accord on December 8, all of the republics except for Kazakhstan and Russia had voted for independence.[34]

These actions were not broadly interpreted to mean, however, that the Soviet Union had been dissolved with no continuing coordinating structure among consenting republics. The draft union treaty published in March 1991 had recognized that the reconstituted Union would consist of sovereign republics, and the "Nine-Plus-One" agreement had renamed the USSR the "Union of Soviet Sovereign Republics." (The word *soviet* means, of course, "council," and suggests a representative system of decision making.) The Treaty on an Economic Community of Sovereign States, which had been signed on October 18, also recognized the "political and economic sovereignty" of the signatories.[35]

On November 14, the day before Yeltsin issued the ten decrees that appropriated key Union structures for the Russian Federation, seven republics had agreed at Novo-Ogarevo, near Moscow, to the text of a Treaty on a Confederal Union of Sovereign States, which would be the legal "successor to the Union of Soviet Socialist Republics."[36] It was agreed that the Union would have a new bicameral parliament and a popularly elected president. The treaty was to be signed shortly and then to be considered by the Supreme Soviets of the participating republics.[37] Anticlimactically, in the wake of Yeltsin's November 15 power play, Gorbachev stated at a brief press conference that the State Council had not initialed the Union Treaty.[38] The dizzying pace of change, which had engulfed what remained of the Union, had been made to order for Yeltsin's "take charge" style.

The economic repercussions of splitting a nation with a complex economy into fifteen independent entities with no advance preparation would be devastating under even the most favorable of circumstances, and those baseline problems are magnified when the country has a command economy that is characterized by not only a high level of centralization but also a production system that has depended, for a number of critical products, on the concentration of production in a few large enterprises rather than a number of smaller, geographically dispersed facilities.

The demise of the Soviet Union had a pronounced negative effect on interrepublican trade. In a 1993 study of the Ukrainian economy, Simon Johnson and Oleg Ustenko note that Ukrainian interrepublican exports amounted to 39 percent of the republic's net material product in 1988, but that the disruption of interrepublican trade occasioned by the dissolution of the USSR contributed significantly to the steep decline in output since that time.[39] In a World Bank study, Constantine Michalopoulos and David Tarr observe that "near chaos characterized the trade and payments in the 15 states" of the FSU during the first half of 1992, and that bilateral agreements among republics did not overcome the problem.[40]

Yavlinskii attributes a minimum of 50 percent of the decline in both industrial and agricultural production in Russia after 1991 to the dissolution of the USSR.[41] The Ministry of Economics of the Russian Federation puts the cost of breakup even higher, suggesting that about 60 percent of Russia's economic decline from late 1991 to early 1994 could be accounted for by the disruption of economic connections among the republics of the FSU.[42] Yavlinskii summarizes the adverse economic effects of this action: "There was immediate—in one moment—not only political but also economic dismemberment of the Union, the elimination of all imaginable organs that coordinated economic activity."[43]

The Continuing Appeal of Dialectical Change

The Yeltsin reformers' determination to accomplish rapid societal transformation repeated a familiar Russian theme. This refrain, sounded loudly in eighteenth-century France, became a staple of Russian radicalism in the nineteenth century and, of course, of Communist revolutionaries throughout the world. "We shall now proceed to construct the socialist order!" Lenin proclaimed triumphantly as he addressed the Congress of Soviets the day after the Bolsheviks took power.[44] Then, after he read his new "decree on peace," the Congress came alive with a long round of applause and spontaneously began singing the "International": "We'll raze to the ground the world of violence, and then we'll build *our* world—a new world . . . !" The militarism, despotism, and deprivation that followed were predictable. "Bombard the Headquarters!" a Chinese poster urged in 1966, as the Great Proletarian Cultural Revolution was launched. The French revolutionaries were likewise unable two centuries ago to establish a new social order with any semblance of orderliness. Fewer people died in the French Terror than in Stalin's, but in both cases the objective was to assure the survival of revolutions that had sought to achieve lightning-quick societal transformations. For Yeltsin, as for Lenin and Stalin before him, the lever of choice was economic restructuring.

Only before the twentieth century could a writer such as Tocqueville have argued that "France alone could have given birth to revolution so sudden, so frantic, and so thoroughgoing."[45] Yet Tocqueville observed that the Revolution failed to achieve its most fundamental goals, "and the nation, at a loss where to turn, began to cast round for a master."[46] David Landes points out that "the series of upheavals and wars that began with the French Revolution . . . brought with them capital destruction and losses of manpower; political instability and a widespread social anxiety; . . . all manner of interruptions to trade; violent inflations and alterations of currency." France, Landes continues, "lost ground in the long run."[47] Thus Theda Skocpol concludes that "France provides poor material indeed for substantiating the notion of a bourgeois revolution that supposedly suddenly breaks fetters on capitalist development."[48] People's minds, even in the intense heat of a French Revolution, "do not change overnight."[49] With all its terror and disruptiveness, Tocqueville insists, the revolution failed to break with the old order.

The Privatization Campaign

At the same time that Yeltsin proclaimed the onset of price liberalization in October 1991, he vowed to "seize the initiative" in enterprise privatization—thus reversing the process of rapid collectivization of enterprises under the Bolsheviks.[50] And on December 29, only four days after Gorbachev resigned as president of the USSR, Yeltsin issued a decree On Accelerating the Privatization of State and Municipal Enterprises.[51]

Whereas Lenin's VSNKh had moved quickly in 1918 to set up regional organizations intended to check *unauthorized nationalization*, privatization head Anatolii Chubais emphasized that the vast network of local property management committees that was quickly organized under the supervision of his State Committee in Moscow would curb *unauthorized privatization*. Reminiscent of VSNKh's stance seven decades earlier, Chubais maintained, as the property management committee network began taking shape, "Now the legal basis for privatization is being established to catch up with the spontaneous process."[52]

And as under Lenin, the Russian reforms implemented by Yeltsin's planners and directed by a central agency achieved dramatic results in a short period of time. In July 1994, Russia's State Property Management Committee (GKI) reported that 70 percent of Russian industrial enterprises had been privatized through the program developed under the leadership of Gaidar, Chubais, and several Western advisers. According to GKI, 21,000 of these larger enterprises had been transformed into joint stock companies through voucher privatization in the "large privatization" (*"bol'shaia" privatizatsiia*) program.[53] (The State Statistics Committee stated in October 1994 that 14,659 had "actually been privatized" by August 1—with shares having actually been distributed.)[54] More than 90 percent of production remained "more or less" under state control, however, when enterprise shares retained by the state were taken into account.[55] Further, GKI data indicated that more than 84,000 small enterprises (those with fewer than 200 employees) had been privatized before July 1 in the "small privatization" (*"malaia" privatizatsiia*) program, totaling 74 percent of Russian small businesses.[56]

Former economic adviser to the Russian government Anders Åslund, citing the GKI report that 70 percent of Russia's industrial enterprises had been privatized by mid-1994, labels this achievement "astounding."[57] Indeed, measured by the yardstick of how many enterprises went through a change in ownership status from 1992 through June 1994, when the voucher privatization period ended, the Yeltsin reformers' success was no less striking, in many ways, than was that of the Bolsheviks from 1918 through 1920, when 80 percent of large-scale enterprises were nationalized. But neither Lenin's 80 percent nationalization achievement nor Chubais's 70 percent privatization milestone signified actual reform success, of course—a fact that Lenin and the Bolsheviks soon learned in the course of their restructuring drive. Existing structures can be dismantled in a variety of ways and quickly refashioned according to a different plan. But what bureaucracies destroy and reorganize, a country's citizenry must accept and be able to manage if the restructuring is to register more than superficial success.

A Closer Look at Restructuring
Under Lenin and Yeltsin

Fruits of Rapid Nationalization Under Lenin

Predictably, in the wake of the Bolsheviks' hurry-up nationalization program, production plunged. In 1920, industrial production had fallen to 20 percent of its prewar level, and agricultural output was only 64 percent of what Russia had achieved in 1913.[58] Deprivation was widespread during this period, and there was an explosion of crime—often born out of hunger.[59] Angelica Balabanoff provides a poignant glimpse of the suffering of these times, the fatalities of which numbered in the millions: "Day by day I could see how material need transformed and deformed human beings and clipped the wings of the young social revolution itself. Here I saw men and women who had lived all their lives for ideas, who had voluntarily renounced material advantages, liberty, happiness, and family affection for the realization of their ideals—completely absorbed by the problem of hunger and cold. . . . I saw individuals who had devoted their entire lives to the struggle against private property, running home with a parcel of flour or a herring, eager to conceal it beneath their coats from the envious eyes of a hungry comrade. The women who owed to the Revolution all their new rights and dignities became suddenly old and worn, physically deformed by their own suffering and incessant worry for their children."[60]

It is impossible to disentangle the diverse causes of Russia's economic chaos in the early days of Bolshevik power. A devastating world war and a protracted civil war had contributed importantly to the economic hardship in which the country was painfully mired by 1920, as had the radical economic restructuring that Lenin had undertaken.

Trotsky had recognized the hazards of aggressively pursuing a radical economic course at that time, but he saw no alternative. Writing in 1920, he argued, "Once having taken power . . . the proletariat is *obliged* to resort to socialization, independently of whether this is beneficial or otherwise *at the given moment*. And, once having taken over production, the proletariat is obliged, under the pressure of iron necessity, to learn by its own experience a most difficult art—that of organizing a socialist economy. Having mounted the saddle, the rider is obliged to guide the horse—in peril of breaking his neck."[61]

The Rapid Reform Imperative Under Yeltsin

Seventy-two years later, Gaidar repeated Trotsky's rationale, insisting in an August 1992 article, "When it is pointed out what Russia was lacking at the end of last year that was needed to create an effective market economy, I want to, not disagree, but add to the list. No, there was no developed, settled private sector, and there were no clear rules for relations between state enterprises and their owners. There was not an adequate environment for competitive, demonopolized market relations. There were no financial institutions to provide efficient redistribution of resources. A labor market was not developed, and labor mobility was constrained by traditions and residues of administrative limitations. Russia did not have its own banking and monetary system, or its own boundaries and customs arrangements. But there was no—absolutely no—time to sit around and wait while all of these preconditions were created. The choice was very clear."[62]

But if Gaidar thought he knew what should be done, he clearly did not know how to set about doing it—even after the price liberalization initiative in January had begun sending the economy reeling.

In announcing his reform program on October 28, 1991, Yeltsin had proposed as his overall goal "to stabilize the economic situation over several months and to begin the process of improving that situation. . . ." "If we embark on this path today," he declared, "we will obtain real results by the autumn of 1992."[63] But Yeltsin did not have a coherent reform program. He had heralded a new path along vaguely articulated monetarist lines (supplied by Gaidar's working group),[64] but he had no map to chart Russia's unexplored economic way. He had abandoned the Economic Community program, which had been developed over a long period of deliberation, in favor of unspecified "drastic economic reforms" whose details had not even been formulated.

Marek Dabrowski, an economic adviser to the Russian government and former first deputy finance minister of Poland, acknowledges that "the Yeltsin-Gaidar cabinet never published any clear formulation of the government programme. . . . But this is not to say that the new government had no comprehensive concept for economic reform at the onset," Dabrowski insists. "Indeed, the concept was drafted by Gaidar's 'team' just before its nomination to government. In October and early November 1991, a special working group, appointed by President Yeltsin and headed by Gaidar, gathered in a government dacha in Arkhangel'skoe (near Moscow) to perform this task."[65]

Thus Dabrowski admits that even the "task" of formulating a "concept for economic reform" was not developed by Gaidar's people until after Yeltsin gave his "drastic economic reform" speech. Yeltsin was a president with a bold proclamation, now in search of an economic program. Its outline would have to be formulated in utmost haste. Nikolai Fedorov, then the minister of justice and a member of the president's State Council, describes a scene at a November 4 round-table meeting of five people, including Yeltsin, when Burbulis handed Yeltsin a proposal for creating "a group in government," to be headed by Egor Gaidar, "which would elaborate, within a week, the first necessary economic measures. The President read it aloud, got to the point about appointing Gaidar, and then looked to see who had signed the proposal. Again, with as much artistic talent as he [Yeltsin] has, he repeated, emphasizing the importance of the name: 'Egor Timurovich [Gaidar's patronymic]—Who is this? What are you proposing? What are you suggesting?' Yeltsin was seriously annoyed, and threw the proposal across the table. Burbulis reddened and hid the papers. We did not decide anything that day, and we did not meet the next day. But on the sixth [of November], a decree appeared appointing Gaidar as a deputy prime minister, and Burbulis as the first deputy prime minister." Fedorov asks, "What had happened, in a day?"[66] Thus Russia's economic future was hurriedly entrusted to "a circle of fellow believers," in Yeltsin's words, with yet another borrowed theoretical vision for a new Russian revolution.[67] Later, Yeltsin's press secretary at the time, Pavel Voshchanov, would insist, "When Gaidar came to power, if he had come with different ideas—not 'shock therapy,' but something else, Yeltsin would [also] have agreed to that."[68]

The "Economic Policy Memorandum" of February 1992, issued *after* the onset of price liberalization, was the first public document prepared by the Yeltsin government that articulated objectives of the program. It was addressed to the International Monetary Fund, (IMF) not to Russia's lawmakers or citizenry. During the four-month period of planning for negotiations with the IMF, the Gaidar team was working to generate international support for the Russian government's economic policy, rather than to build political constituencies at home.[69]

Gaidar was not the first Russian economist to propose macroeconomic stabilization and price liberalization. But he *was* the first in Russia to advocate, and then implement, widespread price liberalization as the first step in economic reform—while monopoly conditions still prevailed—and to believe that the severing of interrepublican ties provided an appropriate prelude to macroeconomic stabilization initiatives. Numerous Russian analysts urgently warned that this approach was certain to further deepen Russia's economic crisis, but they were ignored.[70] Time has shown that these critics correctly anticipated the effects of Gaidar's approach, and that the Gaidar team badly misjudged them. The reformers tried to justify their strategy by insisting that the theory had not been fully implemented. And it had not. Among the Yeltsin entourage, the rush to sieze the moment precluded careful adaptation of macroeconomic stabilization principles to the Russian situation. It is clear from the historical record that the Gaidar team did not take the time to analyze the implications of their plans for either the Russian economy or the larger society. The effects of this narrow perspective were not only economically devastating, but they also extended far beyond the Russian economy, as we will show in chapters two and three—even facilitating the preservation of key elements of the command system that they were so intent on dismantling.

Economic Reforms in the Service of Yeltsin's Political Agenda

A critical feature of the early reform period that retrospective analyses often fail to address is that the economic direction that was so dramatically introduced through price liberalization was geared more toward the achievement of political than economic objectives—and that price liberalization in this context became a cudgel that was intended to, above all else, destroy the old command system. Yeltsin found, in Gaidar's economic plans, a powerful weapon to help him strengthen his campaign against the center and against Gorbachev himself. This point is critical, because it speaks to the rationale that has often been given for strong presidential power to carry out economic reforms.

Whereas analysts often justify Yeltsin's consolidation of power as the reforms continued by arguing that presidential power was serving economic reform, we find strong evidence that the reality was quite different—that the kind of economic reform approach that was initiated under Yeltsin placed economics in the service of his political agenda.

Yeltsin had launched his political offensive in 1989 against the Kremlin Old Guard, following his dismissal by Gorbachev from the Moscow Party Committee post to which he had been appointed (also by Gorbachev) only months earlier. Yeltsin quickly parlayed his image as a David battling the entrenched Soviet Goliath into chairmanship of the Russian Supreme Soviet. A week before he was elected to that position, which served as his springboard to the Russian presidency and ultimately to ascendancy over the man who had dismissed him from his Communist Party post in Moscow, Yeltsin had ignited the chamber with a speech calling for the "real sovereignty" of Russia and rapid political and economic transformation.[71] It was 1990. That formula proved to be so successful for Yeltsin that, following the August 1991 putsch, he was within striking distance of the Kremlin itself. With Gaidar's help he now was well positioned to finish off his old comrades.

Harvard government professor Graham Allison[72] co-chaired, with Yavlinskii, the Joint Working Group that created the "Window of Opportunity" proposal that was presented in June 1991 to President Bush and Secretary of State Baker in the United States, to the other G-7 heads of government, and to Presidents Gorbachev, Yeltsin, and Nazarbayev in the Soviet Union. Their "Joint Program for the Soviet Union's Transformation to Democracy and the Market Economy"[73] was intended to assist in preparations for the meeting between Gorbachev and the G-7 heads of state in London that July. (Gorbachev ultimately proposed a different plan, called by one American official, Allison states, " 'the Pavlinsky Plan'—more Pavlov than Yavlinsky."[74] Such examples of Gorbachev's indecision on the reform front hardly strengthened his hand against the Yeltsin challenge.)

The Window of Opportunity program called for a comprehensive process, from 1991 through 1997, that would create the legal and economic framework for a market economy through institution building, develop "a full program of macroeconomic stabilization" and market reforms, and carry out privatization and sweeping structural reforms. The program proposed both Soviet actions and Western responses.[75]

The Allison-Yavlinskii plan had clear shortcomings. It was too idealistic, proposing a strategy that was not likely to be accepted by the diverse interest groups in the USSR, and proposing a level of Western aid for Russian reform that has since been shown to be unrealistic. While acknowledging "the necessity for *mutual advantage*" for the USSR and the West in any aid program, the "conditionality" provision of the proposal assumed too readily that the economic reform prescriptions of Western financial institutions were the optimal strategies for the Soviet Union; and it would have placed the USSR in the unenviable position of finding itself committed, perhaps too stringently, to the recommended Western approach, once the country became dependent on the aid being doled out "step by step."[76] Further, and perhaps the document's most glaring flaw, the complexity of the country's economic and political problems was not sufficiently reflected in the proposal, as it had not been in the "500 Days" program, which was in many ways its inspiration.

The Allison-Yavlinskii proposal also had a number of positive features, however. It was premised on the idea that both the USSR and Western nations should pursue their own national interests in developing a cooperative strategy for political and economic transformation of the Soviet Union—a principle that Yeltsin's reformers neglected from late 1991 until the December 1993 elections. (We will return to this point in chapter seven.) The proposal underscored the importance of decisive measures to effect economic transformation, but it also emphasized the value of building on the existing production base and connections among enterprises. It was, in short, more a program for constructive economic change than for dismantling the production system that was already in place. It needed additional work, as the authors themselves recognized,[77] and would have required further refinement and elaboration to have served as the principal initial focus for deliberation and action. The perspective it reflected was one of urgency but also recognition of the need for critical and thoughtful scrutiny, from a variety of perspectives, of all details of the reform program that was emerging.

The August putsch derailed this process. When Allison penned his preface that September, following the putsch, he noted: "In the wake of the defeat of the bureaucratic, authoritarian coup, Yavlinksy was chosen as one of the four-man committee to manage the government in the transition and to make recommendations about the new governing arrangements. He was specifically charged with proposing a new comprehensive economic reform program for movement to the market economy and integration into the world economy. That program will bear more than a little resemblance to the economic program for the Soviet Union outlined here."[78]

But Russia got Gaidar, not Yavlinskii, to direct the country's economic course. Later, Yavlinskii would charge that, in creating his new radical reform program, "Boris Nikolaevich and his close circle had very clear political aims." They wanted, he emphasized, to cause "immediate—in one day—both political and economic disintegration of the Union and elimination of all economic structures . . . and to completely isolate Russia from the other republics." Yavlinskii continued, "At the same time, the President wanted to personally lead the economic reform, which meant that it had to be both fast (with the first improvement by the summer-fall of 1992!) and appealing (Make as much money as you want, with no limitations; take as many rights as you want; shorten the working day!). That was a political order. The question was, Who would take responsibility to carry an economic reform program intended to satisfy these political requirements? My colleagues and I have a point of view that is very different in principle. . . . The reforms we had proposed would not have been as fast or as striking, but they would have worked."[79]

Apparently Yeltsin did ask Yavlinskii to head Russian reforms. "In public, I said 'yes,' " Yavlinskii remembered. "But in a conversation with the President's closest circle, and with him directly, I categorically insisted that with such preconditions that [Yeltsin and his advisers] had set as political goals, successful economic reform was not possible in principle. It was necessary to choose—either these political goals, or economics. Then there was a discovery. Another person [Gaidar] came, and said, 'I'll do it.' "[80]

Later, in an interview for *Nezavisimaia gazeta*, Yavlinskii added, "I think that to build, it is not necessary to destroy everything first."[81]

The End of the Cold War and the Beginning of Russian Dependence on the West

The February 1991 *Study of the Soviet Economy*, prepared by the staffs of the International Monetary Fund and other organizations, noted that in 1990 the Soviet Union's external convertible currency debt was small relative to the size of the economy: "9 percent of GDP at the

commercial exchange rate—which is low by international standards."
(The USSR's debt burden was relatively larger, at the time, in relation
to exports.) A worsening in several areas of the economy before 1990
had brought on by that time "severe day-to-day problems of economic
management."[82] And the Soviet Union's economic position rapidly
deteriorated in 1991. A major reason was that republics were withholding tax revenues that were due to the Union. An agreement regarding economic relations between the Union and its constituent republics
was reached in April 1990 and confirmed in January 1991, but republics began to avoid implementing the law by signing bilateral treaties
and economic cooperation agreements among themselves. By April
1991 the Union budget was essentially bankrupt. The projected deficit
level for the year had already been reached.[83]

The 1991 disarray in the Soviet Union created disruptions throughout the economy. Over the course of the year, retail prices for goods
increased by 142 percent, and wholesale prices in industry jumped 236
percent. Production declined by 9 percent, and the fiscal deficit skyrocketed to 31 percent of GDP.[84] It was in this context that the Window of Opportunity proposal was developed.[85] The Window of
Opportunity idea had been labeled a "grand bargain" in a summer
1991 *Foreign Affairs* article by Allison and Robert Blackwill. "We
should recognize that events in the Soviet Union present a historic
window of opportunity," they reasoned. "People in the Soviet Union
have concluded that their society has failed. They believe that the
economic and political democracies of the West have succeeded. They
truly aspire to be a 'normal society.' "[86]

Aid to the USSR would further U.S. security interests, the authors
of the Window of Opportunity initiative believed, while providing resources to the Soviet Union that would facilitate the country's transition to democracy and a market economy. "It may be worth reiterating
what the program is not," Allison writes in his preface to *Window of
Opportunity*. "It is not a *giveaway* of anything to anybody: of Western
money to the Soviets or their soul to us. Rather, if for their own
reasons, they choose decisively the road to democracy and the market
economy, the Program calls for our engagement and support as an
investment in our security."[87]

Underscoring this point, Jeffrey Sachs argued, in a paper delivered
at a June 1991 conference organized by Anders Åslund's Stockholm
Institute of Soviet and East European Economics, "I think it is a kind

of determinist fallacy to think that we should stand back and just let the system collapse, because something good is going to follow in its place. I regard this as a dangerous gamble." His solution? "We are envisaging aid in the order of about 30 billion dollars a year in the first two years of the programme, and then something like 20 to 25 billion dollars a year in the third and fourth year." And he continued, "The only point that I am personally worried about is that the reformers in the Soviet Union do not know there is a way out, because they do not understand that this scale of assistance really would be available under the right circumstances."[88]

But the right circumstances did not materialize. Economist Marshall Goldman suggests in his 1994 book *Lost Opportunity* that "tension developed between Allison and Sachs" over the question of how much to say in public about the likely cost of the Grand Bargain. "Allison did his best to avoid indicating how much the Grand Bargain would cost the West and, especially, the United States," Goldman observes. But as the media began to explore the projected numbers, the Grand Bargain idea faltered at the gate, and Western leaders did not endorse it.[89]

Before year's end, with the dissolution of the USSR, Russia's leading radical democrat took the nuclear briefcase from Gorbachev. And in the wake of the Soviet Union's demise, there was a clear lapse in national interest vigilance by Russia's Foreign Ministry. As Vladimir Lukin, then Russia's ambassador to the United States, highlighted the situation, "The inertia of that time meant that Russia stopped thinking about itself, and Americans stopped thinking about Russia or worrying about winning its support. Inertia led both sides into an easy, mindless existence in which Russia's foreign policy was taken for granted."[90]

But the West did not stop worrying about Russia's debt obligations, which were rapidly mounting. A 1992 IMF *Economic Review* of the Russian Federation noted that during 1991 the Soviet government's "revenue sources were gradually curtailed and dried up completely after the August coup attempt, while expenditure continued."[91] And with the Union broken up, Russia agreed to take on the USSR's debts, although Russia's economic position was rapidly worsening. As the April 1992 IMF *Economic Review* outlined Russia's situation at that time, "The prospects for external assistance are very uncertain, and this uncertainty is endangering the success of the reform process. The dissolution of the former USSR has led several external creditors to cancel or to reconsider the status of commitments made to the former union. In the meantime, there is no scope for commercial borrowing, and reserves are depleted."[92]

Thus infighting between republican and central government authorities in the Soviet Union had done what a protracted Cold War could not accomplish. Moscow had been brought to its knees, and the economic fallout from this internal power struggle was a major factor in Russia's rapid loss of political leverage.[93] Russia was no longer master of its own ship of state but would now look to the West for approval of the reform course that would restructure the country's economy and political system—a development that would have pronounced effects on the character of Russian society itself.

An early indication of this deference to a Cold War rival was seen shortly after the Gaidar reforms began, when the Yeltsin government released its first document outlining the reformers' overall economic plans. In developing its Economic Policy Memorandum prepared for the IMF in early 1992, the Russian government was acknowledging the West's leading role as a participant in Russian reform planning. The Western approach had prevailed in the Kremlin.

Viktor Kremeniuk, deputy director of the Institute of the USA and Canada, summarizes the position in which Russia found itself at the beginning of the reform period: "Under the threat that loans would be denied and requests for debt rescheduling would be rejected, Egor Gaidar was pushed into measures that were not carefully prepared, elaborated, and discussed in the society," Kremeniuk observes. "Of course," he continues, "Gaidar was not at all a passive observer. He himself was eager to create a market quickly in Russia. We would like to believe that he realized how many social, political and cultural obstacles there were on that path—that without careful preliminary work, which could have provided at least a minimal political basis for reform, [the reforms] should not even have been started."[94]

The West did not see it that way, however, and as Russia's lawmakers became increasingly restive during 1992 about the country's economic health in the wake of wrenching price liberalization and accelerating economic deterioration, the reformers found themselves on a collision course with the parliament. The first round ended with Gaidar's ouster as acting prime minister in December. And although Yeltsin made a strong comeback in the April 1993 referendum, this success was short lived. Events of that summer revealed stiffening Supreme Soviet resistance to Yeltsin's uncompromising reform strategy, on the one hand, and growing frustration among the public about Russia's political stalemate, on the other. We will examine these public opinion shifts in chapter seven.

In late August 1993, just weeks before Yeltsin decreed that the Supreme Soviet and Congress of People's Deputies were disbanded, the IMF organized a seminar in Moscow at which IMF spokespeople suggested that the fund would stop its financial support for Russia's reform if Yeltsin should agree to the parliament's budget proposal, which called for a higher budget deficit than the IMF considered to be appropriate for Russia.[95] Stepping up its pressure in mid-September, the IMF warned the Russian government that it should not expect to receive the second half of a loan package that had been promised until Russia "returned to the path of economic reform."[96] On September 16, Yeltsin announced that he was appointing Gaidar to the post of first deputy prime minister for the economy. But the IMF was not placated and soon made known its intention to postpone the award of a $1.5 billion loan because of the Russian reformers' failure to reduce the country's inflation rate and carry out other reforms that the IMF had expected. A September 20 *New York Times* article cites a senior IMF official, who declined to be named, as saying "that his organization was unhappy with Russia's backtracking on reforms during the summer," but also hinting that "Moscow might receive the loan by the end of the year if it displayed a strong and renewed commitment to reform."[97]

Yeltsin's next move came quickly. On September 21 he declared in a televised speech that the Russian parliament was dissolved.

Reported Economic Results: 1991–94

At the time that Yeltsin proposed radical economic reform and requested extraordinary powers from the parliament to carry out his reforms, the official inflation rate was 6 percent yearly. The rate of industrial production dropped 9 percent for the year from its 1990 level.[98] A year later, the economy was in sharp decline, and most of the reformers' economic objectives were decidedly further from realization than they had been before the reforms began. With public dissatisfaction rapidly mounting soon after the January price liberalization, Gaidar claimed, that by the end of 1992, "inflation will slow down to a few percent, the rouble will stabilize and the necessary precon-ditions will be created to attract foreign investment."[99] In June, improvement was nowhere in sight and that month Yeltsin told an interviewer from *Komsomol'skaia pravda*, "I expect prices to stabilize by the end of the year. People's lives will start to improve then."[100]

But whereas Gaidar had predicted, when price liberalization was introduced on January 2, that prices would increase about 3.5 times and then soon stabilize, by year's end they had skyrocketed to twenty-six times their December 1991 level. And Gaidar's projected inflation rate of "a few percent" had become 28 percent per month (3,275 percent yearly) by the end of 1992. The average salary, on the other hand, had increased by only about ten times. Production was declining at a reported yearly rate of 25 percent.[101] For the first time since World War II, the death rate exceeded the birth rate. Infant mortality was on the rise, as were income inequality, homelessness, and crime. An increase in the availability of goods was more than matched by pronounced deterioration in people's ability to buy even essential items. And Russia's foreign debt obligation had risen to more than 112 billion dollars by the start of 1994.[102]

A study by the London-based Centre for Economic Policy Research found that among wage earners in high-, medium-, and low-income categories, all of whom had, overall, experienced significant income growth during the Gorbachev years, real incomes dropped by up to half during the first year of Yeltsin's reforms—and that total real household wealth plunged 86 percent during 1992.[103] Almost all of people's savings disappeared due to price liberalization and inflation. Not surprisingly, the structure of spending changed. Food accounted for an ever-increasing proportion of most families' budgets. Overall, people bought 39 percent less in 1992 than the year before, including 13 percent less meat, 20 percent less milk, 30 percent fewer shoes, and 54 percent less clothing. Further, the foreign investment that Gaidar and privatization head Anatolii Chubais had hoped for did not materialize at a level that even began to approach expectations, and developments in the privatization sphere were not instilling public confidence that the program's most fundamental objectives would be realized, as we will show in chapter six.

Overall, the disruptions visited on the Russian economy by Yeltsin's radical reforms resulted in a reported production decline from December 1991 through May 1994 of 53 percent.[104] (We will discuss inadequacies of Russian official economic data below.) Specialists from the Ministry of the Economy suggested in October that the 1994 fall in industrial output, relative to 1993, was expected to be 25 percent, and that GDP (gross domestic product) would drop another 15 percent from the previous year.105 This steep and continuing decline is not as sharp as the rapid plunge under the Bolsheviks from late 1917 until 1920, certainly; but Yeltsin's reformers did not have to contend with the aftershocks and dislocations of a world war and a protracted civil war. By any measure, the rapid worsening of Russia's economy that is indicated by these figures for late 1991 onward can only be considered catastrophic.

And 1994 would probably not see the decline "bottom out," according to projections of the Ministry of the Economy. In the ministry's "best case" scenario, industrial production would reach its lowest point in late 1994 or early 1995; but in the "worst case" scenario, the economy would not begin to improve until the year 2000. According to the intermediate "likely case" scenario identified in the study, economic improvement would be delayed until 1996 or 1997.106

These figures do not take into account the alarming erosion of Russia's human capital potential after 1991—a subject to which we will return in chapter four.

Advocacy and Analysis in Assessments of Russia's Reform Course

Defenders of radical reforms, in trying to justify Russia's experiment with the short-lived shock therapy initiative and with rapid privatization, often use data bearing on the reforms so selectively that advocacy is more plainly visible than dispassionate analysis. We will illustrate this tendency below and in several subsequent chapters.

Åslund and Sachs, both former advisers to the Russian government, are just two of several analysts who have repeatedly cast Russia's economic nosedive in what we believe to be an unjustifiably positive light, or (particularly in the case of Sachs) directed blame for Russia's economic woes away from the radical reform prescription to other causes. "Data are incomplete and misleading," David Lipton and Sachs stated in September 1992, "and easily misinterpreted to give an overly bleak account" of the costs of reforms. Illustrating a pattern of defense for the radical reform approach that would continue through the time this chapter is being written in November 1994, they concluded, "In our view, these costs are exaggerated."[107]

But when the question is political implications of the reforms, Sachs does a better job than Åslund of identifying the inadequacy of Russia's reform course. In contrast to Åslund, who announced triumphantly in 1994, "A market economy has been successfully created" in Russia, and "Russia has at last become a relatively predictable country,"[108] Sachs continued to worry that "the collapse of Russian reforms" [was] "a serious possibility."[109] Why? Clinton failed Russia, Sachs insists,[110] and the International Monetary Fund lacks the necessary vision to do its job properly.[111] We will indicate in subsequent chapters that a number of analysts both within Russia and abroad shared Sachs's 1994 concern. For Russia and for the world, the political instability resulting from Russia's rapidly deteriorating economic conditions could become the most enduring legacy of radical reforms.

The Production Side

The drop in Russian military production has been highlighted by a number of Western analysts as proof that Russia's industrial production declines are, after all, not so bad. As policy analyst Michael Mandelbaum, for example, puts it, "Russia makes too much of the wrong things." "It is good for the world," Mandelbaum continues, "for Russia to make fewer tanks and missiles. . . ."[112] But Yakov Urinson, first deputy minister of the economy, indicated in October 1994 that most of Russia's production losses were not in the military production sector. Here, Urinson was attempting to do just what Mandelbaum also wanted to accomplish—to put a positive "spin" on production statistics. Thus, he stated that the military production share was "at least 30 percent" of the total production decline. This example is just one of many that show that Russian government officials often share with Western analysts such as Sachs and Åslund a desire to downplay the severity of Russia's economic slide—a point to which we will return below.

A number of articles in the Western press reflect Mandelbaum's perspective. Writing in July 1994 of Russia's production tailspin, *Wall Street Journal* reporter Claudia Rosett contended that, "One point on which market economists largely agree is that Goskomstat's [the State Statistics Committee's] reports of falling industrial production are no cause for alarm, but a sign of economic health." Her rationale was that the Soviet government had historically "poured the nation's resources into producing things for which there was little demand."[113]

That argument does not apply, certainly, to basic food products and wearing apparel. But by July 1994, meat production had declined 45 percent since the beginning of 1992, and milk production had fallen 65 percent. The production of shoes during the first six months of 1994 was 53 percent lower than during that time period in 1993, and this came after a steep decline during the 1992–93 period (a drop in the production of shoes for adults and children of 56 and 73 percent, respectively). The output of men's suits was down 40 percent during the first half of 1994—continuing the pattern of the previous two years. Overall, during 1992 and 1993 the production of fabrics declined 51 percent.[114]

In a September 1994 *Foreign Affairs* article, Åslund explained his basis for arguing that "much of the [reported] decline in Russian production is not real." First, he noted, tax evasion leads to underreporting of both profits and production.[115] He is correct, as numerous Russian analysts have repeatedly observed, that tax evasion, which was widespread in the Russia of 1994, leads to an underreporting of production. The question is, How much does tax evasion actually distort actual production levels? Evgenii Yasin, then head of the Analytic Center in the presidential administration, points out that " 'shadow' business is especially active in the consumer market"—accounting for as much as 42 percent of all goods and services in 1993. "But," Yasin continues, "a part of production, as well, is leaving 'into the shadow.' " He does not know how much.[116] Data for such statements are not available. And what *is* known does not justify Åslund's suggestion that "the depression of the Russian economy is wildly exaggerated."[117]

Even if official statistical data were entirely disregarded in favor of more conservative estimates of production declines, the picture of Russia's recent economic performance would still be dismaying. For example, Yasin states that the shadow portion of the production sphere is smaller, relative to the total, than is the case in the consumer market. (We know of no evidence that this interpretation is incorrect.) But even if shadow production should match the 42 percent figure that Yasin gives for shadow interactions in the consumer market in 1993, the production drop since the Yeltsin reforms began would nevertheless be alarming. And Yasin's estimate is that the shadow economy's share of the overall economy was, in 1992, only half of its 1993 level.

Evgenii Gavrilenkov, first deputy director of the Russian government's Center for Economic Analysis, also emphasizes that underreporting to avoid taxation meant that the actual levels of production in Russian industries were not known. "Unfortunately, no one has the necessary data" to calculate the level of underreporting, Gavrilenkov observed in September 1994, and added, "but I would say that our GDP decline is not 17 or 18 percent but 12 to 13 percent."[118] These are not encouraging statistics—in either magnitude or trajectory—for a country whose *reported 1993 decline* was 12 percent. And Yavlinskii makes the point only slightly differently. "The idea that there is a second economy—that statistics do not take everything into account—is correct," he says. But unfortunately, he continues, even if we knew how to take everything into account, "the decline is still very large."[119]

Åslund also argues, in suggesting that much of Russia's reported production decline is "not real," that electricity consumption figures indicate that the GDP drop from late 1991 through 1993 was overstated. "Universally," he insists in this regard, "electricity consumption is closely correlated to real GDP."[120] That contention is inconsistent, however, with data from the USSR between 1950 and 1980, a period during which the growth in electrical power output and in national income were not closely correlated at all.[121] And other analysts have pointed out that electricity consumption is not a good indicator of production for a number of reasons, including the fact that industrial electricity consumption is more a function of the number of people on the shop floor than of output.[122] International Monetary Fund analyst Vincent Koen and Gavrilenkov provide a better interpretation than Åslund of the significance of electricity production. "The year-on-year elasticity of electricity consumption with respect to actual output may be quite volatile," these researchers note, "and depends on parameters that are hard to quantify."[123]

Both Russian government officials and Western proponents of radical reform in Russia are correct, certainly, in noting that Goskomstat figures do not "tell the truth about the Russian economy."[124] That point is obvious. And production statistics do not identify consumption trends—a point to which we will return below.

Income Inequality, Well-Being, and Aggregate Household Consumption

Whereas Goskomstat's incomplete data related to output would sometimes support too negative a portrayal, at other times just the reverse is true. This means, of course, that careful analysis and balanced interpretations are needed. Several analysts using data periodically collected by the Russian Center for Public Opinion Research (VTsIOM) have charged that Russian government statistics sometimes distort the economic situation in a way that understates negative outcomes for Russia's citizens at the level of well-being and household consumption.[125] For example, government figures are based on a poverty threshold that has been set at an inordinately low level relative to world standards.[126] Further, the Russian government also has consistently underestimated the overall growth in prices. For example, numerous services that were previously available without charge now have to be paid for. The effects of this change on family budgets are usually neglected in official reporting.[127] Additionally, actual prices of goods in stores are often markedly higher than officially reported average prices.[128] Also, frequent delays in wage payments to workers—sometimes as long as several months—substantially reduce the purchasing power of incomes, due to a rate of inflation so high that it is reported in terms of monthly rather than annual increase. VTsIOM national data indicate that, in March 1993, 62 percent of respondents received salaries for the previous month "on time and in full." And by May 1994 this percentage had dropped to 40.[129]

A critical point that is typically ignored by radical reform proponents is that average personal income figures do not take into account the rapidly widening gap between Russia's most and least affluent population segments—and that toward the bottom of the income distribution, purchasing power was substantially lower following the end of the voucher privatization period, relative to the average, than it was at the beginning of the reforms.[130] And the tax evasion that makes production and personal income seem to be more modest than they actually are means also that the income differential between those at the top and those at the bottom of the income ladder is markedly greater than official income figures indicate.

In support of an upbeat interpretation of consumption data, Åslund cites the widely circulated statement that "Real income rose by no less than nine percent last year [1993]."[131] The editors of the *Economic Newsletter* of Harvard University's Russian Research Center do better—as do a number of analysts in Russia. "How real income can go up when inflation exceeds the increase in wages is hard to understand," a March report of the *Newsletter* points out.[132] Sergei Glaz'ev, chair of the State Duma Committee on Economic Policy,[133] accounts for this discrepancy. The growth of income is entirely due to entrepreneurial activity, Glaz'ev finds. "That means," he writes in August 1994, "that the growth of income is occurring in the most well-off social groups."[134]

VTsIOM national survey data add detail to this conclusion, suggesting that for most Russians, purchasing power was not improving by mid-1994 relative to the previous year. According to several VTsIOM national surveys, 80 percent of respondents had to spend more than two-thirds of their family income to buy food—a pattern that was no more favorable than that of a year earlier. In a June 1994 study, only 5 percent reported that their material conditions had improved during the previous six months, but 55 percent stated that their living standards had declined during the period.[135] And 1993, also, had been a year of steep income decline for most Russian people.

Western observers and analysts have repeatedly highlighted positive, but unrepresentative, manifestations of Russia's turn away from the command system, while avoiding discussion of more sobering outcomes and prospects for the future in light of the infrastructure deterioration that has been exacerbated by the reforms. For example, in a May 1994 op-ed article in the *Wall Street Journal*, Radek Sikorski, former deputy defense minister of Poland, wrote that, "not only is Moscow not in its death throes, the city appears to be in the midst of a boom," with "foreign cars, bright posters [that] advertise computers and cat food," and "well-stocked shops" in abundance. Sikorski correctly observed that many Western firms "have more than doubled their sales in the last year," and that many rich Russians can afford to pay premium prices for the services of "Moscow's prettiest prostitutes."[136] And analysts Daniel Yergin and Thane Gustafson accurately noted in a July 1994 *Financial Times* article that "colour is appearing on buildings and in shop windows, enlivening the drabness of even a year or two ago."[137]

In a like vein, historian Herbert Ellison concludes, after an arranged trip to Moscow, Volgograd, and St. Petersburg, "The tremendous positive achievements of the Yeltsin economic reforms are visible everywhere. . . . I returned with a picture of Russian conditions greatly different from the bleak descriptions in our press."[138] Characterizing "the prevailing image" presented in the media as "a severe distortion," Ellison neglects to consider that Russian leaders from Stalin onward have been adept at showcasing their successes while shielding foreign visitors from close examination of grimmer realities beneath a public relations veneer.[139]

Whereas Åslund bolsters his consumption argument by noting the expansion of retail sales ("Previously unavailable consumer goods, such as stainless cutlery, are now in ample supply")[140] and the recent surge in sales of television sets and cars, closer analysis reveals that, for a large proportion of Russian citizens, not only does no new television set seem to be in the future, but there may not even be money for a replacement pair of shoes. And if Western advisers had not grasped the dimensions of Russia's consumption crisis by late 1994, most Russians clearly had. Political analyst Nikita Gololobov reflects the predominant conclusion of those close to Russian public opinion in maintaining that, among "voters and taxpayers . . . nearly everything is viewed as going badly." This public sentiment has been formed "in spite of the government's attempt to manipulate" public opinion, Gololobov continues.[141] We will examine these public opinion currents more closely in chapter seven.

Even Chubais acknowledged in September 1994 the government's public opinion problem. "Reforms have already changed the institutional basis of the society," he emphasized and added, "If today we manage to solve the investments problem, tomorrow everyone will be talking about the 'Russian economic miracle.' " However, he admitted, "What I am saying about the success of the reforms does not match the everyday perceptions of people who have turned out to be in a very difficult situation today at plants that are not operating. And for a person who has not received his salary for three months, my argument . . . is like a discussion about life on Mars. But as a professional economist, I am confident that it is the solution for tomorrow."[142]

Russians have heard similar claims before. But public opinion had by that time become critical in matters of state, and the time of placing blind trust in unfamiliar economic visions had passed. On this point, Åslund is correct. Now, "interests are more important than ideas,"[143] he says.

Finally, consumption trends are not adequately captured by cross-sectional data. Koen and Gavrilenkov observed in November 1994, "It could be argued . . . that the current dynamism of aggregate consumption is not sustainable because it is being paid for by the dilapidation of the capital stock" and "the deterioration of important segments of the infrastructure," which provide the engine for economic growth.[144]

Further Considerations

The questions of how severe the production drop actually was in Russia through the conclusion of voucher privatization, and of how personal well-being was affected by the reforms, had not been settled as 1994 drew to a close. Official figures, self reports, and tax evasion estimates were manifestly unreliable. For our purposes, however, aggregate figures are less important than two less debatable conclusions.

First, the majority of Russia's population were living decidedly less well at the end of 1994 than they had been before the reforms began. Second, the immediate effects of the reforms on both production and consumption did not tell the whole story—and perhaps not the most important part. The structure of Russian production was changing as overall production declined. Output volume in the energy sector declined much less than in other sectors, and declines in civilian goods production exceeded declines in military production. There were severe distortions in the structure of production, certainly, as the reforms began, but the reform course was amplifying these problems.[145]

A profound weakening of the societal infrastructure on which future production and consumption levels depend was visible. The magnitude of these effects will be clarified only after the losses in Russia's human capital potential—brought on by erosion in the educational system and in science, for example—are better clarified. That these losses were already substantial by late 1994 is obvious, as we will show in chapter three. That their ultimate implications may not be measurable for some time to come is illustrated by the course of scientific production from the Stalin era onward. Writing of Soviet science under Stalin, whose record was notable, and of the subsequent declines in a number of specialties, Loren Graham points out that the intellectual costs of Stalinism became pronounced only in the 1970s.[146] And rather than correcting the inadequacies of this inefficient but still formidable system, the first three years of Yeltsin's reforms further crippled it. In comparison with the long-term consequences of the Yeltsin reforms for education, science, and the larger culture, the production declines of the 1991–94 period, whose magnitude is now a subject of careful scrutiny and debate, may eventually be seen as a relatively unimportant development.

2

The Political Dimension of Economic Reform

Interviewer: *"How helpful is an aid arrangement with the IMF and the G-7, from a political point of view? Your critics accuse you of letting foreigners choose your policies. Doesn't that weaken your position?"*

Egor Gaidar: *"The reaction is mixed. For those who anyway support the government, it is a very good sign. It is a very bad sign for those who oppose us. But I think it is generally a good rather than a bad sign for the crucial middle section who could go either way."*

—*The Economist*[1]

The "Western approach," a term we use to identify core features of the economic reform strategy advocated for Russia by prominent advisers and political leaders in the West and generally supported by key financial institutions, has much in common with the perspective that John Williamson describes as a "Washington consensus": a set of economic policy reforms "that Washington urges on the rest of the world." Williamson highlights ten priorities that are central to this orientation, including fiscal discipline, a negative view of subsidies for state enterprises, an "outward oriented" economic policy that emphasizes a competitive real exchange rate and import liberalization, a nonrestrictive policy regarding the entry of foreign direct investment, and the privatization of state enterprises.[2] Added to this list, in the Russian

35

case, was a strong emphasis on price liberalization—one feature that Williamson explicitly excludes from the "Washington consensus" about reform in Latin American countries.[3]

We do not want to imply that the Western approach comprises a seamless web of policy proposals, because it does not. In the Russian case, elements of neo-liberal monetarism were blended with Keynesian perspectives as Russia's reform priorities unfolded. Here, however, we will focus on commonalities among the perspectives of reformers and their supporters more than divergences.

In spite of the manifest economic focus of Western approach priorities, the larger political implications of this approach are at least as significant as the economic prescription it presents. Those political dimensions are the subject of this chapter.

The Western approach was partially implemented beginning in January 1992 but was modified importantly over the course of the year. There were, however, repeated attempts by some Russian officials to bring Russian economic reforms more in line with fundamental tenets of the approach, and through the completion of voucher privatization in June 1994, analysts who served as advisers to the Russian government, as well as Western leaders and representatives of international financial organizations, were continuing to argue that Russian policymakers should more unreservedly embrace reform strategies that would be consistent with the "Western approach."[4]

First Principles

There are two practical reasons why governmental programs for sweeping institutional change should be worked out in a context of open deliberation among diverse interest groups within a country—reasons that internal concerns and issues should be a reform government's first priority. In a general discussion of the "governability" of democracies, Ralf Dahrendorf, then director of the London School of Economics, follows Seymour Martin Lipset in identifying these factors as *effectiveness* and *legitimacy*.[5] First, workable governments must be effective; that is, they must be "able to do things which they claim they can do, as well as those which they are expected to do." And, unless the political context is avowedly authoritarian, they must be legitimate. Governments are legitimate when what they do is judged by the citizenry to be right—or at least, not unacceptable.[6]

The criterion of effectiveness is elaborated by Peter Hall, who points out that "economic policy is invariably a collective endeavor," because it "is the output, not of individuals, but of organizations which aggregate the endeavor of many individuals in particular ways." He continues, "It is an 'organizational intelligence' rather than the intelligence of individuals which ultimately determines such factors as the capacity of the state for strategic thinking or the quality of policy."[7] Put differently, economic policy making is a complicated undertaking, in which a huge number of factors, both economic and noneconomic, must be taken into account. The job is much too complex, with divergent implications for a large number of societal institutions, to be capably carried out by a handful of specialists acting in relative isolation. Systematic deliberation that includes input from a wide variety of groups and a willingness to modify approaches that prove to have unwanted consequences is required if the effectiveness criterion is to be adequately satisfied.

"Legitimacy," Lipset observes, "involves the capacity of the system to engender and maintain the belief that the existing political institutions are the most appropriate ones for the society."[8] Legitimacy is acquired differently in democratic and in authoritarian regimes. Authoritarian control depends heavily on propaganda. Democratic governance, on the other hand, depends more on deliberation and compromise among interest groups with divergent perspectives and priorities. Lipset notes that crises of legitimacy develop during a transition to a new social structure "if . . . all the major groups in the society do not have access to the political system in the transitional period, or at least as soon as they develop political demands."[9] When the subject is economic policy, legitimacy emerges when, in Hall's rendering, "broad coalitions of economic interests . . . converge around specific policy alternatives."[10]

The problem here for reformers is that, as Przeworski suggests, "Outcomes of democratic conflicts . . . are uncertain."[11] But against that uncertainty must be balanced, first, the fact that insufficiently studied, and inadequately debated, proposals for complex reforms cannot possibly take into account all, or even most, critically relevant contingencies, and second, the strong likelihood that a closed process of policy formulation will produce a powerful and potentially disabling backlash if interest groups are free to mobilize and articulate their discontent. The key to making "democratic conflicts" both productive and civil is the building of robust and resilient institutions that can function effectively in an environment characterized by "crosscutting bases of cleavage."[12]

Of course, under conditions of democratic pluralism, not only are the outcomes of deliberation uncertain, but, when the issues are important to a diverse set of stakeholders, initial proposals are unlikely to survive the process of review and debate entirely intact. Further, as Robert Dahl acknowledges, the unequal resources of different interest groups may enable the most powerful ones "to exercise unequal influence in determining what alternatives are seriously considered" and adopted.[13] In short, there are both advantages and disadvantages of the democratic approach to policy formulation. The record of the Bolshevik planning system suggests, however, that a closed approach offers even more disadvantages and fewer positive features.

But the writings of Jeffrey Sachs and Anders Åslund, both advisers to the Russian government until after the December 1993 elections, demonstrate a consistent inattentiveness to these fundamental political requirements for successful economic reform, except in a largely theoretical sense—as well as an overall lack of concern with the critical subject of *political* reform in the larger context of Russia's attempt to transcend its Communist party–dominated past. (We will return to this subject in chapter seven.)

These advisers pay lip service to democratic processes and then proceed to advocate decidedly undemocratic actions in carrying out economic reforms. Sometimes Åslund appears at first reading to favor democratic processes even during "the doldrums of the transitory period."[14] In one paper he asks, for example, "Why is democracy so important for the change of economic system in a formerly socialist state?" And his answer could be a page from Lipset or Dahrendorf. "It is a question of credibility," he answers, and also of legitimacy and of stakeholder interests.[15] He emphasizes that "neither market relations nor property rights will be of much significance without the development of the rule of law," and he adds, "A civil society of a multitude of independent organizations needs to evolve . . . based on grass-roots initiative."[16]

But these caveats are forgotten when Åslund gets down to the real business of economic reform policy. "To create credibility and break inflationary expectations, it is necessary to introduce radical changes," he insists in a 1992 volume (*Post-Communist Economic Revolutions*),[17] and he continues, "Experience shows that people, if they have been properly informed, will accept a democratically adopted harsh stabilization with surprising ease."[18] Yet the brevity of Åslund's nod to democratic processes is soon apparent. In the next paragraph he declares, "A command economy and a market economy are completely alien to each other and no convergence has proved possible. Any intermediate position contains serious contradictions. . . . Little can be done but a full liberalization."[19] Of course, deliberation and compromise always dilute a theoretical ideal, but the alternative to democratic deliberation produces its own set of undesirable problems. A few pages later, writing about the advantages of a rapid pace for reforms, he states, "It is politically easier to have severe measures adopted as a big package. *Greater speed implies less time for discussion*."[20] Thus Åsland highlights the principal advantage of rapid reform: It keeps at bay the consideration of alternatives and compromise.

Overall, the writings of the Russian government's principal Western economic advisers reveal a striking failure to clearly recognize that reform policy making could benefit from the input of groups that represent divergent economic interests. Rather, their preferred strategy is to coopt interest groups so that the imposed reform agenda can be carried out with a minimum of interference from the "outside"—that is, from the diverse constituencies who will have to live with the reforms. They would prefer the input to come from the Western governments and financial institutions who have their own sets of interests.

In an April 1994 report for a World Bank conference, for example, Sachs spoke of the Russian reformers' mid-1992 compromises, which diluted Gaidar's shock therapy program, and concludes, "In my view these compromises were prompted in part by the lack of Western financial aid flows, which induced the reform team *to look inside Russia for broadened support*."[21] To Sachs, for the Russian reformers to have sought support for its policies among the Russian electorate was clearly an undesirable development. We will return to this theme below and in subsequent chapters.

A Toe-Hold for the Western Approach

Sachs's early 1994 assessment of Russian reforms underscores the unprecedented opening that was created during Gaidar's tenure for Western priorities to influence Russian economic policy making.

"Now that [the reformers] are no longer heading the key ministries, there is little the U.S. can do,"[22] Sachs lamented, remembering, perhaps, how very different the situation was when the Gaidar reforms began. Åslund spoke of those halcyon days for his reform vision during an August 1993 interview, recalling, "Back in September 1991, we came to an agreement with Jeffrey Sachs and other specialists that if this team [Gaidar's] should come to power, we would help. And Gaidar's government invited us."[23]

The Western approach to decision making for Russia was successful in dominating reformers' thinking as the Yeltsin reforms got under way partially because Russia's leaders stood to benefit personally by shielding their positions from democratic accountability, and also because the reformers largely insulated themselves from Russian political realities while their plans were being developed. This second factor helps to account for the reform planners' striking misjudgments about the political standing of their reform initiatives among the electorate, which we will illustrate below and in the concluding chapter.

Writing about the Polish experience, Åslund argues that the transition process there "suffered from Poland being the last country in Eastern Europe carrying out democratic parliamentary elections," and adds, "Compromises with a communist-dominated parliament delayed and weakened the reform program."[24] Åslund obviously believes that an electorate long smarting under the privations of Communist rule will quickly embrace his neoliberal theory of reform without strong dissent or, apparently, even prolonged discussion.

Before Yeltsin dismissed the Russian parliament in September 1993, Western advisers were among the most prominent advocates of a preempting of legislative authority by the executive branch. And in late November 1993, just before the elections to Russia's Federal Assembly, Åslund was continuing to emphasize the importance of parliamentary elections as a means of tipping the scales of legislative support in favor of Yeltsin and his reforms.[25] We will see in chapter seven that it did not work out that way.

In our interviews with a broad cross-section of Russian officials and opinion leaders in the summer of 1993 (described in Appendix A), the prediction was consistently repeated to us—from the "left," "center," and "right" of Russia's political spectrum—that any newly elected parliament was almost certain to be a more conservative one. And not because of a "Zhirinovsky factor." At that point, Zhirinovsky's campaign was not yet underway. The chief factor in these predictions was the government's reform program, which was being widely blamed for Russia's economic crisis.

These summer expectations could not take into account, of course, the chilling effects of the new constitution, which gave Yeltsin a degree of power that has rightly been termed "authoritarian." As with economic indicators, Western analysts have often characterized the new Russian constitution in unduly flattering terms. Sachs, for example, stated at the April 1994 World Bank conference mentioned above, "The recent adoption of the new Russian constitution can provide a foundation to achieve" the political goal of "a democratic regime."[26] And in his September 1994 *Foreign Affairs* article, Åslund suggested that the constitution "provides for a parliamentary system with an ordinary division of power between a strong executive and a parliament reduced to a legislative role."[27] Åslund could have more appropriately said that the parliament had been reduced to a largely advisory role, while substantially more legal authority resided with the Russian president now than was enjoyed by the Communist party's general secretaries after Stalin's day.[28] As Robert Sharlet observes, the powers granted the Russian president in the constitution can be compared to the concentration of powers enjoyed by the Communist party of the Soviet Union in Article 6 of the 1977 USSR Constitution[29]—powers that were more comprehensive than those of party general secretaries. We will return to this theme in chapter seven.

"... *this is not a sporting event*"

The predominantly closed nature of Russian reform planning during its critical early months was emphasized by Yavlinskii in October 1992, when he charged that it was not possible even to criticize the government's economic program adequately until July 1992—more than eight months after Yeltsin's announcement that there would be drastic reforms and six months after the introduction of price liberalization. "There were guesses concerning the inappropriateness of the [government's] proposed economic path . . . but the government did not announce [the main features of its] program until July. How could one judge what they were going to do?"[30]

Yavlinskii had maintained, at the time that the Allison-Yavlinskii proposal was being developed in 1991, that the only chance for constructive economic reform was through "negotiations among the [country's] principal political forces."[31] This perspective is fully consistent with our knowledge of how policy change can be effectively carried out in open societies. The achievement of societal consensus "is a long-term, gradual process," Yavlinskii states. "The search for mutually acceptable compromises . . . is not a sporting event—not a race, in which the one who starts first will be able to finish first."[32]

But Gaidar was not willing to follow the path of deliberation and negotiation among interest groups within Russia any more than he had been when the republics of the USSR had been attempting to replace the Soviet command system with a mutually agreed to alternative in late 1991. Then, he had argued that Russia should take leave of that process and follow an independent course. Having achieved that objective, he now wanted simply to circumvent interests *within Russia* that did not mesh with his reform scheme. Writing in August 1992 about the reform strategy that had been adopted earlier in the year, Gaidar stated, "At the beginning of their work, a government usually has more freedom for maneuvering. After that, it diminishes under the pressure of responsibility for unpopular decisions. . . . That is why, from January through March, we tried to use in full measure the political time that we had to make money work . . . and to get the gears of market mechanisms in place."[33]

Thus the Gaidar team justified its relative autonomy and insulation from the critical eye of analysts and interest groups by claiming that haste was necessary in initiating the reforms, a claim that was not effectively challenged. In late 1991, Russia's citizenry and its legislators were weary of the economic indecision that had prevailed at the end of the Gorbachev era. They were exhausted with talk about reform that did not produce reform. They were, in short, primed for radical change. Gaidar, Yeltsin, and the parliament all had a sense of urgency that reform was overdue and needed to begin quickly. The Western approach was presented under conditions that were ideal for relatively uncritical acceptance of its principal tenets among the Gaidar planners. Neoliberal monetarism offered a ready economic "solution" for Russia's economic troubles. And, the West's advisers insisted, the solution must be implemented swiftly.

Åslund illustrates this emphasis on haste in a June 1991 conference attended by several Russian economic planners. Åslund decried "gradualism" as an outmoded type of economic thinking, insisting that "the dominant current of economic theory suggest[s] that a swift and comprehensive change, comprising as many simultaneous measures as possible, is most likely to minimize the social costs of transition."[34] (Elsewhere Åslund suggests that his argument for "fast privatization . . . is probably a minority view" among economists.)[35] In his June presentation, he tried to discredit a more gradual approach to economic reform by linking it with the "old establishment" and "lingering notions of central planning."[36]

As the Allison-Yavlinskii proposal lost its centerpiece status with events that followed the August putsch, Sachs, also, began to strongly advocate rapid restructuring, and in 1992 he was applauding the "remarkable dispatch" of the Gaidar reformers.[37]

The Reformers' Early Privatization Agenda

On November 25, 1991, Yeltsin decreed that, by the end of the year, executives who managed the supply and distribution networks of retail, public catering, and consumer services enterprises throughout Russia were required to reorganize to extricate the enterprises from the system of obligatory relations that had long characterized the USSR's command system.[38] These enterprises were required to obtain a license specifying that they were "juridical persons." But all that the enterprises received was a license. There was no significant amount of training for the alien economic conditions that were being set up by this decree, and there was no plan for facilitating a shift from highly structured relations among suppliers, producers, and distributors to one in which relations could be independently established.

This was the first step toward privatization, according to the government's new plan. Retailers thus gained the "opportunity" to buy goods from suppliers of their own choosing, and producers were granted the opportunity to find their own markets. But, of course, established systems of economic relationships are not transformed through the issuing of licenses, and the greatest opportunities that were signaled by Yeltsin's decree were reserved for established members of the *nomenklatura*, who were well placed to expand their domain of control as barriers were suddenly removed, and for those who were not constrained by ethical standards from improper self-aggrandizement. As Aleksandr Bykov, an official of the Economic Crime Division of the Ministry of Internal Affairs, described this new situation, "Privatization pushed many formerly honest people into questionable activity. . . . A person who managed to figure out, earlier than others, that 'deals' involving state property would not be punished, could make out very well."[39] Economist Larisa Piiasheva characterizes the situation that was created by this Yeltsin decree in similar terms: "Everyone probably remembers what was started at that time. Actually, it was the right to steal."[40]

On December 29, Yeltsin approved, by decree, the Basic Provisions of the State Program for Privatization in 1992.[41] According to this document, small-scale privatization, involving retail, public catering, and consumer services enterprises, was to be started in the first stage, which would occupy the first three quarters of 1992. Approximately 90 percent of these enterprises would be sold through auctions or competition[42]—a major policy deviation—from the privatization legislation that had been passed the previous July but consistent with the general direction that Åslund had endorsed in 1991.[43] This policy shift was announced without any opportunity for public discussion and debate.

In the July 1991 initiative of the Supreme Soviet, which Yeltsin's action superseded, the predominant concerns had been, first, that privatization should effectively address the specific requirements for improved economic performance within each economic sector, and, second, that privatization should be equitable. But Yeltsin's December 29 decree did not allow enough time to seriously prepare for the coordination that would be necessary to facilitate economic improvement, and the price liberalization scheme that was scheduled to take effect on January 2 would wipe out most citizens' savings—thus making it impossible for most of them to participate in this first stage of privatization, which would include many of the more desirable enterprises that were to be privatized.

The prevailing idea among Russian economists at the time that Yeltsin became president was that privatization would lead to improved economic performance by promoting competition and bringing new owners into enterprises. There were a number of different perspectives, however, about who these new owners should be. It was widely accepted that the privatization initiative should take advantage of the money overhang that had resulted from shortages of goods. Citizens with money in the bank that had been accumulated through years of work in a context of shortages could use that money to purchase state property or start new businesses. This idea was seen as a way to compensate the Russian citizenry for forced collectivization and decades of privation during Communist rule. The concept was incorporated into the "500 Days" proposal that had been developed in 1990. And in May 1991 a detailed privatization proposal was prepared under the direction of the newly appointed chair of the State Property Management Committee (GKI), Mikhail Malei. Analysis had convinced Malei's planners that many smaller state enterprises could be bought with then existing personal savings but that most state property could not be privatized for money.[44] One reason was that savings among Russia's citizens were inadequate to purchase such a large volume of property, and the amount that would come from foreign investers was uncertain. A second problem was that public opinion surveys had shown that many citizens did not want to use their savings to buy shares of privatizing enterprises. (Yavlinskii and Stanislav Shatalin had also recognized, in the 500 Days proposal, that personal savings were not sufficient to purchase most property to be privatized, but they proposed that people be allowed to borrow money for property purchases. They had no firm evidence, however, about how many citizens would, in fact, be willing to take out loans for that purpose.)

If privatization could not be accomplished primarily by *selling* state property, then some other method for property distribution would have to be developed. It was in this context that the Russian Supreme Soviet issued the law On Registered Privatization Checks and Accounts on July 3, 1991.[45] This law specified that privatization "investment accounts" would be made available in state banks for all citizens. With these accounts, people could "buy" state property. It was expected that 70 percent of the state property that was to be privatized would be claimed by investment account holders.[46]

Yeltsin had signed the July law, which stated that privatization accounts would be established at the beginning of 1992. He was then still chair of the RSFSR Supreme Soviet. But five months later, on December 29, 1991, President Yeltsin used his special powers to decree that privatization investment accounts would not be set up until 1993—only after a large number of desirable enterprises had been otherwise privatized. The focus of the December 29 decree, and the new privatization plan that the decree approved, was to quicken the pace of privatization—and not in 1993, when privatization investment accounts were to be available for citizens, but beginning in three days' time, on January 1. By January 29 local administrations throughout Russia would be required to have identified enterprises that would be privatized according to the Basic Provisions of the State Program for Privatization in 1992 and to have started the privatization process—without the benefit of privatization investment accounts, and under conditions in which most citizens had just seen their savings largely disappear because of price liberalization.

But how could the first stage of privatization, according to Yeltsin's December 29 decree, emphasize the *sale* of enterprises when most savings accounts were about to shrink drastically in value with the onset of price liberalization? Privatization head Anatolii Chubais answered that question in January 1992. When asked how the government could be sure that the people would have the money to buy enterprises in privatization's first stage, Chubais responded that the savings among the general population would, indeed, be inadequate. But, he continued, "We are taking into account the demand from representatives of the 'second economy' "[47]—that is, demand from people with money that was, in most cases, acquired illegally or through the use of administrative or party connections.

Privatization investment accounts, as conceived in Russian legislative action from July 1991 through June 11, 1992, were intended both to create equity in the denationalization of property and to facilitate economic improvement through the creation of markets and measures designed to dampen the inflationary pressures that could accompany the introduction of a new medium of exchange that was not carefully regulated. A critical feature of privatization accounts, which were to be made available to all Russian citizens, was that they could be used only to acquire shares of state property. They would be registered to named citizens, and only the person named would be able to use an account to acquire privatizing property.

Only after citizens had acquired shares through privatization accounts, and after enterprise stocks could be evaluated on the basis of market demand, would shareholders be permitted to sell their shares at market value, if they so desired, after a period of three years. The three-year holding period was intended to help forestall inflationary pressure that would result from a sudden availability of stocks for which no money had been paid. (Enterprise shares bought for money would not carry that restriction.) And requiring that shares of enterprises not be sold before their market value could be determined was intended to provide a sound basis for investment decisions, as money increasingly came into the market for shares of privatized enterprises.

This would have systematically built confidence among the citizenry in a market economy by creating market conditions in a deliberate, step-wise manner.

It is significant that both Gaidar and Chubais had opposed the idea of privatization accounts from the beginning, according to Petr Filippov, who, before joining the Yeltsin administration, had chaired the Subcommittee on Privatization of the Russian Supreme Soviet.[48] Their view was consistent with Åslund's perspective at that time. In 1991, Åslund had discussed several advantages and disadvantages of voucher distribution of state property and had concluded, "Voucher schemes do not appear viable."[49] They would require an assessment of enterprises, which could not be accurate before markets have emerged, he argued, and they would create political backlash as many newly privatized companies went bankrupt. Åslund also suggested that if property were "given for free," it might not be valued. Chubais adopted the same stance, maintaining, "What blows in with the wind will fly with the wind."[50]

But at some point in 1992, the wind shifted among the privatization planners. By the time that Åslund penned a revision of his 1991 article quoted above, he had decided, "The best option that has emerged in the debate [over optimal privatization procedures] is the distribution of vouchers to most citizens."[51] Voucher distribution, he noted in this revision, had been decided upon by the Russian government. Perhaps Åslund's judgment about the desirability of a voucher plan was influenced by Richard Layard, an economic adviser to the Russian government from the London School of Economics. In 1990, Layard, along with other members of the World Economy Group of the World Institute for Development Economics Research, had prepared a report on the subject of Eastern European economic reform. In the study, they contrasted two approaches to privatization—the sale of state property and free distribution of "at least a substantial part of state enterprises." They concluded, "Most of the arguments against distributing shares strike us as ill thought-out."[52]

But these disagreements among foreign advisers were largely confined to closed-door meetings. It should not be surprising that analysts in Russia such as Yavlinskii voiced dismay that it was impossible to understand the Russian government's early 1992 reform policy. The planners themselves did not know what to do as they were beginning the biggest property giveaway in the history of the world. Gaidar acknowledged in his April 1992 interview with an *Economist* reporter, "In privatisation, there are no clear rules. The most important thing is for us to move as rapidly as possible, and to create a structure of property that will be regarded by most people as more or less just."[53] And, as we will show below, when the reformers did decide among themselves about a plan, they did not want its full details known even by the parliament, which was charged with reviewing and approving privatization legislation.

The Voucher Stratagem

Maxim Boycko and Andrei Shleifer wrote a paper about the Russian voucher program that appeared in a 1993 book edited by two other prominent advisers to the Russian government, Åslund and Layard. Both Boycko and Shleifer served as economic advisers to the Russian government. Shleifer was a Harvard economist, and Boycko was director of the Russian Center for Privatization, an agency of the Russian government under the State Property Management Committee headed by Chubais. Their paper begins by stating, "In accordance with the Decree of the President of the Russian Federation of April 2, 1992 vouchers will be introduced in Russia in the fourth quarter of 1992."[54] But the April 2, 1992, decree to which they refer calls for the creation of "registered privatization accounts in the fourth quarter of 1992"— not the kind of vouchers they describe, which could be sold for cash. The negotiability modification was a significant change, as our discussion will indicate. But this idea was not present in Yeltsin's April 2 decree. Nor was such a voucher utilization plan suggested in the revisions to the July 3, 1991, law On Privatization of State and Municipal Enterprises in the RSFSR that the Supreme Soviet had approved on June 5, 1992. And when the Supreme Soviet approved the State Program for Privatization of State and Municipal Enterprises in the Russian Federation for 1992 on June 11, the law it passed stated that "a system of registered privatization accounts (privatization checks) will be introduced no later than November 1, 1992."[55] The phrase "registered privatization accounts" (*imennye privatizatsionnye scheta*) has an unambiguously clear meaning in Russian: "with the owner's name," or "cheque payable to the person named," is integral to the meaning of the phrase.[56] This denotation is fully consistent with the July 1991 legislation. This owner identification was a critical feature of the privatization accounts plan, because it made the accounts (or "privatization checks") non-negotiable. They could only be used to buy shares of enterprises, which meant that actual privatization would have to precede speculation in future privatization. Pre-privatization speculation was certain to create a buyers' market for negotiable privatization checks, a system that would favor a small number of well-placed and monied interests. For in the aftermath of price liberalization, people with substantial liquidity were in no way typical Russian citizens.

The same day that the Supreme Soviet was approving the 1992 privatization program that had been submitted by the reformers for its consideration, the Yeltsin government's Council of Ministers was hearing GKI's proposal for a different system of privatization that was later implemented.[57] This new proposal, which was presented to the Council by Chubais, made two significant changes in the program being approved that day by the Supreme Soviet. It would remove the recipients' names from the privatization checks, which would make it possible for privatization check holders to sell their checks, rather than investing them in enterprises. Additionally, it would limit the term during which privatization checks could be used, adding further impetus for rapid use of the checks. The Council approved Chubais's proposal, and it was decided that, since the parliament was about to begin a summer recess, the new program would be implemented by presidential decree. *Kommersant* later noted, "The introduction of vouchers is the most radical decision the Russian government has made in creating market structures in the economy."[58]

The idea of issuing unregistered vouchers had been floated as a "trial balloon" before mid-1992 by Dmitrii Vasil'ev, a deputy chair of GKI, when we interviewed him in May. In discussing various methods of privatization, Vasil'ev suggested that "people should not be forced to buy a certain piece of property," adding that more "freedom of choice" would be possible through a procedure in which vouchers were unregistered. Then, "poor people could sell their vouchers to richer ones, and rush to the market to buy sausage." That month he repeated this notion in a *Delovoi mir* interview, saying that "accounts" would be "just a piece of paper," and that "each Russian [could] decide" what to do with theirs—to "either purchase shares" of an enterprise, "or just sell it to another person."[59] But this scheme did not become a part of the legislation adopted by the Supreme Soviet on June 11.

"Miraculously," Filippov remembered in February 1994, "we managed to squeeze through ('*protashchit'*) the Supreme Soviet the first privatization program."[60] But Filippov's memory was faulty. The privatization program that Russia's lawmakers approved was not the one the Russian people got. In July 1993, then chairman of the Commission on Economic Reform of the Russian Supreme Soviet Vladimir Mazaev gave us his perspective on the breakdown of coordination between the executive and legislative branches with the inauguration of voucher privatization. "The parliament was deceived," Mazaev stated. "We approved one privatization program, and Chubais with his foreign advisers created voucher privatization using Yeltsin's emergency powers. The parliament was on holiday, and Yeltsin's people took advantage of that."

The parliamentary discussions that preceded June 11 approval had been lengthy and detailed. A number of critical issues had been debated—as is the case in any parliament when major policy proposals are being reviewed. Gaidar had initially presented the privatization proposal to the Supreme Soviet in March. It had been rejected by the Congress in April, but at the same time the Congress approved a resolution affirming its commitment to the government's course of economic reform. A revision of the program was submitted in May and was approved "in principle." Further discussion followed, and additional modifications were made before June approval. But with Chubais's presentation of a new privatization scheme to Yeltsin's Council, the reformers showed their disregard for the "principles of joint subordination" to which Yeltsin had offered allegiance the previous October when he asked for special reform powers.[61]

The reformers did not want to openly discuss the actual objective behind their voucher distribution proposal, because they were telling the public one thing while pursuing an entirely different goal. Whereas at the time of the parliament's June discussions Chubais had clearly stated, "The politics of the State Property Management Committee are not to further the stratification of society but to let everyone take part in people-oriented privatization,"[62] the plan that GKI had secretly developed was designed to have the opposite effect. And by November, Chubais was not hesitant to advance an entirely different interpretation of voucher privatization's meaning for the Russian citizenry. Now he was not speaking about the "stratification of society," but rather about personal freedom, freedom to cash in on vouchers rather than to participate in "people-oriented privatization." "If he wants to sell his privatization check . . . [for] a case of vodka, so what?" Chubais argued.[63] And in hearings of the State Duma during March 1994, he insisted, "We never had the aim of making every citizen an owner."[64] He thus voiced a view that diverged sharply from the one he had emphasized in public as the first version of voucher privatization was being considered—the version that was presented to, and approved by, the Supreme Soviet.

Our purpose in this chapter is not to evaluate these two approaches to the distribution of state property. But it is important to highlight the type of decision-making procedure that was utilized here. The privatization planners' determination not to discuss the variant that they favored with the Supreme Soviet, at the time that Russia's lawmakers were considering the 1992 privatization proposal, was just one of a number of deliberate maneuvers by the Yeltsin government to neutralize the Russian parliament's authority during 1992 and 1993. Yeltsin revealed the kind of thinking that produced this strategy just as voucher distribution was beginning in Russia. "A presidential decree," Yeltsin declared, "is nothing like Supreme Soviet regulations. It's higher."[65] This perspective was not only *approved* by foreign advisers who were promoting the Western approach among Russia's reformers, but also *recast* in a different light, as is illustrated by the version of this page of history that has been offered by Boycko and Shleifer.

After Yeltsin signed a decree authorizing the new voucher idea on August 14,[66] the Supreme Economic Council of the Russian Supreme Soviet prepared an analysis of this new approach, which the Supreme Soviet had not been given the opportunity to consider. Theirs was a careful study, which inquired into likely implications of Chubais's plan. The Council's report on the voucher program was released September 22, 1992. "Before any decision was made about the program," the report stated, "detailed evaluation was needed of its organizational implications and legal basis. But it seems that the initiators of this program (the State Property Management Committee of the Russian Federation) did not do either. Legally, the [new] program . . . contradicts the RSFSR law On Registered Privatization Accounts and Deposits."[67] Organizationally, the report concluded, the voucher auction plan showed no promise of improving economic performance, but it promised to offer fertile ground for criminal activity.[68] On both counts, this judgment proved to be accurate.

The Politics of Rapid Pace

Several days after the Supreme Economic Council recommended that the sale of vouchers for rubles be prohibited, consistent with the terms of the privatization program that had been submitted by GKI and approved by the Supreme Soviet, Chubais responded. Appearing before the Supreme Soviet, he declared, "It cannot be done—either technically or organizationally. If 150 million people receive checks and want to sell them, it won't be possible to prevent it."[69] The campaign was well under way to whip up popular support for the planners' circumvention of the parliament by trying to paint the parliament as opponents of the people's interests. By this time, a number of radical democrats were attempting to brand detractors of the privatization program as "reactionary forces" who were determined to prevent "the final collapse of the economic base of totalitarianism."[70] The reality of this situation was quite different. Our analysis indicates that the Supreme Soviet, as a body, had undertaken reasoned deliberation on this crucially important issue for Russia's economic future. It was the reformers whose actions at this time were inconsistent with democratic processes, as they carried out a deceptive end-run around the parliament and then launched a blistering propaganda campaign to deflect attention from their strategy.[71]

A fundamental objective of the new voucher procedure was to privatize as quickly as possible. As Filippov put it, "The most basic mistake of the variant with privatization accounts was that it attempted to force everyone to become owners of these accounts *and prevent a rapid flow from hand to hand.*"[72] This rapid-pace strategy was at the heart of the Western approach, as we have already noted. But there is a striking contradiction between the widely accepted *objectives* of privatization, as delineated in the Russian privatization program, and the negative economic and social *outcomes* that could be expected from privatization as it was carried out—at a speed that precluded a smooth transition. We will return to this point in chapters five and six.

Åslund's arguments in *Post-Communist Economic Revolutions* illustrate well this fundamental disjunction. He discusses several reasons for rapid privatization—socialism's loss of legitimacy, for example; the need for a well-functioning market comprising a large number of firms; and the importance of good management for enterprises. "These arguments amount to a strong case for fast privatization," he concludes.[73]

But in reality, the rapid pace for privatization that Åslund and others urged on Russia worked against the realization of nearly all of the objectives he highlights. The legitimacy of socialism among the Russian population was increased as a direct result of a privatization program that most Russian citizens evaluated as not operating in their interests, once they learned how it was actually structured. (We will furnish evidence for this point in chapter seven.) Competition and good enterprise management are both vital to a vibrant economy, but rapid privatization did not facilitate either. It had the opposite effect. Lightning-quick privatization can only be accomplished if people are intimidated or bought off. And in buying off enterprise directors, the privatization program hardly stimulated a drive for better management. We will return to this critical point below.

Layard and the other members of the World Economy Group worry that methodical preparations for privatization can create a "legal no-man's land" conducive to plundering by enterprise managers and bureaucrats. This concern is more persuasive than Åslund's points are. But the rapid privatization that these analysts advocate offers unwanted outcomes, also. Eastern Europe has known problems of the types they describe, certainly—"spontaneous privatization" for self-aggrandizement and dishonest "deals" of many types.[74] But rapid privatization solved none of these problems. Rather, it created a context for rapid fraud and profiteering, along with rapid privatization. A more deliberate approach to the transfer of state property would seem, on balance, to have offered more hospitable circumstances for limiting and rooting out illegal activities associated with privatization.

It is clear that the reformers knew that their program would be attractive to criminal elements in Russia. It is not inconsequential that, with the onset of voucher distribution, the legal requirement that citizens who wanted to use large personal cash reserves demonstrate that their money was acquired legally before buying property being privatized, was nullified.[75] The implication of the new voucher plan for criminal involvement in Russian privatization was obvious to both the reformers and the critics of the privatization program. As Leonid Abalkin, an economic adviser to the Gorbachev government, put it, "I discussed [this situation] with Anatolii Borisovich Chubais, and he himself said that the task is to create a modest number of real owners. Chubais realizes that the owners will mostly be criminally oriented people. But, he said, there are no others now. . . . And without real entrepreneurs and owners, Russia will never get out of the hole. That's why," Albalkin continues, "the model with unregistered checks was chosen."[76]

In a report discussing the relationship between organized crime and privatization in Russia, which we will return to in the next chapter, then Yeltsin aide Filippov acknowledged that "the word 'privatization' has acquired a very clear criminal connotation," but added, "We often have been asked if we are uncomfortable with the fact that, in privatization, there is very active 'laundering' of money that was made through criminal activity. We not only are troubled about this development but also indignant, but what is the answer? To slow down privatization would be a step backward—an attempt to stop the train that has just started gaining momentum on the way to the market."[77]

This situation resulted, to a substantial degree, directly from the Western approach's demand for hasty privatization in the absence of adequate preparation in the political, legal, and cultural spheres. Filippov's "train" was, as a result, on the wrong track, and maintaining its momentum could only distance Russia further from effective reform.

The most basic reason that the reform planners emphasized a rapid pace above all else is that their chief priority was to cripple the command system. The core issue here, then, is *not* between the relative *economic* merits of gradual and rapid privatization for improving the existing system of production and distribution. The dominant justifications for rapid economic reform in Russia grew out of the overriding conviction that there was only a "narrow window of opportunity" to put a new system in place before opposition forces could gather strength to derail the process. As Chubais elaborated on this point when we interviewed him in August 1993, "The parliament started to accept the idea of privatization in 1991, but they'd had enough of it by the end of 1992. We had to work in light of those constraints." Theirs was, then, an almost exclusively political agenda but one unschooled in the requirements of effective political work. We will elaborate further on this theme below.

The Reformers Break Free

After mid-1992, the parliament became increasingly frustrated that the legislative branch was being excluded from review and oversight of the privatization process. GKI was largely shutting out the property funds from involvement in the privatization process, the Supreme Soviet charged. The implication of this perceived usurpation of authority was alarming to many legislators, particularly because the funds were specifically responsible for ensuring "that the state's rights as an owner [were] represented," as the first chairman of the Federal Property Fund, Fikriat Tabeev, summarized the Federal Fund's role.[78] Tabeev continued, "We are responsible, not just for the *fact* of privatization. . . . The Fund is responsible for the economic activity of an enterprise, which means that besides ensuring that the state's interests are realized, the Fund is responsible for the well-being of workers . . . and the competitiveness of an enterprise's output."[79] But as the parliament attempted to review the procedures by which GKI was carrying out privatization, the Committee grew ever more resistant to being held accountable for its actions.

In the April 1993 referendum, the question that concerned the privatization program asked, "Do you approve the socioeconomic policies carried out by the president of the Russian Federation and the government of the Russian Federation since 1992?" Fifty-three percent of the voters said "yes," and both Yeltsin and Chubais quickly turned this referendum result into justification for their growing defiance of Russia's parliament. Following the referendum vote, Chubais's revolt against participation by the parliament in the privatization process was unqualified. "Parliamentary evaluation of the State Property Management Committee is funny," Chubais stated. "There won't be any real influence [from the parliament] on the work of the State Property Management Committee."[80] And he was right.

The Plan to Coopt Russia's Economic Stakeholders

The work of Shleifer and Boycko highlights the Russian government's approach to the political component of policy implementation in the economic sphere. In another 1993 article, "The Politics of Russian Privatization," they describe how "stakeholder interests" (interests of people and groups with existing "control rights over assets")[81] were addressed in the privatization initiative. In their discussion, Shleifer and Boycko fail to consider basic political prerequisites for successful economic reform. This omission is most clearly reflected in their apparent belief that a credible reform effort could be undertaken by buying off groups that have legitimate stakeholder interests, rather than working through the tedious but necessary process of developing meaningful responses to competing interests for the sake of not only equity but the constituency building that is necessary if any large-scale change initiative is to have a chance at long-term success.

The Russian stakeholders with whom Schleifer and Boycko are especially concerned are workers, local governments, managers, branch ministries, and the public. Early in the paper, they underscore their basic perspective on political interaction: "Unless these stakeholders are appeased, bribed, or disenfranchised, privatization cannot proceed."[82] Stalin found a fourth way to proceed with economic "reforms" in the face of stakeholder opposition, of course, and democracies have found yet a fifth way—recognition that a variety of stakeholder claims, even overlapping ones, must be taken into account as policies are being developed.

But the Western approach held that divergent reform ideas should be ignored if possible, and that stakeholder resistance, whenever it appeared, must somehow be overcome. Shleifer and Boycko quickly dispense with worker claims. "To avoid massive resistance to privatization, the government must pay off the workers," they note matter-of-factly.[83] There is no discussion of optimality here, or of the improved economic performance that they hold up elsewhere as a basic reason for Russian privatization.[84] In discussing the three privatization options that were developed in the program, they speak only in terms of "a privatization sweetener" and a level of "generosity" that will provide hope of "getting the workers . . . to hop on the privatization bandwagon."[85] And Åslund's post-factum explanation says more than he may have intended. "The purpose of giving a substantial share of the ownership to workers in enterprises to be privatized was *not based on any ideology or concept of justice*," he states, "but on a desire to facilitate fast privatization."[86]

Shleifer and Boycko turn more heavy handed when the stakeholders at issue are local governments. "The strategy toward local governments is to coopt them into supporting privatization and relinquishing their control rights over firms," they maintain, cautioning, "Given that their claims are often as strong as those of the workers, they will not be cheap to convince."[87] As a way of "putting more pressure on the local governments to privatize," they recommend "starving the local government budgets by not allocating funds from the center."[88] This version of a gentler form of coercion is seamlessly unconcerned with cultivating the local support that is needed for an effective reform effort.

In describing their approach to buying off managers, Shleifer and Boycko emphasize, "Any manager in Russia today can use the program to become rich and remain in control." It may be important to note that Shleifer and Boycko see this element of their program not as a negative feature, but as one of the program's strengths. Their context is a discussion of how "enterprise managers were successfully enticed to cooperate in privatization."[89] Some removal had taken place by the end of voucher privatization, but not much, in relative terms. An estimate that we repeatedly heard in mid-1994 and beyond was that only about 10 percent of the directors of large industrial enterprises had been replaced.[90] The program was consciously structured to produce this result.

Shleifer and Boycko worry about branch ministries, because they cannot identify a fail-safe way to neutralize the potential of branch ministries to interfere with the privatizers' plans. "The ministries will get something [in the privatization process]," they conclude, "but hopefully not enough to stop privatization from going ahead."[91]

Then, Shleifer and Boycko take up the Russian public. "Like every other privatizing country," they note, "Russia must give something to the public for privatization to succeed." They add, "Vouchers played a role in assuring the acceptance of corporatization, since the enterprises needed to offer shares to the public in exchange for vouchers. . . . Something had to be left to the public."[92] But most of the public have not been impressed with these remains, as we will show in chapter seven.

So the stakeholders included in Shleifer and Boycko's analysis were, according to Russia's privatization planners, groups to somehow be bought off as cheaply as possible, or "starved" into submission, or, in the case of managers, rewarded with a frequently undeserved and potentially obstructive pot of gold during the voucher privatization stage of reforms, simply because of their considerable potential for interfering with the reformers' plans. This is how economic reforms were expected to acquire political legitimacy in Russia.[93]

The Roles of Additional Stakeholders

An adequate inquiry into the politics of Russian privatization from 1991 to 1994 must also consider two additional sets of stakeholders in privatization planning. First, a large number of people and organiza-

tions within Russia who worked outside the domain of the state enterprise system had a clear stake in privatization. Some, such as financial
groups and voucher speculators, were afforded new money-making
opportunities through voucher privatization, as were a number of Russian investors who were interested in acquiring ownership in some of
the more desirable properties that were being privatized. Other entrepreneurs who had started businesses before privatization began entered
the privatization debate in the hope of benefiting indirectly from the
reforms surrounding privatization, by influencing legislation in a way
that would be favorable to the business community overall.

Further, outside Russia a number of financial institutions, G-7 political leaders, and foreign advisers had stakeholder interests in Russian
reform. In a 1991 *Foreign Affairs* article, for example, Graham Allison
and Robert Blackwill summarized aspects of "America's Stake in the
Soviet Future." "The fixed point for our compass must be U.S. interests," they began.[94] In arguing that the United States should participate
in "affect[ing] the outcome of the Soviet domestic struggle," they
asked, "Having spent some five trillion dollars to meet the military
challenge of the Soviet Union around the globe, is the United States
(and its allies) to opt out now when the Soviet future is being
formed?"[95] This theme was prominent in the Window of Opportunity
proposal prepared for the heads of government of the Soviet Union, the
United States, and other G-7 heads of state. In his introduction to the
document, Allison emphasized the West's "strategic stakes in Soviet
reform." But the "grand bargain" that was proposed by Allison, Russian economist Grigorii Yavlinskii, and others was clearly aimed at
furthering the national interests of all countries involved in these discussions—the Soviet Union and G-7 nations. Allison summarized the
core of the "bargain" being attempted: "The path of economic transformation Soviet leaders can choose and reasonably hope to succeed in
following depends critically on the extent of Western support. Simultaneously, the extent of Western support depends critically on the program of economic reform that the Soviet Union is prepared to choose
and follow."[96]

But events that came after the Window of Opportunity proposal had
been drafted would fundamentally alter the equation and reshuffle the
players in these discussions. The emphasis on mutual interests among
all national parties, which had been a prominent feature of the deliberations surrounding the Window of Opportunity idea, was replaced by a

new form of dialogue after Gorbachev's resignation and after a number of new participants took key positions in the discussions between Russia and G-7 nations during late 1991 and early 1992. In this next phase, Western interests would be pursued more aggressively, largely unconstrained by the former requirement to balance Western and Soviet interests, now that the USSR was no more and Russia's economy was in deep crisis.

A number of outside players in this new phase would solidify personal and corporate stakeholder interests in Russian reform, as their services to the Russian government provided for them professional recognition and financial gain. Private firms would come on the scene to offer expertise of various types to facilitate Russian economic reform. These activities would often be funded with U.S. dollars—particularly from the U.S. Agency for International Development (USAID). Frequently, the funding levels for this work were quite large, as, for example, when the Washington, D.C., Sawyer/Miller Group received $7 million to develop a television advertising campaign to promote privatization, KPMG Peat Marwick was awarded $98 million in contracts to work with privatized businesses, and when an Arlington, Virginia, consulting firm, Haglar Bailly, received a $20 million contract to "help privatize Russian utilities and encourage them to install U.S.-made equipment," according to a *Wall Street Journal* report.[97] The potential bonanza that U.S.-approved Russian privatization made available for consulting firms quickly became obvious as USAID money began to flow. As John Fialka of the *Wall Street Journal* put it in February 1994, "With so much aid money involved, there has already been a veritable feeding frenzy in Washington," and he adds that USAID "says 1,200 consultants applied to get into the program, a record for the 33-year-old agency."[98]

Conclusion

In sum, interest group activity—both within and outside Russia—importantly influenced the direction of Russia's economic reforms and the priorities of the privatization initiative. Russia's lawmakers were particularly swayed by the claims of enterprise personnel and the administrative bodies that coordinated and supervised enterprises slated for privatization before the Congress of People's Deputies and the Supreme Soviet were dissolved in September 1993. Yeltsin's economic planners, on the other hand, were heavily influenced by the orientations of foreign advisers whose principal emphases were macroeconomic stabilization and a rapid pace for privatization, following the appointment of Gaidar to be Russia's chief economic strategist. In succeeding chapters, we will examine processes through which these different interest groups influenced the direction of Russian reforms from late 1991 through the conclusion of the voucher privatization period.

3

Structural and
Cultural Factors

*Social policy would be much simpler if people from different
cultures were interchangeable robots, responding uniformly to given
situations. But a large body of evidence indicates that they are not. The
peoples of given societies tend to be characterized by reasonably durable cultural attributes, which can have major political and economic
consequences. If this is true, then effective social policy will be better
served by learning about these differences . . . than by pretending that
they do not exist.*
  —Ronald Inglehart, *Culture Shift in Advanced Industrial Society*[1]

*It is fully in keeping with the capital concept as traditionally
defined to say that expenditures on education, training, medical care,
etc., are investments in capital. However, these produce human, not
physical or financial, capital.*
              —Gary S. Becker, *Human Capital*[2]

The government officials and advisers who developed Russia's economic reform strategy failed, most fundamentally, in not adequately
recognizing that radical economic reform is not just about economics—that market transactions take place in political, organizational,
and cultural contexts that are relatively enduring. Far from being extra-
neous to economic relations, these factors importantly shape the economic sphere and constrain actions within it. For example, structural
arrangements that influence work relations, and therefore motivation
and productivity, must be understood if economic improvement is to
be realized through reform, and the developmental basis of ongoing

interorganizational patterns cannot be ignored if effective structural transformation is to be accomplished. In Russia, interorganizational relations remained integrally bound up, as the reforms began, with the bureaucratic structures of the Soviet era. When these structural and historical factors are studiously examined as economic proposals are being created, obstacles to the realization of reform objectives can be identified, and avenues of opportunity that are presented by these specific societal features and configurations can be exploited in the pursuit of effective reforms.

The importance of taking into account these noneconomic factors at the beginning of the reform period in Russia was recognized by a number of analysts. A 1992 World Bank Country Study, *Russian Economic Reform*, emphasized that "Russia's transition to a market economy requires a thorough-going institutional transformation in virtually all spheres of the economy and society," and that "institutional reform within the public sector must transform the state, and simultaneously encourage the growth of a civil society capable of perpetuating and preserving the economic space for private enterprise."[3] Stephen Haggard and Robert Kaufman highlight a key justification for this emphasis. "When economic reform is viewed over the long run," they suggest, "the biggest challenge is not simply to initiate new policies but to sustain and consolidate them so that they gain credibility among economic agents."[4] Radical planning, John Friedmann emphasizes, is "not merely normative" but also includes "a strong analytical element" and necessitates "a knowledge of institutional constraints" and "an ability to assess and evaluate alternative solutions."[5]

Planners do not arrive at the stage of political articulation with an empty plate. And during preliminary reform planning, it is vital that overarching structural and cultural features of a country be brought into the deliberations if a proposal is to be developed that can usefully guide reformers' work at the second, political articulation, stage— when the proposal is exposed to the unblinking eyes of divergent interest groups.[6] At that point, the comprehensiveness and balance of preliminary planning will be judged by representatives of the people who will have to live with the reforms, and some of its inevitable omissions will be challenged. If these deliberations proceed constructively, more corrections than distortions will be introduced into the proposal.

There is nothing novel about our emphasis on the embeddedness of economic relations in a larger network of political and social arrangements, as is illustrated in the 1992 World Bank Country Study cited above. The fundamental importance of these interrelationships is well established in the literatures of comparative political and cultural studies and organizational analysis. Structural and cultural dimensions of a nation are critically important to the operation of its economic sphere, this literature indicates, and must be taken into account if programs aimed at restructuring complex and long-standing economies are to be viable. In mainstream economics, also, this perspective has achieved increasing acceptance. We will elaborate on these points below.

Our objective in this chapter is not to provide a comprehensive enumeration of critical noneconomic factors that should have been taken into account in Russian reform planning. This should be a task for a multidisciplinary collaborative team—and is the kind of preliminary, detailed analysis that the Gaidar planners should have commissioned at the beginning of their work. Our more modest goal is to identify examples of noneconomic factors that are so basic and important as to confirm our contention that the Russian reformers quite clearly neglected even the most fundamental building blocks for effective reform planning in a world where economic relations are closely tied to other societal structures and processes.

Economics and Society: Contrasting Views

Beyond the Rationality Assumption

Inadequacies of the simplifying assumptions that characterize neoclassical economics have repeatedly been highlighted. "The economic approach is clearly not restricted to material goods and wants, nor even to the market sector," Gary Becker argues in *The Economic Approach to Human Behavior* (1976), adding, "Moreover, the economic approach does not assume" that people "can verbalize or otherwise describe in an informative way reasons for the systematic patterns in their behavior."[7] This perspective both extends and refocuses Karl Polanyi's insistence that the economy is "embedded in non-economic institutions"[8] by recognizing, as Jack Hirshleifer puts it a decade later in *The American Economic Review*, that "economists will . . . have to become aware of how constraining has been their tunnel vision about the nature of man and social interactions. Ultimately," he suggests, "good economics will also have to be good anthropology and sociology and political science and psychology." Why? Because "the model of economic man has indeed been productive, but only up to a point."[9]

And for a large number of contemporary analysts, this recognition has taken firm root. The key conclusion that follows—a perspective that is now widespread in the social sciences and philosophy—is that the economic, political, social, cultural, and psychological dimensions of human life are intertwined. Philosopher John Rawls, following the tradition of Rousseau and Kant, is critical of the unqualified economic rationality assumption, arguing that "the more evident and easily applied principles of rational choice do not specify the best plan" for action in actual decision-making situations[10]—partially because a social contract among individuals takes precedence over personal utility-maximizing strategies.[11] Sociologist Amitai Etzioni maintains that "a new conception of how people make choices" is emerging—a perspective that recognizes that economic decisions "are boxed in by emotion and values."[12] And Cornell University economist Robert H. Frank finds several important deficiencies in "the standard economic model of rational choice." People are often *not* efficient processors of information, as Herbert Simon has demonstrated,[13] and judgment errors are often systematic. Further, Frank emphasizes, "We are creatures not only of reason but also of passion."[14]

The "emotions," "values," and "passions" that Etzioni and Frank identify are located in a larger cultural framework by Paul DiMaggio, a sociologist in Yale University's School of Organization and Management. Among several proofs DiMaggio provides for his statement that "Culture influences economy at the organizational as well as the individual level," he revisits Donald Roy's 1954 study of a Chicago machine shop, where management's dysfunctional interventions into the workplace resulted from the managers' seeming "to have been blinded by strongly held cultural conceptions of organization."[15] In short, their behavior in the economic sphere was importantly influenced by cultural factors.

Underscoring this point, economist Robert Heilbroner emphasizes that the kinds of social obligations and activities that result in "economic" production vary from society to society.[16] Observing that the idea of exchange is at the center of market mechanisms, Heilbroner examines "the psychological basis for the exchange relationship" and, in the spirit of Kant and Rawls, concludes (citing Locke) that "market society, with its linchpin principle of impersonal, equal-valued exchange, presupposes" subordination to a social contract that may often be at variance with "rational maximizing" behavior.[17] Thus, for Heilbroner, "insofar as [economics] accepts as final the analysis of social movement in terms of unexamined 'economic' forces," the discipline remains "an ideology—a belief system."[18]

Henry J. Aaron, director of economic studies at the Brookings Institution, observed in 1994, however, that this broader conceptualization of the relationship of economics to other spheres often is not yet employed in policy analysis. Taking issue with Becker "that the standard [economic] model is capable of extension to encompass the full range of human actions," Aaron argued instead that if the adequacy of economists' policy work is to be improved, economists must "rely less slavishly on the insights of theory" and "abandon a measure of disciplinary chauvinism" in favor of a more empirically grounded and interdisciplinary approach.[19]

"Strict and Orthodox" Macroeconomic Reform: Basic Requirements

Whereas the stream of economic thinking represented by Aaron's perspective requires that the relationship between a country's economy and other spheres be taken into account in reform planning, followers of the Western approach have adopted a very different planning strategy. Their goal from 1991 through 1994 was to force into place as many policies as political circumstances would bear that were consistent with their overarching economic theory, disregarding as completely as possible specific features of the economic, social, and cultural environment of Russia in which these neoliberal reforms were being planted.[20] Politics, they recognized, was a limiting factor; but they did not recognize *how* limiting, or how to generate long-term political viability for reforms, as we indicated in chapter two. And beyond this inadequacy, proponents of the Western approach believed that they could steamroller their proposals to realization in spite of other societal barriers as well. Preserving the theoretical integrity of their reform idea, they insisted, should take precedence over any other considerations.

Anders Åslund, for example, believes that the "frequent references to the unique nature of Russia" by Russian economic planners "undermine attempts to move in the direction of a market economy."[21] Åslund has repeatedly stated his belief that for Russia to extricate itself from its economic crisis, the country's "macroeconomic stabilization program should be as strict and orthodox as possible."[22] And writing in 1993 of his Russian colleagues who formulated economic policy from late 1991 onward, Åslund argued, "Being armed with appropriate theory, they are working in the Russian government and outside of it, striving to apply it to existing conditions in Russia. Thanks to the efforts of such Russian economists as Egor Gaidar, the Russian economy can develop very quickly, *in spite of its past.*"[23] In a like vein, Jeffrey Sachs insists, "The lack of experience and of a democratic tradition in Russia . . . cannot serve as an argument to justify a more cautious approach to market reforms. . . . The success of the reform depends on the stability of currency and its convertibility."[24] Throughout their tenure as economic advisers to the Russian government, these key participants in Russian reform planning consistently held to this position. And, the rapid pace of reforms that they advocated for Russia effectively precluded serious attention to noneconomic factors that shape economic relations in a country.

Gaidar accepted this point of view without reservation, although the level of "shock" that he applied was less extreme than most Western advisers had urged.[25] "We proceeded from fundamental laws of economic behavior of *homo sapiens*," Gaidar stated in a February 1994 article. "And it turned out that these laws work in Russia, with our [country's] specific character, as well as they work in Argentina, Korea, the Czech Republic, Slovakia or Australia."[26]

Below, however, we will suggest that inadequate attention to the ongoing societal forces that sustain long-standing institutional features of a country risks reproducing, in a reconstituted form, the very characteristics that reformers are trying to transcend. The Soviet bureaucracy succeeded for decades in prevailing over Gaidar's "fundamental laws of economic behavior," and its roots were deep in every facet of Russian life when the Gaidar team began their work. It was a mistake for the reformers to think that they could wish away the hold of this powerful system largely through an attack on federal-level coordination units, the introduction of macroeconomic stabilization measures, and privatization. Ministries can be abolished by decree, certainly, and ownership hurriedly transferred from state to private hands. But such "reforms" do not speak to the larger problem of how to create conditions that will sustain market relations among a citizenry steeled in very different patterns of both organization and thought.

Autocracy, Hierarchy, and Seismic Change in the Russian Tradition

The Russia inherited by Lenin's Bolsheviks had been, from the fifteenth century onward, notably autocratic in comparison with nations of Western Europe. And along with one-person rule there developed a multidimensional and extensive apparatus for central administration. There were hierarchies of state service, of riches and taxes, and of ethnicity.[27] Peter used the tsars' autocratic power and the bureaucracy they had created (which he significantly strengthened) to launch Russian industrialization according to his personal vision, and from Peter's day until 1905, Teodor Shanin observes, "all the major changes in the political structure of the tsardom of the Romanovs were to come neither from 'below' nor from the 'outside' but from its very top, and were put to work by the state officialdom."[28]

Russian history illustrates the tenacious hold that these trends can establish over time and the opportunities for alternative development paths that are often thus forgone. Russia was little affected by the social and cultural ferment that accompanied the Protestant Reformation or the political effects of the French Revolution, which reverberated throughout Western Europe. There was no conflict between church and state in Russia, where the church was officially subordinated to the state, and Russia therefore failed to benefit from the creative tension and robust civil society that this conflict helped to stimulate in Western Europe. James Billington characterizes the turn to "social thought" in Russia from the 1840s to the 1880s as "in many ways an artificially delayed . . . Russian response to the rich ferment of reformist ideas in France," but the movement it signaled, away "from the blue skies [and] into the kitchen,"[29] did not succeed in loosening the grip of Russia's oppressive bureaucracy. When revolutionary reversals finally began, and Russia was forced to submit to the erratic visions of a new class of autocrats, Russia's hierarchical tradition found even more decisive expression under Lenin and Stalin.

The Renewal of Autocracy Under Yeltsin

The August 1991 putsch brought a startling end to Bolshevik rule but no relief from top-down administration in the political sphere. Rather, the democratic reforms that had been initiated under Gorbachev, which finally lifted the Soviet legislature above its rubber-stamping function in compliance with executive power dictates, were sharply reversed. As the government's reform planners increasingly faced resistance to their economic proposals among Russia's legislators, they ultimately rejected all attempts at legislative oversight, consolidating power in the executive branch. Finally, a new legislative structure and constitution were born out of confrontation and violence, and not surprisingly, Yeltsin acquired sharply increased powers. This development resuscitated, in the Russia of 1993, key features of the Soviet-style system that had prevailed before Gorbachev's 1989 reforms—reforms that had offered the promise not only of facilitating a separation of executive and legislative power but also of promoting the development of a civil society. "State Duma" was an historically appropriate name for the new parliament's lower house. Whereas the Imperial Duma had been an advisory body to the tsar, the State Duma elected in December 1993 became a body distinctly subordinate to presidential power.

Not surprisingly, this replay of the Soviet and imperial past was manifest, not only in Russia following the demise of the Soviet Union, but throughout a large portion of the former Soviet Union (FSU). As political scientist Philip Roeder observes, "Russia's lurch away from the balanced powers of its previous constitution reflects a broader pattern of post-Soviet political evolution toward authoritarian regimes."[30] But Roeder's analysis shows that the experience of the Soviet period did not consign the republics of the FSU to authoritarianism. At the beginning of 1994, Roeder finds, three of these republics seemed "to be on paths—albeit precarious paths—toward inclusive, competitive democracies."[31] Turning away from authoritarianism in these republics, however, had required a deliberate and persistent effort to break free from institutional shackles and familiar decision-making procedures of the past—an effort that was thwarted in Russia by Yeltsin and his supporters.

New Life for an Old Bureaucracy

Yeltsin not only repeated the autocratic responses to political challenges that had been a characteristic hallmark of Bolshevik leaders and tsars who preceded him, but he followed them in enlarging bureaucratic structures to enforce his dictates. The government bureaucracy mushroomed under Yeltsin. Zhores Medvedev points out that, although the population of Russia is just over half that of the USSR, and the Council for Mutual Economic Assistance, the Warsaw Pact structures, the government of the USSR, and the organizational apparatus of the Communist Party of the Soviet Union (CPSU) have all been dissolved, very few of the people who had staffed the bureaucracy of the Soviet Union were put out of jobs. Virtually all of the administrative buildings of the CPSU and the USSR remained in the hands of Russian bureaucrats following the breakup of the Soviet Union. "The bureaucratic apparatus in Russia, in comparison with that of the USSR, did not shrink but rather grew in size—by 20 percent, according to some estimates," Medvedev states.[32] The central bureaucracy of the RSFSR/Russian Federation increased by 2.4 times from 1991 until the end of 1993.[33] Aleksandr Pochinok, vice chair of the State Duma Budget Committee, acknowledged in an April 1994 interview that, although "there are no longer any Soviet Union structures, the number of ministries and departments is about the same. But there are even more bureaucrats."[34]

Not surprisingly, most of these bureaucrats were the same people who filled similar roles in the Soviet era. Olga Kryshtanovskaia, a researcher at the Institute of Sociology in Moscow, has documented the survival of the "old Party nomenklatura" among Yeltsin's army of elites. Her research group has interviewed "almost all" living members of the highest levels of Soviet and party nomenklatura. They found that, in early 1994, 75 percent of the members of the Yeltsin presidential administration had come from the Soviet-era nomenklatura. Thirty-seven percent of these individuals had held political positions under Brezhnev, and an additional 38 percent had climbed the political ladder under Gorbachev. A large number of these members of Yeltsin's circle, then, were seasoned veterans of the Soviet-era administrative system. This body of presidential appointees had grown by 1994 to the point that it equaled the size of the government—that is, the entire executive branch outside the presidential administration. In the government (executive branch), 74 percent came from the Soviet nomenklatura, and among regional political elites 83 percent were nomenklatura members.[35]

It was to be expected, of course, that members of the nomenklatura would be well represented in any post-Soviet political configuration. These people were, after all, the most experienced and knowledgeable people in Russia about political and economic matters. But if the objective were to transform the old command system into a trimmer and more responsive one, deliberate and comprehensive measures were required to break the old organizational mold. As management analyst

John Child observes, in rigidly hierarchical systems organizational learning tends to be low, partially because of information closure, which inhibits adaptability to changed external conditions.[36] Adaptation must be planned, and restructuring must be directed toward fundamental organizational reorientation if persistent patterns are to be changed in a progressive direction.

But that was not what happened. Instead, Yeltsin's tendency was to restore within his administration the kind of hierarchical structure that had been a central feature of Communist party rule, and throughout Russia, the bureaucracy flourished. Political analyst Anatolii Kostiukov observes that, "In the process of commercialization of everything and everyone, the bureaucratic office became one of the most profitable of today's industries."[37] This development has been examined by a number of Russian analysts and political observers—and not just by Yeltsin's political foes.[38] Even Gaidar acknowledged this trend, observing in February 1994, "The bureaucracy is very quickly acquiring its 'classic' forms."[39] Gaidar continued, "Today, state bureaucrats have a very specific ideology—the ideology of cynical bureaucratic decadence." He added that these officials do not have any global aims for the state. Rather, "their aims have a very private character—to strengthen the role of the state for the sake of getting rich quickly at the state's expense. It has always been that way," he notes, "but as a *secondary* goal. Today, this goal is becoming predominant."[40]

In our interviews with Russian government officials, opinion leaders, and prominent business people, bureaucrats were repeatedly cited as being principal beneficiaries of the government's economic reform program—particularly members of the former nomenklatura. "The nomenklatura and the mafia have benefited more than anyone else from privatization," a Moscow property fund member emphasized—highlighting a linkage we were to hear again and again from the most knowledgeable people in our study. Most of the privatization officials we interviewed in all our research cities and at all levels of government made this point, as did a number of other officials and community leaders. "We have already seen, in Smolensk, the formation of mafia-nomenklatura 'clans,' " a well-known opinion leader maintained. "They will be the ones who will share all the privatized property among themselves." We will return to this theme in a later section of this chapter.

A privatization specialist in the Sverdlovsk oblast suggested, further, that many of the difficulties that were being experienced by privatizing enterprises were a result of nomenklatura resistance to restructuring that would diminish their power. "But these people are also the chief beneficiaries of privatization," he added, "along with directors and criminal groups. All except ordinary people are now taking advantage of privatization to grab state property for themselves." A Voronezh business leader was just one of many who made the same points. "Newly privatized enterprises are having problems because they have been 'captured' by racketeers and mafia members," he maintained. "All the power remains in party nomenklatura hands." There was widespread agreement among our sample of officials and other leaders that, in privatization, Russia was getting the worst of two worlds—inequitable property distribution, and ownership by people who, in a large proportion of cases, were poorly suited to their new roles.

Gaidar wants to pin the blame for these developments on the partial implementation of his monetarist-inspired reform plans,[41] but, ironically, his 1994 critique highlights an outcome to which his program importantly contributed—the consolidation of power among bureaucrats. His retrospective analysis fails to confront the inevitable consequences of a reform strategy that was, from the beginning, highly centralized—consistent with Yeltsin's overall executive approach. Rather than developing a reform program aimed at trimming bureaucratic structures, the Russian political and economic reformers chose instead to expand them, in keeping with the traditions of their Soviet and Russian past. They had a reason beyond mere habit. A monolithic bureaucracy was required, they believed, to pursue the dominating *political* objectives of their economic program—to solidify executive power that was being justified by the government's stated commitment to radical reform, and to quickly destroy what remained of the Soviet-era economic control system that had begun to unravel conspicuously as early as 1988.

"We are ready to unveil Big Privatization," Anatolii Chubais announced with the beginning of price liberalization in January 1992. "We have worked out the required tasks for privatization in regions, oblasts, Moscow and St. Petersburg."[42] The first task was to assemble the 50,000-plus government personnel who would be required to implement the program. As political scientist Lev Timofeev described this transfer of the reins of Russia's bureaucracy from one set of hands to another, "All the managerial strings for property, including the process of privatization, . . . remained in the apparatchiks' 'corporation.' "[43] And now, Timofeev wrote in May 1994, "the 'corporation of apparatchiks' remains in charge of the life and future of the country . . . and [is] using reforms in [its] corporate interest."[44] The apparatchiks "are supporting initiatives and creativity only in their own circle, only for their own people, and only within the framework of their bureaucratic organization," Timofeev insisted.[45] Analyst Yakov Gilinskii concurs, arguing, "I am confident that the current powers . . . will never voluntarily agree to real reform. They will do their best to stay in charge. They will maintain all the obstacles . . . to retain all the 'handles of power' in their own hands."[46] Political analysts Yurii Burtin and Grigorii Vodolazov characterize this reconstituted economic arrangement as one of "nomenklatura capitalism."[47] Not only did most of the players remain the same, but Gaidar's reformers were also soon replicating the decision errors that had been a hallmark of Soviet planning—mistakes that were often directly attributable to excessive centralization.

A Truncated but Hardy Hierarchical Structure

What was lost in Russian bureaucracy under Yeltsin was the firm and extensive control from the top that, during the Soviet period, coordinated all lower-level structures. The state apparatus was not systematically transformed or downsized. Rather, piecemeal procedures were undertaken to patch together vital connections that were imperiled by the sudden demise of the Politburo-headed command system. The Central Bank of Russia partly filled the shoes of *Gosbank*. Along with the elimination of *Gosplan* and *Gossnab*, the system of branch ministries was abolished as the Yeltsin-Gaidar reforms began, but a number of departments soon began to emerge that replicated the organizational form and functions of the old branch ministries in important details. And the State Property Management Committee, however, developed a rigidly centralized structure, whose directives were enforced from the federal to local levels.

But for the most part, the Yeltsin-Gaidar attack on the Soviet command system left lower-level hierarchical structures—the regional and local bureaucracies—solidly in place and fully functioning. The reformers mistakenly believed that they were breaking with the familiar Soviet order through their focused assault on federal-level control and coordination mechanisms. This control system was already beleaguered in 1990, and it was further undermined by Yeltsin and other politicians who were fanning separatist sentiments at the republic level in 1991. Then it was partially decapitated in accordance with the government's economic program under Gaidar's leadership. As David

Lipton and Sachs approvingly summarized these developments in 1992, "Within a short period of eight months, almost all centralized operations of the command economy ceased."[48]

In their 1992 report, Lipton and Sachs suggested encouragingly that, in the wake of the dissolution of the command economy's centralized operations, "new commercial structures are developing rapidly," and "spontaneous market activity is evident."[49] Gaidar's assessment of early 1992 trends is similar. "In the first months of 1992, a serious step was taken," he states. "Especially important was a methodologically new advance in Russia's history. The state did not spur people as it had in the past, but rather slackened the reins. And the invisible hand of the market began pulling the wagon out of the mud."[50]

"The ideology of the reform that we started in 1991," Gaidar wrote later, was "to raise the country, not through strengthening the muscles of the state, but just the opposite—by weakening the state bridle, reducing the power of state structures. *The withdrawal of the state must open up space for organic development of the economy.*"[51] Predictably, what Gaidar's strategy actually opened up was space for regional and local bureaucracies to consolidate power below the federal level, space for further disintegration of the economy, and, as we will indicate below, space for the "organic development" of organized crime.

Historian German Diligenskii describes this process pointedly.[52] "The political situation that appeared in Russia after the disbanding of the Soviet Union led to a strengthening of the role of the apparatus in the system of power," he observes. "Bureaucrats at all levels now feel themselves increasingly independent from any kind of supervision. The Communist Party, which had been the authority to which members of the apparatus were accountable, finally left the stage. As a result of the conflict between the highest executive and legislative powers, . . . the apparatus received an unprecedented 'free hand'—the possibility of acting according to their own will."[53]

Aleksei Demichev was a regional Communist party boss until the August 1991 coup. Disillusioned, he left his position to become the general director of a joint stock agricultural company. In an April 1994 article, Demichev argued, "We need laws to regulate relations between production and bureaucrats in the state apparatus—bureaucrats who were never before so numerous and powerful. . . . Those former 'administrative command' bureaucrats we are cursing at now were better than today's 'democratic' ones."[54]

In October 1993 Yeltsin, after having thrown off legislative-branch checks on executive power at the federal level, furthered the reconstruction of the Soviet-style system of executive authority at the regional and local levels as well. First, he called on the soviets (elected legislative bodies) at all levels to cease their activities voluntarily, blaming them for the slowdowns of executive initiative that inevitably result from a separation of executive and legislative powers—"dual power," in his words. A series of decrees followed, granting regional and local executives the authority to develop procedures for elections to new representative bodies at their levels. These representative organizations, however, would have substantially reduced powers. Thus, Yeltsin reinstituted the Bolshevik system of giving executive officials control over elected bodies of "people's representatives." High-ranking regional executives were made accountable directly to Yeltsin.

In light of these developments, Gavriil Popov, former Moscow mayor and chair of the Russian Movement for Democratic Reform, wrote in May 1994, "Everything we see now, we remember from our past. It was a fundamental feature of the Soviet system to merge, to fuse together, executive power and representative power. . . . Before our eyes is now appearing the prospect of a regime in which bureaucrats, without the help of the CPSU and without a 'front' of Communist slogans, will hold all the power."[55]

In sum, the complex system of bureaucratic authoritarianism created by the Communists was transformed under Yeltsin, beginning in 1991, into a new variant that lacked the controlling influence and accountability requirements of recent Communist leadership in the Soviet Union.[56] A number of players participated in this development. Yeltsin had repeatedly demonstrated his preference for authoritarian control, and Western leaders supported him in those tendencies—perhaps thinking that a Yeltsin ensconced in Russia's presidency would be in the West's near-term interest, while ignoring the enormous danger to both Russia and the world of a reinvigorated system of nomenklatura control freed from the constraints of Communist party domination—even one professing democracy and scrambling to take advantage of opportunities for private ownership. Such a development, in a country largely unschooled in democratic governance, not only ensures that equity concerns will have no firm standing and that a reform program will be likely to work against national economic improvement, but also discredits both the prevailing power structure and the idea of democracy among a large number of citizens, while raising troubling questions about future foreign policy directions of a government largely driven by opportunism. The economists, also, who believed that their theories could be applied without thoughtful reference to Russia's existing institutional arrangements and cultural traditions, share major responsibility for the creation of an economic reform program that facilitated the resurgence of bureaucratic authoritarianism in post-Gorbachev Russia.

From State Planning and Corruption to an Explosion of Organized Crime

A study of crime in Russia that was prepared under the direction of Yeltsin aide Petr Filippov and released in early 1994 concluded that at least 70 percent of privatized enterprises and commercial banks had some type of connections with organized crime. The study found that, unlike Western Europe and the United States, where the activities of organized crime are generally restricted to certain types of products and services, "In Russia, organized crime controls all kinds of activity."[57] A report of the Ministry of Internal Affairs to the Russian parliament in May 1994, noting that thousands of joint stock companies and hundreds of banks were under the control of organized crime, concluded that entrepreneurship in Russia had become a haven for criminal operations.[58]

Viktor Iliukhin, the chair of the State Duma Security Committee, examined the political as well as the economic dimensions of this problem in a May 1994 report. In the economic sphere, Iliukhin stated (citing a Russian Academy of Sciences study), "55 percent of capital and 80 percent of voting shares [of enterprises] are in criminal hands, Russian and foreign." (Iliukhin's reference to foreign criminal investment highlights a trend in which foreign money is increasingly being "laundered" through Russian businesses.) "Crime has become a national disaster in Russia," Iliukhin continued. "It is also politicized, and aims to seize leading positions of power. Today, crime groups influence executive decision making at all levels, and they are trying to influence the legislative process as well."[59]

And in a May 1994 U.S. Senate committee hearing, Louis Freeh, director of the Federal Bureau of Investigation, broadened this sketch, noting that Russian organized crime was by that time involved with international crime groups in drug trafficking, had been found to be involved in illegal activity in the United States in cooperation with La Cosa Nostra, and, it was feared, might at some future time participate in the arming of terrorist groups with nuclear weapons or weapons-grade nuclear materials.[60]

Stephen Handelman, a visiting scholar at Columbia University's Harriman Institute, notes that "the mixture of unbridled capitalism, organized crime and official chicanery has produced a crisis of governance" in Russia.[61] Handelman recognizes that "Russian policymakers committed a fundamental mistake" in trying "to develop a free market before constructing a civil society in which such a market could safely operate."[62] Yet he is unwilling to directly confront the implications of this planning error and instead dilutes the plain message of his observation by stating that "A reversal or slowdown of reforms is the goal of the former Soviet establishment"—thus shifting his focus away from the obvious fact that the rapid pace of reforms is heavily implicated in the problem he is highlighting. Handelman appropriately traces important historical roots of organized crime in Russia today to the behavior of Communist authorities in the Soviet period. But corruption in the Soviet command system was just one of the features of Russian society that Gaidar's Western advisers urged the government to largely ignore in formulating their proposals, in favor of a transition scheme that neglected Russian structural and cultural realities.[63]

The inevitable difficulties that would attend Russia's move toward a market economy in the context of a corruption-riddled bureaucratic control system were well recognized long before the Gaidar reforms began. Thoughtful Russian analysts had repeatedly emphasized the necessity of providing for mechanisms to work against the spread of corruption and crime in the transition. The Shatalin-Yavlinskii 500 Days proposal, for example, devoted explicit attention to "the criminal economy," and after observing that it was "built into the official economy" as well as involving "clandestine economic activity," the program proposed explicit actions to face the problem head-on as reforms were pursued.[64] Similarly, the Allison-Yavlinskii "Program for an Organized Return to the World Economy" (Window of Opportunity) called for systematic but urgent institution building that would provide the legal and societal foundations necessary for "a normal market economy."[65] But Gaidar's approach was largely to ignore this tangled web and even to clear a path for criminal involvement in reforms, as we noted in chapter two.

Mark Masarskii, a prominent Moscow business leader, describes the predictable result of this approach among state bureaucrats. Today, he argues, "bureaucrats are preoccupied with the idea of exchanging power for property," adding that until the state "stops behaving criminally in the business sphere, the whole of Russia's economy will remain criminal."[66] It was in that light that Vasilii Lipitskii, then chair of the executive committee of the Civic Union, observed in 1993 that "there were real alternatives which could have produced better results and reduced the possibilities for abuse. . . . Perhaps the opportunity for abuse [afforded by the Gaidar program] *caused them* not to select another alternative," Lipitskii added.[67]

Vladimir Ovchinskii, a lawyer and analyst for the Ministry of Internal Affairs, summarizes the consequences of the Gaidar team's approach. As the strict system of state control disappeared, he suggests, "the system fell apart, and criminal authoritarian structures filled the vacuum.[68] . . . We are on the brink, after which we may become a criminal state. The situation is critical, because the leadership in the economy is virtually in the hands of organized crime."[69] And Nikolai Petrakov, one of Russia's most prominent economists, insists, "We have not created a market. Instead, a monopoly criminal economy emerged from our totalitarian one. The 'new rich' appeared—as I identify them, 'the capitalists of Gaidar's conscription'—people who do not need a civilized market at all. They don't want competition, . . . and they love weak [political] power."[70] Consistent with this perspective, among our general population sample an overwhelming 82 percent thought that mafia and crime groups were benefiting substantially from the privatization program. (Table B–7.5; Appendix B).

In our interviews with Russian government officials and other leaders, we found that the distinction between legal elites (nomenklatura) and criminal elites was widely becoming blurred, as was differentiation between "legal" and "illegal" business activities.[71] "There are hardly any honest people in business today," a privatization specialist told us. A nationally prominent policy maker emphasized, "Industrialists and mafia groups are connected now. Honest people have been pushed out of business just as democrats have been pushed out of politics." And an okrug soviet deputy in Moscow said, "Everything is in the hands of corrupt bureaucrats and the mafia." The chair of the board of directors of a large Moscow bank told us that the chief obstacles to effective privatization were "ineffectiveness of the legal system and corruption." "What groups are benefiting the most from privatization?" we asked. His reply was unhesitating and, by the time of that midsummer 1993 interview, one that we had come to expect: "The mafia and 'shadow' groups." Such perspectives were not the exception but rather were predominant among the officials and business and opinion leaders we interviewed. As a Smolensk privatization official put it, "New ownership arrangements are springing up everywhere, interlaced with criminal structures."

The Socialist Culture of Work and Transition to the Market

The tendency of rigidly hierarchical systems to inhibit organizational learning within administrative bureaucracies has a counterpart in socialist work organizations, where, as Hungarian economist János Kornai observes, the paternalistic relations that exist between the enterprise and the state reinforce values of solidarity and security, the priority of collective interests over individual interests, and the distribution of income according to work.[72] Sociologist Tat'iana Zaslavskaia writes of the same phenomenon in Russia, but with a harder edge: "Long years of a passive alienated existence have undoubtedly left their mark not only on the present behavior of people as regards the economy but also on their habits and values—in other words on their social quality as workers. Once they had become accustomed to an irresponsible attitude to their jobs, workers gradually lost all their professionalism and habits of intensive, purposeful work and became used to being idle and showing no initiative. Alienation and indifference, irresponsibility and sluggishness, scepticism and cynicism became the norms of social conduct and were accepted as received standards of behavior."[73]

Survey research data collected by the Russian Center for Public Opinion Research (VTsIOM) supports the main directions of Zaslavskaia's indictment. VTsIOM analyst Zoia V. Kupriianova summarizes the results of an August 1993 study of the work force in Russia, stating that the general pattern she found reflects a "passive orientation toward success" in which hard work and honesty are not highly valued and work motivation is low and seems to be declining.[74] And a study by Liudmila Khakhulina and Aleksandr Golov, which compared data sets collected by VTsIOM in 1989 and 1993, found that most 1989 respondents did not expect hard work to generate success, and that this expectation had declined further by 1993.[75] The surest route to success, most people believed, was through special connections or questionable behavior. In the study, responses of individuals who had experienced substantial recent improvement in their material well-being were separated from the overall sample for part of the analysis, and indeed the most prevalent avenues for success, among these self-reports, were consistent with prevailing public stereotypes.[76] Similarly, a comparative study carried out at the University of Michigan with data from 1991 and 1993 found that, whereas 67 percent of United States respondents believed that hard work leads to economic improvement, only 21 percent of Russians had that opinion.[77]

"A mass psychology of people as robots has been created" through seven decades of totalitarian administration, economist Yurii Shishkov argues. These people "are ready to do what they have been ordered to do, but they have not been able to think independently, to make decisions, or to take the risk of responsibility. . . . Most people in the society have forgotten how to think and act independently, and they can neither harness the winds of competition nor endure a continuing struggle to improve their well-being—preferring instead a meager but dependable existence on the rolls of the state."[78]

Our four-city research has repeatedly provided evidence consistent with Zaslavskaia's and Shishkov's assessments—even outside the state enterprise system. Respondents we have interviewed who manage joint ventures, joint stock companies, foreign firms, and private Russian businesses, as well as directors in state enterprises, have often echoed the complaint of Yakov Vartanian, the managing director of a Moscow joint venture. After describing a chronic accounting problem in his company, Vartanian continued, "Accounting is a minor frustration, though, compared to managing the work force in our production facilities. Our workers can't make decisions on their own. It's the result of more than seven decades of 'Don't do this. . . .' "[79]

The persistence of such patterns does not create a societal straitjacket that would prevent the development of a market economy, certainly, and the general characteristics of a country do not describe traits of its exceptional members. Further, to even identify a coherent set of closely held general features of a society is no simple matter. Anthropologist Victor Turner states the problem well in noting that "the culture of any society at any moment is more like the debris, or 'fall-out,' of past ideological systems, than it is itself a system, a coherent whole."[80] Yet national experiences and organizational arrangements clearly do result in a number of orientations and behavior patterns that characterize substantial proportions of a country's population, and if a reform program is to secure the level of public support necessary for its survival, it must appeal to the values and strengths of more than a small fraction of unusual individuals. In matters of politically viable economic reforms, which must satisfy diverse constituencies in a reasonably short time period, "a little leaven" does not go far. Rather, it is likely to give unrealistic encouragement to policy dead-ends. Even if the organizational linkages of command economic systems could be severed quickly or recast, the behavior patterns, values, and norms that were adaptive under the former economic conditions would not thereby be automatically realigned to fit the changed environment. It is a long way, culturally, from the kinds of paternalistic relations Kornai identifies to societal arrangements that effectively nourish the values of competitiveness, risk-taking, and entrepreneurship that are basic to capitalist economic organization.[81]

And having a *desire* to adapt to new economic arrangements, as was clearly the situation among a large proportion of the Russian population at the end of 1991, does not provide the tools or means for shaking free from patterns in which most citizens have long been immersed. Policy-oriented economists who ignore this fundamental fact can expect to see their reform plans quickly founder on shoals that have already been definitively mapped by a number of researchers. "The problem lies not in assuming that human actors are rational, in some reasonable sense of that word," Farmer and Matthews point out, "but in the assumption that all rational actors are the same."[82] Important reasons that they are not can be found in the divergent structural arrangements and historically shaped behavior patterns that characterize the accustomed ways of life in different cultures.[83] We know too much about the workings of culture for Gaidar's narrowly directed faith in the "fundamental laws of economic behavior of *homo sapiens*"[84] to be the guiding principle for radical economic reform. Gaidar and his advisers did not understand, or were unwilling to acknowledge, that principles gleaned from economic behavior in relatively stable systems of the West were an inadequate guide for confronting the vastly different processes that are called into play, and considerations that must be taken into account, when the task is radical economic change in Russia.

Economic Transformation in Theory and Practice

We are not concerned here with the normative question of how far an authoritarian state should ultimately go in divesting itself of control over the economic sphere of a society, but rather with the practical subject of what it must do, along the way, to ensure that its divestment goals are not derailed because of a failure to lay the necessary tracks, after adequately preparing the roadbed, so that the journey may be successfully completed. The two considerations are logically and empirically separable, and we have attempted to keep them unentangled in assessing the Russian government's economic change initiatives.

How can the state best facilitate adaptation from a command economy to a market environment? This must be the central question of reform planning in a context such as the Russia of late 1991. Gaidar's approach, as we have shown, was to favor swift elimination of state control over a broad spectrum of economic relations, in keeping with "Chicago school" dictates. He followed Milton Friedman scrupulously in decrying gradual economic transformation in cases such as the one Russia presented in 1991.[85] Friedman hopes for a world characterized by "voluntary co-operation among individuals in which each man is free to use his own capacities and resources as he wills in accordance with his own values so long as he does not interfere with the right of others to do likewise."[86] But he is unwilling to recognize that purpose and planning are required for reformers to move inadequate and inefficient economic systems toward that goal—that monetarism does not itself furnish a useful blueprint for pursuing radical societal change. Unwilling to shed a narrow view of social relations that is thoroughly dominated by economic considerations even under conditions of massive societal restructuring, Western approach proponents tend to simply assume, along with Friedman, that the state of nature to which humans and their organizations will quickly revert when released from the fetters of authoritarian state domination will predictably be consistent with the neoclassical ideal.

Columbia University economist and Harriman Institute director Richard Ericson acknowledges more pointedly than several Chicago school proponents that a country's economy cannot be entirely restructured without grave implications for its larger system of values, customs, and institutional arrangements. Unwilling to dilute the monetarists' prescription for swift change, no matter what the cost, he argues, "Only the wholesale complete replacement [of these features] opens room for an alternative, market-based system to begin to function. Thus, the primary implication for reform arising out of the nature of the traditional economic system is that *any reform must be disrup-*

tive on a historically unprecedented scale. An entire world must be discarded, including all of its economic and most of its social and political institutions, and concluding with its physical structure of production, capital, and technology."[87]

On the positive side, Ericson at least acknowledges that the kind of rapid transformation that Western advisers urged for Russia would have momentous and sinister consequences for the country's social institutions, its production system, and its technological position in the world. On the other hand, Ericson's proposal to purposefully discard "an entire world" is a millenarian idea that has never led to the kind of result he hopes for. When, in 1992, the societally disruptive forces of the Gaidar program were unleashed in Russia, along with "echo" price reforms in most other CIS republics, Ericson identified some of their first effects: a high inflation rate, the severing of trade relations, an "ongoing collapse of production," "regional semi-autarchy," and a weak ("but hearty") nonstate sector.[88] These outcomes had a practical dimension, in his view. "Growing disruption has, at least to a point, a positive role to play," he argues, adding, "indeed, for systemic transition it is probably good that the prospects for an early recovery are poor. There is much that must be destroyed in the physical structure of capital, production, and interaction before market oriented activity becomes viable and self-sustaining. . . . A Schumpeterian 'whirlwind of creative destruction' is necessary."[89]

Ericson's appeal to Schumpeter is misplaced. The "creative destruction" that for Schumpeter is "the essential fact about capitalism" bears no relationship to the assault that was waged on Russia's societal institutions beginning in 1991 in the name of economic reform. The process that persistently "revolutionizes the economic structure," was, for Schumpeter, one that, "*from within* incessantly destroy[s] the old one, incessantly creat[es] a new one."[90] Nothing in Schumpeter's writing reflects a taste for the kind of willful *political* destruction of major societal institutions in pursuit of a theoretical idea that is central to Ericson's perspective. "The essential point to grasp," Schumpeter emphasizes, "is that in dealing with capitalism *we are dealing with an evolutionary process*."[91] And Schumpeter's discussion of economic "transitions"—from capitalism to socialism, for example—in no way resembles the "creative destruction" idea highlighted by Ericson.

Ericson believes that, under the circumstances of massive societal dislocation that he wants to see develop, markets would somehow "naturally arise in response to the needs of economically autonomous actors."[92] But the historical record tells us that what is likely to naturally arise first, under such circumstances, is a stage ready-made for demagogues who can effectively play to audiences that have been primed for authoritarianism because of economic turmoil and widespread societal dislocations. Of course, markets will also eventually arise—a point we will return to in chapter seven. The question for reformers, however, is more complex, and must inevitably confront the issue of political and societal implications of reform strategies.

Kornai's perspective about the necessary path to "a free economy" differs sharply from that of Chicago school proponents—and is notably more consistent with our knowledge about the prerequisites for effective change in the real world. In writing about privatization, Kornai maintains that the state "apparatus is obliged to handle the wealth it was entrusted with carefully until a new owner appears who can guarantee a safer and more efficient guardianship. The point now is not to hand out the property, but rather to place it into the hands of a really better owner. A precondition to this is that genuine private entrepreneurial motivation should gain ground and take hold."[93] Sociologists Robert Hamblin et al., state this principle in broader strokes: "When mastering new tasks, organizations and collectivities gradually acquire expertise that is fundamental to social adaptation."[94]

Consistent with this reasoning, John Friedmann identifies three major forms of planning, which correspond in general to three different states of political systems. Allocative planning is oriented toward system maintenance. Innovative planning is directed toward evolutionary change. Radical planning aims for structural transformation.[95] But radical planning—the variant that the Gaidar team wanted and needed to carry out in Russia—does not connote single-minded pursuit of an ideological vision that is blind to surrounding social forces. Rather, its "radical" nature derives, Friedmann emphasizes, from the scope and ambition of the aim to set aside and replace "the existing structures of domination and dependence."[96]

Åslund responds to Kornai's position by arguing, "Our assessment is that state management is in far more precarious shape; the financial proceeds are less important than macroeconomic performance; our requirement of a critical mass of private enterprises casts doubt on the possibility of breeding good entrepreneurs before privatisation. Strong owners are desired, but is it realistic to believe that they will surface in

a relatively distorted market?"[97] But if state management was inadequate, the management of privatized enterprises in Russia at the conclusion of voucher privatization was, overall, no better and was
arguably worse. (We will return to this point in chapter five.) Further,
macroeconomic stabilization was not achievable according to the program undertaken by the Gaidar team, with the political and structural
realities that it neglected. And Åslund's fear that good owners would
not surface if they were sought deliberately could certainly not be
quelled by the hasty ownership transfer program that he favored. In
sum, then, the Russian experience during the period of interest in this
book provides substantial support for Kornai's perspective.

The "Western Approach" in Two Phases

Only three years before Ericson began advocating a massive demoli-
tion strategy for Russia's social institutions and production system, his
assessment of the potential for less extreme approaches to reform had
been strikingly more positive. In 1988 he had suggested, in a RAND
Corporation report, that "changes and reforms (perestroika) under
Gorbachev" might have a chance to "change the nature of the system"
in which the military dominated the country's "priority-driven command economy." He had not considered that likely "to happen in the
near future, if only because of 'brakes' on reforms (e.g., state orders
[goszakazy] and ceilings [limity]) in place for the transition period."[98]
But at that time he had identified no insurmountable barriers to constructive, market-oriented change in the Soviet economy. Similarly, in
a 1989 article that appeared in the Journal of International Affairs,
Ericson had urged that the Soviet economic reform initiative "must
become much more radical in conception ... in order to provide a
consistent framework" for entrepreneurship and economic improvement.[99] But he had concluded that, although economic transformation (ekonomicheskaia perestroika) was a risky undertaking, "As
Gorbachev and his associates have argued, the most effective Soviet
foreign and security policy consists of a program of domestic renewal
and economic reform."[100]

Ericson had made no mention, in these analyses in the late 1980s, of
his conviction in 1991 that "an entire world must be discarded." That
was clearly not Gorbachev's ekonomicheskaia perestroika plan, which
Ericson had highlighted approvingly in 1989. And as recently as 1990,

Ericson was maintaining that "Nobody, in East or West" knew how to undertake reform of the Soviet economy. "There is no experience, there is not even a theory," he had acknowledged, "of the successful transition from a command economy to a market economy."[101] But a year later, he not only had a theory, but he had also acquired such confidence in his newfound perspective that he was willing to advocate discarding most of Russia's social institutions and structures of production and technology in pursuit of it.

Yet in 1991, before the Western approach caught hold among Russia's policy makers, Ericson was attempting to put the most favorable possible face on his call for cataclysmic disruption in every sphere of Russian society, suggesting, "[although] a period of serious economic deterioration seems inevitable, . . . it might be cushioned by aid from the West."[102] And, he was insisting, although "the ultimate configuration of institutions and interactions is unknowable" in the wake of the reform-induced societal chaos he envisioned, the preferred orientation at the edge of the abyss "is to abandon the Faustian urge to control, to know in advance, and thus to allow economic outcomes to arise naturally as the unpredictable consequences of market interaction."[103]

A year later, however, Ericson's prognosis was both firmer and more grim. Now, he was predicting that a likely consequence of the Gaidar reforms would be "the formation of a set of semi-autarkic regional economies." This development "would undoubtedly involve the economic breakup of Russia," he continued. Then he described an "optimistic" scenario in which Russia might recover to its 1987–88 level of output by the year 2002, but adds, *It may be too optimistic to assume that the federation will hold together peacefully, even in the more optimistic scenarios.*"[104] His conclusion? Russia could disintegrate "into a stagnant, quarrelsome economic morass." This outcome is what "Western policy must seek to avert through deep interaction, not thoughtless money, *even if the former proves to be an impossible dream*," Ericson now maintained.[105] With this "impossible dream" ending, he plainly clarifies the political significance of his economic solution for Russia. A very possible outcome of reforms in a neoliberal mode, he suggests, was not the creation of a market society in Russia at all, but rather the dissolution of Russia itself.

The turning point from upbeat to pessimistic forecasts among foreign advocates of the Western approach seems to have come in the aftermath of Gaidar's appointment to direct Russian economic reforms. Åslund had applauded Gaidar's monetarist perspective in June 1991,[106] and in Gaidar, Yeltsin adviser and future state secretary Gennadii Burbulis found an economic planner who was willing to push the "Russia first" political stance that was the defining characteristic among the so-called Young Turks being assembled for Yeltsin's team.[107] Thus the "crusading phase" for neoliberal monetarism had ended in victory—thanks largely to the country's reflexlike revulsion, following the August putsch, against the already weakened Soviet command system.

Whereas in June 1991, Åslund was hoping that his version of radical economic change could somehow be initiated by coopting, persuading, or defeating (in his words) the Soviet policy apparatus and military,[108] with the ill-conceived putsch the Soviet apparatus and military had unexpectedly defeated themselves. Back in June, Åslund had made several negative remarks about Gorbachev and had suggested that "he could stay on only as President with limited powers . . . and for a short period," but Aslund quite obviously had no clear notion of how a transition might be realized to a political situation that would be more to his liking.[109] And in the wake of the failed coup, Gorbachev had hurt his own cause as the country's center of gravity. Whereas Åslund was worrying in June that "the government is stuck in populism" and needed "a source of legitimacy to overcome this tendency,"[110] Yeltsin's defiance of the putsch perpetrators gave him a virtual carte blanche to spearhead radical change.

With Gaidar at the helm of economic planning, price liberalization was quickly launched in January 1992, accompanied by a hastily devised program to initiate widespread privatization. And after overnight price liberalization had become an historical fact and the economy was in freefall, and with massive privatization underway shortly afterward, proponents of the Western approach lost little time in modifying their earlier ideas about the larger implications of their reform strategy for Russia.

Back in 1991, while still in search of a reform torchbearer among the Soviet leadership, Åslund, for example, had recognized that the measures he advocated would entail "huge social costs," but he had added, "It is an open question how large these costs will be."[111] Tempering the severity of this prediction, he had noted that the Polish and Czechoslovak citizenry "accepted the consequences [the 'shock'] with surprising calm," and emphasized, "Poland offers an illuminating example of *how fast the necessary transition can be.*"[112]

A rapid journey from the hardships of the reform period to the benefits attending the economy was the scenario Åslund had consistently promoted during 1991's "crusading phase" for the Western approach. "The main issue is to cross the rousing river as fast as possible in order to reach the other shore and establish a firm foundation for the construction of a new market economic system," he stressed in a January 1991 paper, drafts of which were presented at two Russian institutes. "Hence, speed and scale are far more important than, for instance, revenues from privatization," he urged at that time.[113] And Lipton and Sachs, in their classic 1990 *Brookings Papers* article on shock therapy in Poland, argued, "A *rapid* transition to a market economy ... will permit the Eastern European economies to overcome some of the thorniest problems of transition."[114] But in mid-1992, with Russia's economy now reeling from Gaidar's January 1992 shock, the notion of a rapid transformation, which Åslund and Sachs had so pointedly advertised only a few months earlier, seemed to have been forgotten. Now Åslund was predicting that "economics in Russia will need a complete change of generations, if market-oriented economics is to take over."[115] At the same time, he took comfort in observing, "There is little doubt that [Russia's] high inflation will sweep away most of the command economy institutions," and said that "the failure of stabilization" can thus "hardly stop the liberalization"[116]— presumably for the benefit of future generations, if all should go well. But, Åslund now conceded, "a long period of restructuring is necessary."[117] And Åslund's "rousing river" of transition had become, in 1992, decidedly more tumultuous. "Russia today is to be compared with Weimar Germany in 1922," Åslund warned. "There are frightening parallels."[118] Sachs's prognosis in the Polish case was also somber by 1992. "Several years must pass before the fruits of reform are widely evident," Sachs was now saying. "The intervening period has been called 'a valley of tears.' " As consolation, he asserted, "The time in the valley depends on the consistency and boldness of the reforms," and added, "If there is wavering or inconsistency in economic measures, it is easy to get lost in the valley."[119]

What gains could Russia realize if the hazards Åslund underscored were successfully navigated, and if Sachs's "valley of tears" were crossed in a timely manner? "If Russia becomes really successful," Åslund was suggesting by 1992, "it might come to resemble the United States near the end of the 19th century."[120] But Russia could not be confident, from Åslund's 1992 vantage point, of actually being able to achieve this sharply scaled-down vision of a "radiant future." "It would be wrong," Åslund stated, "to imply that Russia's relations with the outside world would follow a predictable course if only it undertook a proper change of economic system," because financing "is far from predictable. . . . Financial flows are by no means given, and they can be very small or palpable."[121] In the same vein, Sachs continued to warn of a Russian calamity without "large-scale Western assistance"— assistance that ultimately was not offered at the level that had been expected during this critical phase of reforms.[122]

In this second, "settling-in" phase of Russian reforms, then, Western approach proponents began preparing the ground for a possibly disastrous ending to Russian reform, culminating in a Weimar Germany–like devolution or even the demise of the Russian state. The Russian federation "is not sustainable as a state," Jessica Eve Stern suggested in a 1994 article.[123] She discussed a series of explanations for the "centrifugal forces" that she saw as prevalent in Russia. Economic regionalism was a key factor—a process that had been strengthened "by the extreme divergence in the effects of the market reforms implemented beginning in 1992 on wages and prices in different parts of Russia."[124] Further, Stern argued, the rapid pace of change in Russia, combined with "incessant fighting among branches of power," had produced a "cohesiveness vacuum," and "little is left to hold the country together."[125] For Stern, Russia's chaotic economic and political situation offered a singular opportunity for the United States to press for "projects that affect the West's vital interests," such as cementing the fragmentation of former USSR republics, realizing the "destruction of chemical weapons" and securing the deactivation of weapons "located in politically volatile regions."[126] Yes, the West should provide economic assistance, Stern insisted, "but assistance should be made conditional on behavior that the West finds acceptable."[127] Thus Russia's economic and societal distress, and even the country's "inevitable" dissolution, can be turned to the West's advantage, she believed.

A number of other analysts have also suggested that the Russian center might not hold. In a January 1993 article, for example, political scientist Peter Reddaway argued that "Russia is on the brink of coming apart,"[128] and in September 1993, C. Fred Bergsten, director of the Institute for International Economics, speculated that "over the next century or so" the world might see a major global reconfiguration, including a "Northeastasia" economic unit "encompassing parts of *for-*

mer Russia and China, but centered on unified Korea."[129] This development, Bergsten suggested, could result from the former Soviet Union's recent status as a "drop-out from the higher-income club."[130] When Lynn Nelson spoke to Bergsten about the basis for his "world without Russia" scenario, he responded that he had "just thought it up." Some other Washington, D.C.–based economic and defense analysts we spoke with during the first half of 1994, however, had developed similar ideas. The president of one institute devoted to the study of strategic questions told Nelson, for example, that the Bergsten scenario "is completely consistent with our thinking, too."[131]

The onset of these Western prophecies of worsening economic, political, and social conditions in Russia cannot be attributed to an unanticipated and unwanted demise of the Soviet Union, for as we noted in chapter one, the Gaidar reformers *sought* this outcome. Western advisers also supported this policy direction, and to our knowledge, no advocate of the Western approach has spoken against it.

But Åslund and Sachs have ready answers to the question of why Russia had fallen so precipitously from commanding the center of the USSR's superpower position to having arrived, only a short time later, at the brink of national ruin. "The problems are not so much caused by swift change as by the tardiness of the transition," Åslund believes.[132] "The insufficient price liberalization contributed to the survival of the actual command economic functioning for several months."[133] For Åslund, the political requirements of constituency building and the negative social and structural consequences of an almost instant turn to Western approach policies should be ignored for the sake of "strict and orthodox" application of his macroeconomic stabilization ideas. And Sachs, after noting in April 1994 that "Russia is in such a deep state of crisis that its new democracy and social stability are at risk," concluded, "To overcome these risks, the Russian Government should embark on a policy of rapid stabilization."[134]

A principal theme of this work is that the priorities of Western approach proponents were misplaced during the period under study here. A more harmful failing than "insufficient price liberalization" was inadequate *planning* for liberalization—and for privatization. The "deep state of crisis" to which Sachs refers, and the inability of Gaidar to "stay the course" with a reform program that ignored critical political, structural, and cultural factors that were integral to the reform process, should have come as no surprise.

Some analysts, such as Reddaway, contemplate Russian disintegration with alarm and apprehension. But others reveal, through their projections, a great deal about the lengths to which they would have Russia go in pursuit of the neoliberal policy direction they have advocated. We believe that Russia's strengths tend to be underestimated in these analyses. We do not anticipate a breakup of the Russian federation—a subject that is outside the focus of this book. What we do expect is heightened nationalism and growing distrust within Russia toward those in the West who would knowingly see a nation dismembered in the pursuit of a controversial economic vision.

4

Contrasting Economic Priorities in Russian Reform

*That which remains unacknowledged [in economics], as I have
tried to make clear, is the substratum of beliefs that causes us to
structure our perceptions in terms of an "economy" rather than a
sociopolitical order.*

—Robert Heilbroner, *Behind the Veil of Economics*[1]

*What kind of market liberalism is it, which destroys the agents of
the market?*

—Mark Masarskii, "Ia skorbliu po pogibshim predpriiatiiam"
(I Am Grieving Over Lost Enterprises)[2]

"Strengthening the ruble became the main priority of the first stage of
reform, by firmly applying the brake of financial stabilization," Gaidar
wrote in August 1992.[3] The Gaidar reform program, by accepting the
promise of eventual gain through strict macroeconomic stabilization
policies, developed a strategy that leaders of Western governments
consistently avoid. Gaidar chose to advocate stringent monetary policies, under conditions of acute economic crisis, that were aimed at
achieving long-run goals with an unknown time line. And the efficacy
of this transitional strategy for a country whose economy and production system had been distorted by decades of central planning was also
unknown. Monetarist theory was of uncertain utility for effectively
confronting a situation in which markets did not, for the most part,
exist. John Maynard Keynes highlights the practical danger of such an

approach: "*In the long run* we are all dead." Keynes continues, challenging economic planners to shed the comfortable confines of pure theory, "Economists set themselves too easy, too useless a task if in tempestuous seasons they can only tell us that when the storm is long past the ocean is flat again."[4]

In August 1992, Gaidar attempted to distance himself theoretically from the Chicago school following accusations that he had succumbed to Western influences that were working against Russian national interests.[5] "Russia never had a policy of shock therapy," he insisted later.[6] "We could not. We were not able to simultaneously, immediately, correct all the serious structural macroeconomic and financial imbalances. . . . We never attempted to stabilize the exchange rate, because we lacked the necessary currency reserves." Our reform, he repeated, "can never be put into the traditional scheme of 'shock therapy.'"[7] Jeffrey Sachs, also, was insisting in 1994 that "'shock therapy' did not fail in Russia. It was never tried."[8]

This argument is a red herring. *Shock therapy was not "tried" in the same way that communism was not "tried."* They were not "tried" only in the sense that Russian realities in both 1917 and 1991 were badly out of line with the theoretical assumptions that inspired the Marxist agenda for a communist society, on the one hand, and the Yeltsin reformers' program for radical transition, on the other. In sharp contrast to Sachs's retrospective 1994 interpretation, in 1992 he was crediting Russia with having "embarked with remarkable dispatch on a program of radical economic reforms" that had already "created an enormous opening" for market relations.[9] Similarly, Anders Åslund was applauding Russia's reformers at that time for having "launched its daring transition" with the immediate tasks of liberalization and macroeconomic stabilization. "The focal point" of the stabilization effort, Åslund continued, "was to *balance the budget* in the first quarter of 1992." And, he added, "Their very impressive attempt succeeded amazingly well."[10] Shock therapy was indeed being tried by Russia's reformers in early 1992, and the unqualified praise from recognized shock therapy proponents in the West attests to that plain fact—one that was later explicitly acknowledged by Åslund himself.[11]

Later, Sachs would attempt to account for the failure of shock therapy by directing substantial blame toward the West for failing to provide needed foreign aid, as we noted in chapter one. Observing that the Russian government "surely faced daunting issues, with little experience," Sachs adds, "The West could have usefully pushed towards solutions together with financing." But, he continues, "There was not a single Western loan in support of the Russian budget in the first six months of 1992, and in practice almost no such loans during the first 18 months of reform." Thus, he concludes, "The Russian stabilization efforts were gravely weakened following May 1992, through a combination of lost resolve, political missteps, and the absence of international supports."[12]

It is no justification for shock therapy advocates, however, that their theory did not mesh well with constraints that prevailed in Russia. A key to effective policy is to anticipate such impediments, rather than to use them as excuses in the aftermath of policy misjudgments. Any economic reform strategy whose success depends on massive injections of foreign assistance must be judged as poorly suited to today's political situation.

Apparently having missed key lessons of the first two years of post-Soviet history, Gaidar continued to believe in 1994 that the primary focus of Russian reform should be financial stabilization. "First of all," he wrote, "financial stability is necessary—the stopping of inflation and the growth of prices. . . . Such stability not only brings a person immediate psychological relief and makes his life predictable, but it also makes it possible to develop long-term plans. . . . It [financial stability] is the key to the overall stability of the country. From that will follow economic revitalization."[13]

Outside Russia, also, Western approach proponents still were failing to acknowledge in 1994 the utopian character of the economic course they had advocated for Russia. "The so-called shock therapy approach to stabilization . . . is desirable," Sachs told participants in an April 1994 World Bank conference, "because it offers the most realistic chance of avoiding a political catastrophe."[14] But one need only recount the political turmoil in Russia from early 1992, in the wake of shock therapy's initiation, through September 1993, when Yeltsin forcibly shut down Russia's duly elected parliament, until December 1993, when Vladimir Zhirinovsky's ultranationalist message was shown to have found fertile soil, to see a few manifestations of the "political catastrophe" that resulted from the initiation of the shock therapy experiment in Russia. Pereira, Maravall, and Przeworski aptly summarize the political requirements of economic reform in a democratic context, suggesting that if reforms "are to proceed under democratic conditions, they must enjoy continued political support through the democratic process." They continue, "A sound economic strategy is a strategy that addresses itself explicitly to the issue of whether reforms will be supported as the costs set in," rather than trying to excuse loss of support for reforms as an effect of irresponsible populism. This "typical argument of economists," they maintain, "is just bad economics."[15]

With the obvious failure of shock therapy in the democratizing context Russia knew during the early 1990s, its proponents were now trying to salvage its beleaguered image by claiming that shock therapy was not really implemented in its pure form. Marxists have often rationalized in the same way, of course, in trying to account for the failure of communism in Russia. Would shock therapy advocates now suggest that their approach is appropriate only under conditions of rigid authoritarianism? Are they willing to sacrifice democratization for their economic prescription—in the short run? It should not be necessary to highlight again the many historical proofs that short-term concessions to authoritarianism have repeatedly resulted in entrenched tyrannies—in numerous cases with market-based, not socialistic, economic systems. Economic development is no guarantee of democratization, as a number of analysts have shown.[16]

The Macroeconomic Stabilization Imperative

Defenders of Russia's radical reforms have continued to avoid confronting the implications of their attempt to utilize a standard formula for rapid macroeconomic stabilization in Russia—a formula that had been developed in contexts that diverged importantly from the Russian case on a variety of dimensions.

"The *planned economy* was specially created to function without money," economist Grigorii Yavlinskii argues. "That's why it does not react to stringent macroeconomic policy the way it is described in textbooks."[17] Monetarists have a straightforward and simple solution for long-term inflation, for example. Print less money. "Always and everywhere," Milton Friedman insists, "long continued inflation is . . . a monetary phenomenon that arises from a more rapid expansion in the quantity of money than in total output."[18] Yavlinskii maintains that to effectively confront inflation, monetaristic measures must be applied, but in conjunction with other initiatives. "Our position," Yavlinskii's

YABLOKO faction stated in April 1994, "is that inflation in Russia has primarily an institutional, and not a monetary, character." Thus, "Purely monetary methods to fight inflation must be supplemented with real reform that can eliminate the causes of inflation," YABLOKO insisted.[19]

There are a number of important institutional sources of inflation in the Russian production system, according to Russian analysts. Evgenii Yasin, former head of the Analytic Center in the Russian government and subsequently appointed economics minister, pinpoints three: monopolism of enterprises, the wide gap between internal and world prices, and inappropriate enterprise behavior growing out of long experience in the Soviet command system. For example, price liberalization, rather than resulting in a leveling of prices, produced chaotic growth under circumstances in which enterprise directors often continued to apply accustomed methods in an altered economic environment. And research has found, Yasin notes, that the chief criterion of success for many directors continued to be "preserving the working collective and creating for it the best possible life conditions."[20]

Was monetary policy responsible for these results? Yes, Sergei Glaz'ev emphasizes. Glaz'ev, a deputy in the State Duma, had been a minister of foreign economic relations before he quit the government in September 1993, following Yeltsin's decree dissolving the parliament. Glaz'ev insists that the reformers should have known that market conditions cannot be created overnight when appropriate market behaviors have not been learned.[21] Such factors as these, in combination, account for the failure of monetary policy to achieve the results that were intended, Yasin maintains. He continues, "The monetary part in our inflation—the part that can be eliminated through strict monetary policy—is a fairly small part of the total."[22]

Yavlinskii emphasizes another critical factor contributing to Russia's spiraling inflation: the burden that many enterprises carry, held over from the Soviet period, of providing housing, medical care, educational instruction, child care services, and several other kinds of benefits to their workers. In a study of Nizhnii Novgorod's enterprises, Yavlinskii found that "most of the state and post-state enterprises spend up to 80 percent of their profits to support the social infrastructure. That is why the first step on the way to structural transformation," he insists, "has to be the separation of the social infrastructure from state and post-state enterprises."[23] But there is no place in the monetarist reform formula for such *micro*structural details as working out new arrangements for housing, medical care, and education among enterprise personnel. When these analysts see persistent inflation, they can see only money supply distortions in the long run, and they have no suggestions for confronting pressing near-term problems of enterprise structuring. Gaidar, for example, acknowledged in 1994 that the "problem of the social sphere of enterprises," in which both enterprises and their personnel "have unavoidably been trapped," was not addressed in the reform program he initiated.[24]

Government subsidies are a major source of inflation, of course, as these analysts recognize. On the one hand, there is widespread support among Russian economists for a decisive reduction of the government subsidies that help to sustain Russia's distorted production system. But, on the other hand, they insist, it is necessary for the government to be involved in measures to promote economic improvement. The subsidy reductions, they suggest, need to be thoughtfully applied. Russia's radical reformers argued against substantial government participation of this kind, however, thinking that it would promote resource misallocation, dampen investment from other sources, and lead to a variety of other negative outcomes.[25] Gaidar's planners accepted this monetarist outlook unreservedly. Sergei Vasil'ev, who was considered the chief ideologist of the Gaidar team, is indistinguishable from Friedman on this point. "The government must limit its activity in the economic sphere to the maximum extent possible," Vasil'ev insisted in an April 1994 interview, "and let the market, money, and entrepreneurs work."[26]

Although the Gaidar planners failed to realize their objectives, and the program was quickly compromised, the Chernomyrdin government formed after Gaidar's departure attempted to maintain a reformist image that would be pleasing to the West—while the state bureaucracy expanded and amid clear signs that branch ministries were winning their struggle to acquire renewed powers.

It was in this context that the Russian government prepared a budget proposal for 1994, a budget draft that would be submitted to the International Monetary Fund for review before being delivered to the State Duma. When Russia's lawmakers were finally shown the budget proposal, Yavlinskii was one of many who objected to its priorities. "The draft for the federal budget does not conform to the necessary priorities in economic and social policy," the April statement by the YABLOKO faction argued.[27] "[The government planners] are ignoring the most pressing problems of the present situation: the overall decline in production and the payments crisis." The statement continued, "They are not taking into account the most important elements of economic reform: structural transformation, support for entrepreneurship, reorganization of inefficient enterprises, industrial policy, demonopolization, and social policy."[28]

The Yavlinskii faction was one of several in the State Duma that found the budget proposal wanting and urged that it be reworked. Several consultations ensued with representatives from the Council of Ministers, but the government insisted that the budget had to be approved without modification. Ivan Rybkin, speaker of the State Duma, then called the prime minister in search of a solution to the impasse. But, according to Rybkin, Chernomyrdin was unwilling to consider a compromise. There is a demand that the budget *appear to have been approved* by April 20, Rybkin reported back to the lawmakers. It was April 14. In just six days negotiations were to begin on the $1.5 billion loan package that had been held up, partially because the IMF had disagreed with the 1993 state budget proposed by the Supreme Soviet. Chernomyrdin's government did not want to displease the IMF again, whatever the concerns of the Russian legislators about misplaced priorities. The IMF was clearly a great deal more concerned with deficits and inflation rates than with priorities regarding economic reinvigoration. Minister of Economics Aleksandr Shokhin addressed the State Duma on April 15. In concluding his speech, Shokhin urged the deputies to approve the budget proposal "according to the *instruction of* the head of the government."[29]

Following the address, a *Moskovskie novosti* correspondent asked Shokhin what his real goal had been in the speech, because its heavy-handedness had offended even lawmakers who *supported* the budget proposal. Shokhin responded that he was doing his best to get the parliament to approve the proposal (or to appear to approve it, which is what happened that day), because it would give Russia the opportunity to receive the $1.5 billion IMF credits.[30]

Yavlinskii urged that the budget proposal be disapproved because, he said, "Its current form means that the Russian economy will remain the same as it is now," with continuing stagnation and production declines.[31] His objection was that too much emphasis was being placed on financial stabilization, through tax increases and reduced government spending—at a time when he believed that state investments needed to be increased to help restore Russia's production capabilities. The budget "is too severe for our ill economy," he insisted.[32] He favored a governmental policy, he explained, "whose essence is not self-elimination [from the economy], but the opposite—active involvement by the government" in a broad spectrum of areas.[33] "This is the only way to realize financial stabilization," Yavlinskii maintained. "The main lesson from the experience of the past two to three years is that the state must play an essential role in the transitional period. . . . Macroeconomic stabilization as the goal, which was put ahead of everything else, was a mistaken strategy from the very beginning."[34]

Yavlinskii had been arguing this point from the early days of Gaidar's reforms, once the outlines of the government program became clear. He insisted in mid-1992 that, "Under present conditions, financial stabilization can be only a temporary state, and one that can be achieved only at a very high price—a sharp decline in the standard of living and a deep drop in production." Russia paid that price, at a markedly higher level than the reformers had predicted. Yavlinskii continued, "But it is these two factors in combination [a sharp decline in living standards and a deep drop in production] that are the most important preconditions capable of bringing *a recurrence of imbalance* in a short period of time. Therefore, economic policy should be reoriented toward *long-term* financial stabilization."[35] Yavlinskii's perspective was that the government's policy, which had been urged on Russia by the IMF, would in actuality lead to a heightened budget deficit, as Russia's economy worsened because of inappropriate attention to investments that could improve production.

Gaidar, in contrast, called for an overall reduction in government expenditures during 1994. "We must take the difficult path of reducing state expenditures to slow inflation," he argued, repeating the usual monetarist prescription. "The core of the problem in this situation is extremely simple," he believed. "With the existing level of inflation and level of taxation, no economic growth is possible."[36]

But Yavlinskii insists, "It is not possible to achieve macroeconomic stabilization before a real private sector appears in the economy—before structural and institutional changes are brought about."[37] The sequencing he would prefer—with structural adjustment and institution building *preceding* macroeconomic stabilization—has characterized his approach from the 500 Days program through the Window of

Opportunity proposal and his more recent analyses. In May 1992 he published a critique which noted that financial stabilization had not occurred and pointed out reasons for the failure. "From the start, the economic policy of the Russian government has not had a conception of institutional transformations in the economy [beyond privatization]," he objected, and added, "Furthermore, such a conception was declared to be, if not of minor importance, then at least of secondary importance."[38]

In his 1992 critique, Yavlinskii had elaborated on these points. "There is one extremely important circumstance that calls into question the effectiveness of the direct use of recipes from the neoliberal school of economic thought in reforming a 'post-plan' economy. This conception initially assumes the presence of a functioning market econom. . . . An accelerated changeover to 'playing by market rules even before the game itself starts' (for example, freeing up prices without an anti-monopoly policy) in an essentially nonmarket economy will not lead to an accelerated transformation of the latter into a viable market economy but to its destruction, including the destruction of the few spheres that could have formed the framework of a future effective market economy."[39]

Glaz'ev holds the same perspective. "We have not created the mechanisms of a market economy which make monetaristic policy effective in developed countries," he stated in November 1993, shortly after he left his government post.[40] "In our situation, strict monetaristic policy can have only one effect," he continues: "a very deep decline in production. . . . The introduction of standard [macroeconomic] measures for transition to a market economy did not take into account the structural disproportions and existing 'rules of the game' on the micro level. As a result, the standard macroeconomic policy that has often been attempted in countries with market economies produced unexpected effects that were quite opposite from those that had been anticipated."[41]

Concentration and Structural Distortions in Production

At the end of the Soviet period, industrial production was highly concentrated—in most sectors, in only one or a few enterprises. The 1991 report by the World Bank, et al., *A Study of the Soviet Economy*, illustrates this feature of the Soviet production system in noting, "For

87 percent of the 5,885 products included in the machine-building sector, a single producer accounts for all deliveries" to *Gossnab* (the State Supply Commission). "A similar picture emerges from disaggregated Goskomstat data," the report continues, "which indicate that some 30–40 percent of Soviet industrial output is composed of goods produced on single sites. For example, single factories produce 100 percent of sewing machines, 97 percent of trolley buses, 100 percent of cooking equipment, and so on."[42] Russian industry at the end of 1993 revealed a similar pattern of concentration. About 2 percent of industrial enterprises produced more than 40 percent of all industrial products,[43] and more than 80 percent of all production in most sectors came from one or two enterprises.[44]

Most of these enterprises were large—substantially larger than their counterparts in Western countries.[45] In late 1993, almost 90 percent of Russia's industrial potential was concentrated in enterprises with more than ten thousand employees each.[46] Further, some appeared to be "significantly oversized," according to *A Study of Soviet Economy*, with capacities that greatly exceeded demand for their output. The production system was weighted down with the output of heavy industry and resultingly inadequate production capacity for consumer products. And the military-industrial complex was overbuilt relative to other sectors.[47] Eighty percent of the USSR's military production facilities were on Russian territory.[48] In late 1994 more than seventy Russian towns whose inhabitants worked almost exclusively in military production and research still remained closed.[49]

The tendency in Soviet and Russian enterprises "toward huge scale and extreme concentration" clearly resulted from preferences of central planners.[50] In Russia's vertically integrated system, not only was there often only one producer of a product, or only two or three, but there was also often only a single buyer. This situation did not change substantially with liberalization and voucher privatization of enterprises. Thus, "most [production] enterprises still cannot choose the suppliers for the raw materials, machinery, parts and other supplies for production," Glaz'ev observes.[51] With the beginning of price liberalization, this structure invited unchecked inflation through monopoly pricing.

With such prominent structural distortions in its production system, and the disruption of supply and distribution networks that was brought on by the collapse of the Council for Mutual Economic Assistance (CMEA) and the subsequent dissolution of the Soviet Union, a continuing downturn in production was to be predicted in 1992. After the demise of CMEA, Soviet exports to former CMEA members dropped by 57 percent, and imports fell by 63 percent.[52] And with the dissolution of the USSR, linkages in Russia's production and distribution system were further disrupted. The Russian government's economic reform program, rather than responding to this emergency with measures to ease the precipitous slide in production, exacerbated the production crisis by bringing on further dislocations with a privatization initiative for which enterprises were ill prepared. The results of these shocks to the production system were predictably catastrophic.[53]

As Glaz'ev observes, "There *had* to be a structural crisis, and it was natural that it was accompanied by a decline in production, because a large part of industry was oriented toward defense production. But a crisis should produce something new—not just reduce output in sectors that are not economically efficient. It should also create conditions for the flow of capital and resources in directions that would increase economic efficiency and facilitate the introduction of new technologies and the modernization of enterprises."[54]

According to the State Antimonopoly Committee, at the end of 1993 about seven thousand production enterprises continued to enjoy monopoly positions at either the federal or regional levels, in spite of the fact that a central objective of the government's economic program was to reduce monopolization.[55] Leonid Bochin, head of the State Antimonopoly Committee, argues that the actual prevalence of monopolies was even higher at year's end than official figures indicate. Under new government regulations, to be considered a monopoly an enterprise now must control 65 percent of the market. In 1992 that percentage was 35—a level of market control consistent with international classification norms. Thus, official data show, the number of monopoly enterprises was halved in one year simply by changing the definition.[56]

A principal method of breaking up monopolies in the government's privatization program was to allow individual departments to privatize. Thus, for example, a transportation department of a production enterprise could set up its own autonomous transportation company. Rather than addressing the problem of product competitiveness directly, this procedure often contributed to production declines by making it more difficult and expensive for a production enterprise to do its necessary work. And the heart of the monopoly problem—the absence of a competitive environment for the main products of *production* enterprises, not just for the services of ancillary departments—was skirted. Yeltsin adviser Petr Filippov recognized this deficiency, in retrospect: "All our attempts to scale down enterprises, to separate off transportation departments, or typography departments, did not produce any positive effect."[57]

Yurii Yaremenko, director of the Institute of Economic Forecasting, maintains that, "The principal defect of the course we are now on is that obvious and specific characteristics of the Russian economy were ignored. . . . The structural and technological disproportions that characterize our economy produce features of our economic environment that prevent the rise of a "self-starting market."[58] Economist Mancur Olson frames the problem similarly, arguing that "a thriving market economy is not, contrary to what some say, simply the result of 'letting capitalism happen'—not something that emerges spontaneously out of thin air. It requires a special set of institutional arrangements that most countries in the world do not have. The most prosperous countries happen to have these institutional arrangements, but they take them for granted. These arrangements are usually overlooked in ideological debate and in scholarly research."[59]

The effect of this narrow vision was that production was adversely affected by the monetarist-inspired reforms across a broad spectrum of economic sectors. As Glaz'ev points out, with the introduction of Gaidar's reforms, "production declined almost everywhere"—not just in military production or other overbuilt sectors.[60] Economist Stanislav Shatalin underscores the point. "I want to emphasize, first, that the decline in production does not have a structural but rather a universal character," he wrote in early 1994, "and second—and most importantly—that it struck the most progressive, high-technology branches of production."[61] And even the country's "loss-making enterprises using backward technologies and obsolete equipment . . . are not positioned haphazardly," Yaremenko insists. "They form complete chains, and by leaving them to their own devices we are rending the system of economic links and immeasurably aggravating old shortages."[62]

Production Improvement or a Focus on Raw Materials Export?

In light of defining features of Russia's production system at the beginning of the reforms, Yaremenko argues, the economy "needed to be prepared structurally, or parallel steps needed to be taken to build market relations and accomplish structural transformation." He continues, underscoring a critical priority for Russia that the West's monetarists seemed intent on ignoring: "Under no circumstances should the fruits of the long-term industrial development of the country have been lost, but just the opposite. They should have been productively used." The cost of neglecting this accumulated potential will be immense, Yaremenko maintains. "I am deeply convinced that, as long as there are internal resources for structural and technological transformation, there is a future for our reforms. But if they disappear, the reforms have no future."[63]

The revitalization of Russia's production system is a key priority among nearly all Russian analysts. "Accelerated deterioration of whole industries is a direct route to overall economic collapse," Yaremenko maintains. Therefore, "Economic policy must once again make production the top priority in decision making"[64] to counter the process Glaz'ev describes as a "very strong tendency of growing deindustrialization of the country and irreversible degradation of our scientific and industrial potential."[65] Yavlinskii's prognosis for the alternative is grim. "Russia with its resources and human potential has to be a modern industrial country," he insists. "The approach from the position of vulgar liberalism today leads to hypertrophic growth of the primary sector and the gradual elimination of processing industries. We are confident that this tendency has to be stopped."[66]

But Åslund faulted Russia's economists for their "extraordinary emphasis on production," attributing this emphasis to the persistence of "old Marxist values."[67] Such attempts at misdirection could not succeed where they counted the most, of course—among those who were not ready to witness a continuing erosion of Russia's production potential. By 1994 Åslund was insisting, "the structure of Russia's total exports will change toward larger exports of raw materials."[68] With such statements a part of the public record, it should not be surprising that a widespread conclusion in the Russia of late 1994 was that the radical reform agenda had included making the Western world safe from the potential competition of Russian production while exploiting the country's natural resources.

Investment Requirements and
Barriers to Investment

Improved production depends on investment, as economist Leonid Abalkin recognizes. The sharpest crisis is in the investment sphere,

Abalkin wrote in July 1993, which to a great extent predetermines long-term tendencies toward further declines in production.[69] In most branches outside the military-industrial complex, a large proportion of production equipment was old in 1993, and much of it was obsolete. By one account, depending on the sphere of production, between 60 and 100 percent of equipment was worn-out.[70] (Among enterprises in the military-industrial complex, the situation was typically better.) Workplace injuries and fatalities were increasing, as was environmental damage due to equipment failures. There were thirty-two major accidents involving ruptured oil and gas pipelines in 1993, for example, and experts were predicting even more in coming years. Accidental radiation exposure was on the rise, as were disasters involving ships and trains resulting from equipment malfunctions. Fires and explosions due to aging hardware were increasing in frequency.[71]

According to the Center for Informational and Social Technologies of the Russian government, the volume of capital investment in industry needed to be increased by a factor of at least two, on a yearly basis, just to keep present equipment running, and levels of investment would need to be raised by a factor of four to achieve significant economic improvement.[72]

Of course, a substantial proportion of production operations worked against economic recovery. Some of their output was not needed, and some production facilities needed to be extensively modernized. Gaidar's Institute for the Economy in Transition estimated in the spring of 1994 that 58 percent of Russia's existing industrial capacity should not be supported with continuing investment,[73] and Stanislav Assekritov, the first vice president of the Reforma Foundation, estimated at the same time that only about 16 percent of the country's industrial facilities were capable of producing goods that would be competitive in the world market.[74] This situation underscores yet another reason for sharply increased investment—not only to replace old and obsolete equipment but also to transform production methods in a large number of enterprises. But the trend through the end of voucher privatization was in the opposite direction. From the beginning of 1992 until mid-1994, the level of capital investment dropped by 65 percent, with the sharpest decline being registered in the production sphere.[75] And the trajectory was not encouraging. During the first six months of 1994 total capital investment declined 27 percent in comparison with the first six months of 1993, and in the production sphere the drop was 37 percent.[76]

Neither the Russian government nor its citizens invested substantially in Russian industry during 1993. Instead, it is estimated that during that period between $15 billion and $25 billion was taken out of the country.[77] Capital flight, which had been ominous before October 1993, increased further with Yeltsin's shelling of the Russian White House and accelerated even more with Zhirinovsky's December election success. Harold Malmgren, a former U.S. trade representative, suggested at the beginning of 1994 that about $2 billion per month may have been leaving Russia by that time.[78]

Foreign investment in Russia by mid-1994 was disappointingly low through the end of voucher privatization. For comparative purposes we will highlight the situation in China, where foreign direct investment commitments rose from $7 billion in 1991 to more than $100 billion in 1993, while actual disbursements jumped from 1991's $3.5 billion to nearly $25.76 billion in 1993.[79] In contrast, according to deputy economics minister Yakov Urinson, total foreign investment in Russia by the end of 1993 totaled $2.7 billion, an increase of $1.4 billion for 1993.[80] Foreign investment in Russia was only 10.5 percent of the amount invested in China at the end of 1993. And even worse for Russia, mid-1994 data suggested that perhaps as little as $1 billion in new foreign investment would be forthcoming in 1994,[81] although some analysts were speculating that with the post-voucher stage of privatization the 1994 level of foreign investment might match that of 1993.[82] Chubais continued to make optimistic predictions,[83] but Yasin termed Chubais's estimates excessively high[84]—as they had been during the voucher privatization phase.

Adding further gloom to this unfavorable picture is the fact that nearly half of the foreign investments in Russia during the first quarter of 1994 were in oil and gas. This kind of investment, which was oriented toward extraction and exportation, was not the type Russia needed most to improve its production system. Overall, Russia had attracted only about 0.1 percent of foreign investment worldwide by the beginning of 1994, and less foreign capital was invested in Russia than in Hungary ($5.6 billion) and Poland ($3 billion), for example.[85] Urinson noted that more foreign money had been invested in tiny Estonia (population 1.5 million) during the first six months of 1994 than in Russia.[86] In 1993, United States firms invested $7 billion in China—10 times more than the $700 million invested by U.S. businesses in Russia.[87]

There are obvious reasons for Russia's poor showing. Russia's economy was in disarray, and the country had become politically and socially unstable. Not surprisingly, then, *Euromoney*'s March 1994 country risk rankings, which periodically compare the risk of capital investment in different nations, placed Russia 138th out of 167 countries in the study.[88] In contrast, China's *Euromoney* ranking (38th place) was higher than that of *any* East European economy. And a February 1994 study by the research department of *The Economist*, which compared the credit-worthiness of twenty-six "emerging economies," ranked Russia 25th—just ahead of last-place Iraq.[89]

In August 1993 we interviewed Aleksandr Radygin, head of the privatization department in Gaidar's Institute for the Economy in Transition and one of the authors of the Russian privatization program. Radygin acknowledged that "Gaidar had some illusions about the possibility of attracting foreign investors. In some ways, his was a theoretical scheme," Radygin said. "The reformers had expected that with price liberalization there would follow an effective anti-inflation policy, and along with privatization these developments would create the best conditions to attract foreign capital."

Pausing to note that these expectations were not realized, Radygin continued, "It's hard to imagine that any economist could propose a better sequence that would have worked. The low level of foreign investment is the most painful point for the Russian government," he added. "But it's difficult to evaluate Gaidar's program. There's nothing to compare it with."

Russian Reform and the Entrepreneurial Spirit

Elsewhere, we discuss the Russian government's neglect of the non-state business sphere beginning in late 1991.[90] A stream of legislation that was passed in the USSR during the late 1980s had established principles for cooperative enterprises—a development that was justified by Soviet leaders as being consistent with the goals of communism. By the time of the August putsch, more than 111,000 cooperatives were in operation. (Many more than this were registered but not operating.) The cooperative sector accounted for 6 percent of the Soviet Union's gross national product for 1991—about seventeen times more than the cooperative contribution had been in 1988.[91] Seven million people were working in cooperatives.[92]

Most cooperative owners had actually wanted to be private business people, however, rather than participating in the building of "socialist enterprise."[93] (In this study, when we refer to "private" enterprise, we are speaking of new businesses, not privatized enterprises.) On December 15, 1990, a law was approved in the RSFSR, On Enterprises and Enterpreneurship, which specified several legal forms of property ownership, including private enterprises.[94] By 1991, most people who were beginning new businesses in Russia were private entrepreneurs, not members of cooperatives,[95] and the number of private enterprises was growing rapidly.

But this trend was halted abruptly when Gaidar took the reins of economic reform. New business start-ups lagged after the Gaidar reforms began, outside the shadowy realm of sidewalk kiosk enterprises. Production was particularly hard-hit. Russia's encouraging potential for new production enterprises at the end of 1991 had been sharply reduced three years later. "As soon as Gaidar came to power he became an opponent of entrepreneurship," Mark Masarskii maintains. An adviser on entrepreneurship to the Moscow government, Masarskii had become a prominent business leader during the Gorbachev era. Gaidar the academician had written favorably about the salutary role of entrepreneurs in an economy, Masarskii notes, and before joining the Yeltsin government he had been a strong supporter of Russia's entrepreneurial pacesetters. But Gaidar the economic planner did not take into account the crippling effect of price liberalization and new tax policies on entrepreneurship. These measures drove many private firms out of business.[96] Ironically, the actual number of small businesses declined during 1992—the first (and only) year that Gaidar headed the reform program.[97] "It is paradoxical," Masarskii suggested in January 1993, "that under the 'market-oriented' government last year we [business people] were much worse off than under the 'non-market' government" in recent years.[98]

Gaidar's inattention to the entrepreneurial sector during the period that he headed the economic reform program is widely recognized. We heard this complaint repeatedly from political and business leaders and specialists we interviewed in 1993. "Gaidar never paid attention to the entrepreneur," Constantin Zatulin emphasized when we interviewed him that July. A prominent Moscow businessman and State Duma deputy following the December 1993 elections, Zatulin expressed frustration that Gaidar seemed not to think it important that conditions be created that would be favorable toward private business activity. "He showed no sign that he saw entrepreneurship as being critical to economic reform," Zatulin said.

Economist Nikolai Shmelev maintained when we interviewed him in June that "Gaidar, Chernomyrdin, the Bolsheviks—*all* have artificially kept a lid on the natural energy of entrepreneurship"—which Shmelev described as "the energy of mushrooms breaking asphault." In a *Nezavisimaia gazeta* interview three months later, Shmelev charged that the reformers "have not changed anything" in the private sphere. "They made it even worse, somehow, than it used to be. . . . You could be put in prison for private activity earlier, but economically it isn't any easier now. There was a lot of talk, but the current powers continued to control—even worse, they made more difficult— the process of securing authorization to open a business."[99]

"To open my own production enterprise today would be as difficult as sixty years ago," Shmelev told us in our interview. "Gaidar talked about promoting private initiative, but he did nothing."

Masarskii insists that Gaidar understood from the beginning that state policy toward private entrepreneurship would have a dampening effect. "But Gaidar and I have different interests," Masarskii emphasizes. "He represents the interests of the state. That means the 'apparatus.'" Gaidar represents "the power which is above the society and outside it—the power which has suppressed the civil society until now. . . . State priorities are different from the priorities of a civil society."[100]

In our interviews with Russian business and opinion leaders, the net of blame for these developments was cast well beyond Gaidar's circle of Russian reformers. Viktor Shchekochikhin, president of the Russian Union of Private Owners, told us in July 1993, "The post-Communist regime which is declaring its commitment to the market doesn't want to see private entrepreneurship develop. These people want to create pseudo-entrepreneurs," Shchekochikhin insisted—"nomenklatura entrepreneurship. *Gosplan* entrepreneurship is developing."

Shchekochikhin continued, "It is shocking that the World Bank and the European Bank for Reconstruction and Development *said* that they were creating a special fund to support entrepreneurship. But," he emphasized, "they don't work with entrepreneurs. They go through state structures, which aren't interested in promoting private business. In practical terms, Western help doesn't often reach private entrepreneurs. And it's the same with the foundations that were organized according to government decisions," Shchekochikhin added. "They only *pretend* to support private entrepreneurs." He was referring in particular to Gaidar's All-Russia Association of Private and Privatizing Enterprises, which was created before the April 1993 referendum.[101]

As for the privatized sector, Shchekochikhin told us, "It is still close to the state sector—closer to it than to the private sector. Private entrepreneurs have nothing to do with privatization." And he elaborated in detail on his interpretation of Anatolii Chubais's privatization program, arguing that "it achieves only one goal: to divide property into parts, which is just a continuation of the old socialist idea." The privatization planners neglected what should have been their main priority in privatization, Shchekochikhin suggested, which is how to create a real market and real entrepreneurship through the distribution of these vast holdings. "That is an entirely different issue from the one they addressed."

Noting that hardly any new production enterprises were started in the private sphere during the last half of 1991 or in 1992, economist Vladimir Tikhonov, a member of the Presidential Council, explores the reasons. At first, Tikhonov states, the primary culprit was the inaccessibility of production materials outside the state sector. Therefore, most of the capital of new entrepreneurs was kept in the monetary sphere.[102] At the beginning of 1992, many private entrepreneurs thus had large reserves of capital that they wanted to invest in production enterprises,[103] but this capital lost most of its value nearly overnight, with Gaidar's price liberalization. Further, the Russian government's tax policies changed abruptly under Gaidar, and his value-added tax scheme was so burdensome for small businesses that many were forced to close. Writing about this development, Tikhonov maintains that "many new entrepreneurs, because of unbearably heavy taxation, went into the 'shadow' economy."[104]

Shmelev maintains that "the democrats not only failed to develop ways to stimulate private sector activity, but they have not even created conditions that would allow the private sector to be secure from the intrusions of bureaucrats and criminal groups. They came up with the most foolish tax system in existence . . . the same with bank loans. If it is not possible to stop inflation now, the state must recognize that it is necessary to support the private sector—not just in words, but in reality."[105]

But that did not happen. Irina Khakamada, a deputy of the State

Duma and former general secretary of Konstantin Borovoi's Party for Economic Freedom, emphasized in mid-1993, "Until now, market reforms were . . . 'carried from above.' But entrepreneurs—the representatives of small and medium-sized businesses—have received only crumbs."[106]

This situation had not improved significantly by late 1994, although entrepreneurship continued to be prominently encouraged with words, as it had been from the beginning of the Yeltsin-Gaidar reforms. Yeltsin established the Council on Entrepreneurship, an independent think tank composed of Russian business executives, in March 1992. It was ostensibly created to provide a business perspective for government decision making, but its advice was largely ignored.[107]

Ivan Kivelidi, chair of a resuscitated Council on Entrepreneurship in 1993, observed that two earlier incarnations of this organization had existed previously—under Gorbachev and under Yeltsin. "But it turned out that, always, we played the role of 'housekeeper's children.' Everything that we worked on went into the trash can," he complained. Kivelidi became a businessman in 1987, when he organized a cooperative and turned his first small business into an empire. In this July 1993 interview, he asked, "Do our leaders actually support entrepreneurship as a way of life, as a system of values?" He continued, "Until now, it seems that [the Council's] ideas have been only slogans for politicians, for whom free entrepreneurship is an abstract idea, and even dangerous. It is a threat to their existence."[108]

In this context, initiatives have been announced that had the stated goal of promoting entrepreneurship but that, Kivelidi argued, were created for the benefit of "quick bureaucrats who seized a piece of our proposal in order to find 'a warmer place' for themselves." He then provided an example to support his charge. "Recently, the government announced that a Center on Entrepreneurship Development is being created, and a bureaucrat has already been put in charge of it." The center is being created as a clearinghouse for Western investors, Kivelidi stated, and the officials in charge of the Center will wield substantial power. To find the richest people in our country today, he suggested, a person should look among bureaucrats, "because they have a fast-selling product which is in great demand—their signature. It gives them the opportunity to enrich themselves, while preserving an image of legitimacy."[109]

The trend Kivelidi decried in 1993 seemed to be continuing a year later. During May 1994, Russia's government completed a document aimed at showing support for small businesses. The Federal Program of State Support for Small Entrepreneurship proposed "to create good economic, legal, and organizational conditions" for small business.[110] But details of the program did not live up to its billing. "It seems that the initial goal of those who developed the program was not as much to support entrepreneurs as to support those bureaucratic structures that want to continue leading and managing entrepreneurs, the same way they used to oversee state production," analyst Leonid Lopatnikov insists.[111]

By this time, there were several government organizations devoted to entrepreneurship at the federal level. There was a Federal Foundation to Support Entrepreneurship and Develop Competition. There were also four departments in different federal ministries that were intended to encourage private business. But rather than advancing overall entrepreneurial activity, these different bureaucracies seemed to be working at cross purposes. "If a draft of a bill was prepared by the Antimonopoly Committee, the Ministry of Economics would *never* agree with it," Alla Aloian of the Federal Foundation observes.[112] Lopatnikov describes this situation in similar terms, maintaining that the Federal Program was intended more to create an image of supporting entrepreneurs than to actually provide meaningful impetus to the development of the entrepreneurial sector.[113] He pinpoints a critical reason for the competition among ministries for oversight of entrepreneurial activity, observing that the Federal Program of State Support for Small Entrepreneurship describes one of the principal coordination tasks of the state as "attracting foreign investments in small business."

"Is any comment needed?" Lopatnikov asks.[114]

"In spite of its repeated declarations," Aloian maintains, "the government does not consider the development of small business as one of its priorities." In highlighting deliberations within the government that surrounded development of the Federal Program that was worked out in May 1994, Aloian charged that it "was not discussed with much interest."[115] Ivan Grachev, chair of the Subcommittee on Small Business of the State Duma, underscores this point, stating that the "people who represent and implement state power today in the country still do not understand the role of small business in a market economy. They see it as something secondary. This characterizes state power as a whole in both branches."[116]

As Lopatnikov summarizes this problem, "The attitude toward small entrepreneurship during the past two years was, indeed, the Achilles' heel of governmental economic policy. Tax relief and other privileges which used to give the initial impulse to the creation of thousands of small . . . firms were eliminated."[117]

Adding detail to this point, Andrei Orlov, president of the Academy of Economics, describes a study of entrepreneurship that he headed in the spring of 1994. Orlov found that all levels of taxation, from local to federal, collected from 80 to 90 percent of reported profits from private businesses.[118] "With today's level of taxation," analyst Yakov Gilinskii stated in March 1994, "every enterprise and every businessman has to hide income to avoid taxes." The result of this situation was predictable. "Now, almost all private and most state businesses in all spheres—production and retail—are under the 'roof' of organized crime," Gilinskii charged, adding, "It is not possible to work and not break the law. . . . The criminalization of the economy is, to a great degree, the result of repressive activity of the state itself."[119]

In a similar vein, Nikolai Efimkin, director of a joint stock company in Ekaterinburg with both production and retail branches, suggests that "everything possible has been done to annihilate this activity [entrepreneurship]. We all realize that entrepreurship is being carried out in a criminal-like environment. But it is difficult not to support those business people who are saying, 'We are ready to work with racketeers, because they charge up to 10 percent.' The state takes up to 90 percent and with fines and a variety of sanctions, it takes even more."[120]

Tax rates were only one of the problems. "The results of tax policy are made even worse by repeated changes in tax regulations, in export-import tariffs and duties," Moscow business leader Mark Goriachev adds.[121]

Further, Russia's licensing requirements and regulatory provisions directed at private businesses threw up a formidable wall against new business starts. Orlov argues that state policy toward small businesses was oriented toward maximizing revenue not only for the state, but also for state bureaucrats through the maze of regulations that invite bribery. It lacked a workable strategic plan for furthering entrepreneurship, he suggests.[122] An illustrative example of the proliferation of licensing requirements can be seen in the fact that, as of mid-1994, a department in the Moscow city government that was devoted exclusively to licensing entrepreneurial activity just in Moscow had a full-time staff of more than one thousand people.[123]

The director of the State Antimonopoly Committee's Moscow branch, Oleg Novikov, observes that licensing requirements in Moscow "create barriers to any entrepreneurship activity in the city." These licensing requirements do not protect consumers, Novikov argues.[124] When we interviewed him in June 1993, he interpreted such impediments as strategies to preserve monopoly control. "There is monopoly at every level of government," he insisted, "and people want to keep it that way." Aleksandr Ioffe, chair of the Moscow government's Council of Experts on Small and Medium-Sized Businesses, maintains that "the absolute power of bureaucrats takes away people's desire to be entrepreneurs even before they begin planning to own private businesses."[125] "Small business in the capital city develops mainly today through the support of the 'shadow' sector of the economy," Ioffe suggests, "because of the tradition of bureaucratism and extortion" that continues in Russia today.[126]

An additional problem faced by entrepreneurs is the virtual impossibility, in Yeltsin's Russia, for entrepreneurs to secure long-term loans at interest rates that are manageable. And this situation, which applied effective brakes to entrepreneurship, was clearly part of Gaidar's agenda. "After the [April 1993] referendum, it became possible to increase control over monetary and budgetary policy," Gaidar stated in August 1993. "In particular, it was then possible to direct the Central Bank to increase interest rates—something that we were unable to do from May 1992 until April 1993. [Following the referendum], the interest rate was raised from 100 percent to 110 percent, then 120 percent. Now it has reached 170 percent—about the current level of inflation. *Unfortunately, the process is slow. We would, of course, prefer a more radical solution,*" Gaidar indicated.[127] Thus the government severely constricted the lifeline of the entrepreneurial class that could generate the competitive vitality, and tax revenue, that drives a market economy.

A month before Gaidar wrote of this strategic "success" in getting interest rates up to the level of inflation, economist Vadim Medvedev, head of the Economic Analysis Group in the Gorbachev Foundation, wrote of the effect of these interest rates on private business. Loans were too costly for most entrepreneurs to use them for capital investment, Medvedev insisted. Further, banks were very reluctant to make loans for longer than three months—which made it virtually impossible to use loans to invest in production.[128] Efimkin noted in May 1994,

"Credit policy has come to a dead end. Small enterprises—with very few exceptions—have stopped taking out loans. . . . But they cannot survive without loans."[129]

These considerations led Yavlinskii to argue that "the government must, with extreme urgency, create a system of state and private banks to provide long-term loans."[130] Foreign advisers could have provided valuable counsel to Russian financial specialists socialized in the ways of Gosbank, but that was not one of their priorities. Indeed, the high-interest strategy that was encouraged by Gaidar was entirely consistent with the Western approach.

Most Russian economists agreed with Ioffe that "only the state is able to start the engine of entrepreneurship, to supply money for small businesses."[131] At the time that the 1994 budget proposal was being discussed, Yavlinskii's YABLOKO faction objected that the portion of the budget aimed at supporting small business was less than 0.01 percent of the total. In the budget proposal "the share of state expenditures for institutional transformation is extremely low," the April YABLOKO statement pointed out. "The urgent tasks for economic policy today are institutional and structural transformation. From this point of view, the 1994 budget does not provide the necessary vehicles to realize the most important economic priorities." If a pressing goal is to bring down inflation, vastly increased support for small business is necessary, YABLOKO argued, because an important source of inflation is the weakness of the private sector.[132]

An appropriate Western contribution to Russian reform could have been to offer input that would have helped Russian planners develop measures to strengthen entrepreneurship in 1992 and 1993. Tikhonov told us in July 1993 that Sachs and Åslund had managed to convince Gaidar that price liberalization was needed late in 1991. It should have been possible, along the way, to have discussed with him requirements for hardy entrepreneurship, but apparently they did not. And their writings of that period offer no evidence that entrepreneurship was one of their central concerns.

The problem here is that processes through which institutional and structural transformation of any kind can be effectively accomplished were largely unknown to monetarists and the other foreign advisers who worked with Russia's reform planners. Sachs's "main pillars" of economic reform for Russia gave no standing to the urgent need for initiatives that could have promoted the private business sector. Instead, Sachs took heart that Moscow's "kiosk boom" provided good proof of "spontaneous market activity." What Sachs was seeing here, without recognizing it, was the spontaneous creation of conditions that were ripe for mafia activity. But Russia needed more from entrepreneurs, than imported soda, fruit punch, and candy. It needed production. That was not part of Sachs's agenda.[133] And Åslund, who has a great deal to say about stabilization and privatization of state enterprises, finds the subject of entrepreneurship uncompelling, except to complain that entrepreneurs often had to pay bribes.[134] By trying to treat an infant market as if it were a mature one, these advisers encouraged the squandering of an extraordinary opportunity that had developed by late 1991 to promote vigorous expansion of Russia's private sector. As Masarskii describes this situation, "During the last two years, due to the efforts of our monetarists, hundreds of thousands of enterprises in the private sector were destroyed—enterprises that could have become the basis for efficient production. I grieve for those young plants that were trampled. What kind of market liberalism is it that destroys the agents of the market?"[135]

But in 1993, Western governments and international financial institutions began to insist more urgently that Russian leaders intensify their attention to entrepreneurship. This stepped-up emphasis on private business came at the time that Yeltsin was trying to generate support for the upcoming April 1993 referendum, where Russian voters were to express their overall opinions about the Yeltsin reforms. U.S. president Bill Clinton joined this campaign, agreeing to hold summit talks with Yeltsin only three weeks before the referendum and promising both a "new democratic partnership" and new U.S. aid for food, housing, and entrepreneurship.[136]

The G-7 leaders soon rallied behind this effort to bolster Yeltsin's credibility at home, pledging an aid package of about $28 billion a few days later. United States officials emphasized, at the time that the aid program was announced, that "the package could unravel if Russian President Boris Yeltsin fails" to win the referendum. The $500 million in seed money promised by the U.S. was made conditional on matching contributions from other countries totaling $1.5 billion. Britain also agreed to provide technical assistance to develop industry, and Japan promised to furnish advisers for creating small businesses in Russia.[137]

Although Yeltsin won the referendum, most of the aid was not forthcoming. Sachs estimated in January 1994 that perhaps $4 billion of the $28 billion announced in 1993 had actually arrived.[138] But the entrepreneurship component of promised Western assistance remained a high-profile topic. By mid-1994, U.S. House leaders Richard Gephardt and Robert Michel were complaining, in a memoramdum to Secretary of State Warren Christopher and Secretary of Defense William Perry, that "A strong sense of urgency . . . is conspicuously absent in the delivery of our assistance to Russia."[139] And during the same period, Capitol Hill testimony was praising the potential of Clinton administration proposals for programs to encourage Russian entrepreneurship. For example, in a hearing of the House Appropriations Committee on May 10, Assistant Secretary of State Strobe Talbott highlighted the Clinton administration's "special emphasis" on providing support for new production and retail firms, and Representative Robert Livingston compared Russia to "a burned-out forest," whose young entrepreneurs "are like the seedlings coming up through the ashes. . . . We want to make sure that they are cultivated and encouraged to whatever degree possible," Livingston continued, "and I guess that's really the essence of our program of assistance to Russia."[140]

Russian leaders got the message, and it was widely believed by Russian analysts that the continuing, if unenthusiastic, attention to entrepreneurship in the Russian government was partially a response to this pressure from the West.[141] But the Russian government kept its primary focus on large enterprises, business leader Aleksandr Volovik maintains, "it is easier to keep them in check."[142] A report prepared by a panel of prominent economists for *Novaia ezhednevnaia gazeta* at the end of 1993 goes further, concluding that, although the command system was swiftly demolished with Gaidar's reforms, no satisfactory alternative system was created. Instead, the state bureaucracy came to see "in the emerging entrepreneurial class a threatening competitor."[143]

Igor' P'iankov, the president of a Moscow joint stock company, describes the outcome in vivid terms: "Business in Russia is very different from business in the West. An entrepreneur 'over there' ascends the stairs. Here, he hauls himself up a rope made from barbed wire."[144]

Research and Development at Risk

A shrinkage in the number of scientific personnel after the demise of the Soviet Union was inevitable as production was redirected away from its strong emphasis on defense. At the end of the Soviet period, about 80 percent of the work of scientific personnel in the USSR was connected with the defense sector,[145] and about 70 percent of the USSR's scientific capacity was located in Russia.[146] Defense industries have long been the principal repository of Russia's best high-technology scientific production. High-technology civilian commodities, such as computers and even television sets, continue to be produced in defense enterprises, along with radar equipment and fighter jets. In 1993, 80 percent of the output of Russia's military-industrial complex was for the civilian sector. These enterprises produced 100 percent of television receivers and 90 percent of the refrigerators made in Russia, for example.[147] Overall, it is estimated that the defense sector performed about 30 percent of Russia's civilian research and development activity in 1993.[148]

This nesting of civilian science and technology—particularly high-technology R&D—in Russia's military-industrial complex requires that conversion in the defense sector be carried out thoughtfully, if innovation is to be sustained and improved. But this was not a high-priority item on the Western advisers' agenda or on Gaidar's. As Sasun Karapetian, an economist at the Institute of Management, characterized this situation in 1993, "Conversion in the military-industrial complex has a rather symbolic character up to now. No state program to change the output of enterprises and scientific organizations in the military-industrial complex has been worked out."[149] And in late 1994, it was still correct to characterize conversion efforts in this tangled but critical sector of the Russian economy as largely spontaneous, and "inadequately thought out."[150]

The results of this poor planning have been dismaying for Russia's scientific research and development community. In January 1993, Shatalin's Reforma Foundation and the economics department of the Russian Academy of Sciences issued a report evaluating the first year of reforms under Yeltsin. Observing that not even one goal of the stabilization policy had been achieved, the report charged that "tendencies leading to the destruction of the economy are gaining momentum," among the most important of which are "the erosion of research and technological potential, and a massive brain drain."[151]

A 1994 report of the Organisation for Economic Co-operation and Development (OECD) discussed the brain drain resulting from emigration and the movement of scientific personnel into other kinds of work within Russia. The OECD study suggested that perhaps 10 percent of Russia's scientists and engineers had already been lost through emigration and added that the impact of this movement "is not measured by numbers alone, as the emigrants leaving are in many cases people with international reputations and with marketable skills." In general, the report continued, "It is to be feared that certain highly reputed scientific 'schools,' such as some in theoretical physics, will disappear, due to the dispersal of their personnel abroad."[152]

It is recognized by both Russian and foreign analysts that a large amount of Russian technology is not competitive in the world arena. More than 70 percent of all scientific workers, and of expenditures for scientific research, are in "branch science"—scientific work that was controlled by ministries in the Soviet system.[153] The focus of branch science is largely applied, and branch science and technology organizations grew in the Soviet Union as much because of bureaucratic interests within the ministries as a result of real R&D needs in the society. In September 1993, a report on science and technology was released by the Ministry of Science and Technological Policy that stated, "Branch science needs to be fundamentally restructured and reoriented toward the market." The report explained that "not more than 10 percent of branch science is competitive at the world level."[154]

Yet a core of Russia's large branch science capacity is important to Russian production. OECD's 1994 report noted that "spontaneous reorientation" in the branch S&T system "carries the risk that organisations capable of succeeding in more stable market conditions may disappear, leading to an unnecessary erosion of the nation's research capability." The study further suggested that "if potentially viable elements of the branch S&T system are to be saved," then "strategically important S&T organisations" will have to receive "at least transitional state support."[155]

The good economic news for Russia in late 1994 was that, consistent with IMF guidelines, inflation had been reduced to a monthly rate of 5 percent. The bad news was that the Russian government's fixation on meeting inflation targets was, as many Russian economists saw it, propelling Russia swiftly and surely down the road toward Third World status. "By the end of the year," Glaz'ev predicted, "the Russian economy will finally have a new structure—that of developing countries."[156] Glaz'ev warned, "Irreversible deindustrialization of the country is proceeding full-speed," and he added that the process has already gone so far that, "We will never be able to restore a large part of our high-technology production. We have already lost critical reserves that were necessary for future economic growth."[157] Major blame for this development, according to many Russian analysts, should be attributed to the erosion of the country's R&D capability, which according to the OECD report cited above, "may well be [Russia's] principal treasure" next to its abundant endowment of natural resources.[158]

With Russia's scientific activity shrinking "spontaneously," production followed a course of "primitivization" during the 1991–94 period. Innovation waned as investment declined and R&D programs were cut. This trend was intensified under Chubais's privatization drive, as large production units were often broken up into smaller, autonomous enterprises. Demonopolization would be good for competition, of course, if it were carried out in a way that would facilitate *competitiveness*; but the Russian way of enterprise fragmentation typically had the opposite effect. These breakups were carried out in the absence of a market structure or adequate market choices. Even worse for long-term economic vitality, the new smaller firms lacked the resources necessary to acquire the technological knowledge that had been provided in the larger enterprises to which they had been attached formerly. As Glaz'ev details this process, the breakup of production enterprises into smaller units, without careful prior planning, "is especially harmful for complex production systems. It destroys them. It provokes the new owners to simplify their production."[159]

This trend could have primarily near-term implications, if Russia's R&D potential could be put "on hold," in the way that corporations lay off assembly line workers until business picks up. But science does not respond well to such shocks of discontinuity. Vladimir Fortov, chair of the Russian Foundation for Basic Science,[160] surveys the prospects for science in late 1993. "We are catastrophically losing our scientific leadership and our scientific training institutions," Fortov warns. "The level of scientific studies is dropping, as is the production of scientific journals and books. Young people are leaving science and technology for business or to go abroad." The number of graduate students studying in institutes of the Russian Academy of Sciences dropped from two thousand in 1991 to just over one thousand in 1992, and to fewer than eight hundred in 1993.[161] Agreeing that Russian science has traditionally been overstaffed, Fortov continues, "The paradox is that we are losing, not only the 'excess,' but the focal points as well."[162]

Evidence for Fortov's contention could be found not only in previously mentioned signs that some highly reputed scientific 'schools' might soon disappear, but also in funding trends. OECD estimates that, once figures are corrected to correspond to OECD norms, R&D investment was approximately 1.4 percent of GDP in 1991, which "places Russia at the level of the OECD country average."[163] But actual expenditures (not amounts budgeted) for basic science in 1992 were a great deal lower than in 1991—dropping to one-third of their 1991 level in just one year. And the loss of support for basic research was much more harmful than is suggested by these overall figures, because at the same time that total funding for science was rapidly shrinking, allocations within the budget that went for research were being cut even more drastically. In 1991, 50 percent of the money allocated for basic science was used to pay the direct expenses of scientific research, beyond the costs of salaries and overhead. In 1992, only 3 percent of the sharply reduced budget for science was for such direct research expenses—or 1/50th the funding level of a year earlier.[164] The rest went to salaries and overhead costs. And salaries for scientific personnel were very low.[165] In early 1993, salaries in the scientific sector were 30 percent lower than in the country overall, but in the late 1980s they had been 20 percent higher.[166]

Disinterest among Western advisers in Russia's R&D capability has an obvious rationale. A high level of native technological and scientific expertise is not necessary for raw materials export. The Russian government's neglect of this worsening problem, however, is more difficult to understand. YABLOKO's objection to the 1994 budget proposal was partially based on government inattention to this area.[167] As Khakamada states this criticism, "Spending for basic research and support for scientific-technological progress is unjustifiably low. It is probably the country's only hope for competitive potential, not counting raw materials."[168]

In the Russia of 1994, the government was almost the only sponsor of scientific activity. There were only a handful of foundations to support scientific work, and those that had been formed had inadequate resources. There were few private research institutes. Because of these considerations, Yaremenko insists that it is "impermissible" to sacrifice the country's research and development potential to the "imperative" of "the deficit-free budget."[169]

Lessons from Poland and China

An outline of Western approach priorities for post-Soviet reforms was furnished in Lipton and Sachs's first 1990 contribution to the *Brookings Papers on Economic Activity*, where they outlined their "ideas about the basic strategy for a package of comprehensive reforms" for Eastern Europe in general, and particularly Poland.[170] In presenting their economic logic, Lipton and Sachs noted that repressed inflation "is a fundamental factor in many of the deepest economic problems" of these countries, including "chronic shortages, poor export performance, the weakness of private firms trying to compete with state firms, and even the widespread corruption of state managers." But, they continued, these problems are often not as intractable as they seem. "A strong dose of macroeconomic austerity" can substantially alleviate many of them.[171]

It has turned out that those Russian economists were right who insisted that the Western approach was certain to prove unworkable in placing primary emphasis on macroeconomic stabilization. Western economists have often charged, not without cause, that most Russian economists lacked their own level of knowledge regarding the principles of market economies. Yet many Russian economists, also with sound evidence, have argued that Western advisers tended not to understand well the institutional structure and other societal features of command economies. Thus, in the former Communist countries that have attempted the shock therapy approach, inadequacies of the formula have inevitably required that it be quickly revised—but with severely damaging economic and political fallout along the way.

While urging on Russia lessons from the early Polish experience, shock therapy advocates demonstrated an impenetrable disinterest in China's reform efforts, arguing that the Chinese case was uninformative for the Russian situation. That neglect will be the focus of our analysis below.

John McMillan and Barry Naughton describe a feature of the Chinese economy that is of critical importance for the Russian situation. "All the institutions of the planned economy [in China] were developed as component parts of that system," they observe. "They are mutually consistent, but incompatible with a true market economy." What would be the effects of shock therapy in such a situation? "A big-bang transition can indeed cause the interconnected socialist system to collapse," McMillan and Naughton acknowledge, adding, "But there is more to moving to a market economy than just removing government controls. New institutions must be created."[172]

In retrospect, McMillan and Naughton conclude, China's impressive economic reform achievements resulted from a "massive entry of non-state firms," a "dramatic increase in competition, both among state firms and between state firms and non-state firms," and "improvements in the performance of state-owned firms resulting from state-imposed market-like incentives." Thus, they suggest, "China shows the potency of the fundamental market forces of entry and competition. China's example does not however, justify *laissez-faire*: the state must monitor firms during the transition."[173] And as for privatization, they argue that the Chinese experience shows that "rapid privatization need not be the centerpiece of a reform policy."[174]

Shock therapy proponents virtually ignored all of these lessons in Russia. Although it can reasonably argued that the Russia of late 1991, following Yeltsin's assault on Soviet Union structures, was in a poor position to pursue a gradual reform course, we know of no evidence that Western advisers or political leaders discussed with either Yeltsin or Russian economic planners the hazards of the separatist course that Yeltsin unilaterally announced on October 28, 1991, which would include "a one-time changeover to market prices." And this proclamation of a new direction for Russia alone, which, as we have shown, violated Russia's treaty commitment with other republics, coming weeks ahead of the Minsk Accord declaration that the USSR had been disbanded—weeks during which the Gaidar team spent considerable time working with Western advisers. Indeed, these political developments seemed compatible with the Western advisers' perspective on how reforms should be initiated; Yeltsin had, with his offensive against the USSR, contributed to the wrecking of the state-organized economic linkages, which, as they saw it, could not be destroyed any too quickly.

Even after the breakup of the USSR, lessons from the Chinese case would seem to have been at least as valuable as lessons from Chile in helping to formulate a viable reform course for the now-fragmented economic system in Russia, since China had, after all, a command economy that resembled that of the USSR on a number of key dimensions. The positive economic effect in China of the entry of large numbers of private and cooperatively owned enterprises was apparently unpersuasive to the Russian planning team, which made no strong effort to stimulate new business start-ups, as we have shown. The Chinese example did not mesh well with key elements of the Western approach, and the creation of a competitive environment in Russia was seen as less important than measures to reduce the budget deficit.

In an October 1993 paper, Sachs and Wing Thye Woo summarize their arguments against looking to the Chinese experience for insight into optimal reform strategies for Russia and other countries of Eastern Europe and the former Soviet Union (EEFSU). Their presentation illustrates the slips in logic and failure to furnish tenable supporting evidence that are hallmarks of ideologically driven analysis. Here, will review central points in their argument.

It is correct, as Sachs and Woo maintain, that in China "the transfer of workers from low-productivity agriculture to higher-productivity industry" was simpler than the kind of structural adjustment required in the EEFSU because industry in the EEFSU "is overbuilt" and "virtually all workers [in the EEFSU] before 1992 were in jobs heavily subsidized by the state."[175] But Sachs and Woo do not recognize that these are arguments *against*—not *for*—shock therapy in Russia. Their point suggests that in Russia, *even more* studious attention to reform mechanisms was required than was needed for China—attention specifically geared to Russia's particularly thorny industrial production problems, which were not as severe as those in China.

Overall, Sachs and Woo's attempt to discount the Chinese case because of the considerable differences between initial reform conditions in China and the EEFSU is too facile. Of course, it is important to identify dimensions of national economies that render them more or less comparable with other nations undergoing transition. Sachs should have done more of that, rather than rigidly applying his perspective from Poland, for example, to Russia—and attempting, in the process, to discredit more studied and situation-specific approaches to economic reform.

Our intent here is not to support the Chinese approach or to force parallels between the economies of Russia and China. But we find it notable that Western approach proponents who have been involved in Russian reforms sometimes seem to develop their comparisons among economies in transition more from a position of advocacy than of inquiry. It is that tendency with which we take issue in the discussion below.

There are clearly a number of factors that render hazardous certain types of comparisons between Russia and China, and also between Russia and Poland. Not only was Poland's economy so different from Russia's at the beginning of reforms as to make a uniform approach to marketization in those two countries highly suspect, but Poland's experience with shock therapy was not enviable. Were the sharp declines in GDP (12 percent in 1990 and 7 percent in 1991, according to standard estimates) and industrial output (22 percent in 1990 and 15 percent in 1991)[176] inevitable results of economic reform, or rather the unnecessary effects of an inadequate reform approach? Poland's economy improved in 1992 and 1993, with a GDP increase of 1 percent in 1992 and 4 percent in 1993. The road back from the economic damage inflicted by shock therapy was thus certain to be long, even in a country characterized by an "intense desire to rejoin the economies of Western Europe," as Lipton and Sachs described the situation in Poland in 1990.[177]

Andrew Berg and Sachs counter by arguing that "the overall decline in 1990 GDP was much smaller than the official estimate."[178] They contend that output was mismeasured and that consumption declines were modest.[179] Shock therapy's defenders like to emphasize that salaries were widely underreported because of "the vast black economy," and to highlight the rapid rise in the purchase of big-ticket items such as automobiles in Poland.[180] But these factors do not mitigate the clearly negative effects of shock therapy for a large proportion of the Polish population. Following the introduction of the "big bang," private sector activity soared, but real incomes dropped much more sharply than had been expected.[181]

If, as shock therapy proponents want to suggest, the economic picture was bright in 1992 and 1993, why were reform candidates being defeated at the polls? In September 1993, the electorate voted into office a parliament dominated by former Communists and a Communist-inspired agrarian party. These candidates had campaigned on a promise to soften the harsh effects of economic reform while continuing to move the country toward a market economy. Sachs may score debating points in the United States by claiming that "calls for gradualism" are "based on naive interpretations of shaky statistics,"[182] but this stratagem clearly would not play well in Poland. A nation whose citizenry

was, in general, enjoying the fruits of newly realized economic pros-
perity—from new cars to thriving black market businesses—would not
have been expected to banish the goose that was bringing them such
golden benefits.

Consistent with 1993 Polish voting patterns, a public opinion study
reported in April 1994 by Bronislav Geremek, chair of the Committee
on International Relations, found that only 20 percent of respondents in
Poland continued to support the reforms.[183] This was in sharp contrast
to survey results in 1989 that found 70 percent in favor of economic
reform.[184] And Poland's political situation remained tense and unpredictable in 1994. As President Lech Walesa's popularity continued to
slide,[185] disagreements with the Polish parliament in April prompted
him to threaten its dissolution.[186]

Further, as Kazimierz Poznanski points out, successes that have been
enjoyed in Poland's economic course since 1990 are attributable "in large
part, to the fact that many shock therapy policies have been softened, if
not reversed."[187] The bottom line is that, in Poland, Western approach
proponents do not have a good example to support their position.

With such a disappointing reform record as Poland's for the Western approach, it would be prudent for reform planners to search wher-
ever they can to identify promising leads that might produce improvement over this undistinguished example of neoliberal initiatives. In this
context, China's experiences could be viewed as a source of potentially
useful information rather than being reflexively rejected as largely ir-
relevant to other settings. China shows that it is more than theoretically
possible to promote market development without wreaking havoc on
an economy in the process. But even in 1994, Sachs was still attempting to characterize the debate in Russia over "the relative merits of
shock therapy versus gradualism" as, in reality, a choice between "a
sensible and consistent financial policy" (his) and a more gradual approach that was being proposed "by a bitter and corrupt Communist
opposition."[188]

Other research has reached very different conclusions from Sachs
and Woo's about the potential value of the Chinese example in informing economic reforms elsewhere. Gary Jefferson and Thomas Rawski,
for example, recognize that "China's industrial gains of the past 15
years are partly attributable to favorable initial conditions. But," they
continue, "the contrast between China's trend of buoyant increases in
industrial output, real wages, employment, and exports and the perfor-

mance of industry in states that have attempted to accelerate the pace of institutional change is too large to be explained solely by differences in initial conditions."[189]

Naughton observes that although "some features of the Chinese experience" have been "intriguingly positive," while some have been "clearly negative," the literature of economic reform includes only "a few diffuse characterizations of the Chinese process," which are circulated "without much critical reflection."[190] An important reason for this situation, of course, is the power of incompatible paradigms over the minds of analysts who are committed to a particular one. As Thomas Kuhn points out in *The Structure of Scientific Revolutions*, "The proponents of competing paradigms practice their trade in different worlds," and "practicing in different worlds, the two groups of scientists see different things when they look from the same points in the same direction."[191]

"Unfortunately," Sachs insists, "there is little in China's experience that is directly applicable" to the Russian case.[192] But we find little evidence that Western approach proponents have earnestly tried to assess the validity of Naughton's argument that the economic changes taking place in China "form a virtuous cycle of reform."[193] Are there, as McMillan and Naughton contend, "specific characteristics of the centrally planned system that can be used to initiate a step-by-step reform process"? Might they be correct that "once a crack is opened in the monolith that is the centrally planned economy, cumulative forces take over and prise the crack open ever more widely"?[194]

This perspective is the antithesis of Sachs and Åslund's position— the position that they held not only in 1994 but also before the Soviet Union's demise in December 1991. "The examples of harm caused by gradualism in the transition are ample," Åslund contends.[195] But his evidence does not live up to its billing. He argued in 1992, for example, that "gradual deregulation gives economic crime an unnecessary and very dangerous boost."[196] The unfolding of events in Russia suggests that the opposite has been true there. Russia's hurry-up privatization scheme, so warmly praised by these analysts, is deeply implicated in its epidemic of organized crime, as we pointed out in chapter three. And Sachs's contention that a more studied approach would allow "rear-guard actions by old power structures" to "succeed in derailing key reforms"[197] is equally unsupported by results of the actual course of reforms in Russia. Contrary to Sachs's claim, it was the haste of reforms, particularly, that opened the door to nomenklatura profiteering from privatization and the consolidation of power by the old Soviet bureaucracy in the wake of the rapid destruction of prevailing linkages in the political and economic systems.

"There is no guarantee," economist Josef Brada contends, "that the evolutionary approach, which requires the long-run co-existence of a large Soviet-type system with a small, nascent and fragile capitalist system in a single economy will eventually result in a triumph of capitalism over socialism. Indeed, just the opposite is to be expected, as the economically and politically powerful state sector will act to marginalize or wipe out small capitalists."[198] But contrary to Brada's expectation, the private sector was flourishing in China during 1994. In Russia, on the other hand, after the failed attempt at shock therapy, entrepreneurs were struggling to regain the toe-hold that seemed stable before the Western approach intervened.

Sachs and Woo continue their argument by maintaining, "China's two-track liberalization facilitated the flow of peasant agricultural workers to new sectors. . . . Subsistence agricultural workers are delighted to move, since the wages in the new sector are higher than in subsistence agriculture." EEFSU "state-sector workers, however, may prefer to remain in the state enterprises even though their productivity would be higher in the new firms," they add. But they offer no empirical evidence to support this critical hypothesis. According to their logic, "As long as the subsidy to state-enterprise workers is greater than the difference in productivity in the two sectors, state workers will not voluntarily leave their jobs for the non-state sector."[199] It would have been more informative, however, for Sachs and Woo to have considered ways that private sector development could be, and has been, encouraged by reformist governments. Their hypothetical reasoning on this point cannot obscure the obvious attraction of nonstate business in both Russia and Poland, as well as in China, when real entrepreneurship is allowed to develop.

Unlike the situation in China, Sachs and Woo insist, market reform in the EEFSU necessarily involves a decline of industry "because of the excessive size of heavy industry in the EEFSU, and the corresponding underdevelopment of the service sector."[200] Of course that is true, but the statement does not speak to the real question here. Would the decline be greater with a situation-specific approach than with "big bang"? They do not say. Available evidence, however, makes a strong case for the superiority of a more studied approach over the "big bang" in minimizing productivity declines.

"Economic planning was far more deeply entrenched in the EEFSU than in China," Sachs and Woo note, and "the specificity of state planning was far greater in the EEFSU." Further, "regional governments were given greater autonomy in China than in the EEFSU."[201] Again, this is an argument for a more thoughtful and studied approach in the EEFSU, rather than for overnight attempts at liberalization and hurry-up plans for privatization. These analysts offer no evidence to suggest why they propose a different interpretation of these historical and structural differences.

Because of gradual decay in economic performance during the 1980s, Sachs and Woo observe, a policy of "decapitalization" was followed in the EEFSU, in which "the physical and financial capital stock was simply allowed to run down." To sustain consumption levels, in all of these countries an extreme foreign debt crisis developed.[202] But contrary to their reasoning, a large debt obligation would seem to be an argument for the smoothest possible transition—one that would be oriented toward minimizing productivity declines and the kind of political instability that would deter massive foreign investment. The Russian government's attempt to follow the Western approach had the opposite effects.

"On almost all fronts," Sachs and Woo maintain, "the state-enterprise sector in China has continued to perform poorly. It is heavily loss making." In citing "several recent studies of the Chinese experience," Sachs and Woo emphasize the relatively lower level of performance of state-owned enterprises (SOEs) compared to those in the nonstate sector, while ignoring two other critical factors.[203] First, China's two-track program was intended to reduce the state's relative contribution to industrial output, and it has. Naughton reports that "the SOE share of industrial output declined from 78 percent of the total in 1978 to 48 percent in 1992, the first year in which SOEs did not produce the majority of industrial output." Further, SOE output grew 7.7 percent annually between 1978 and 1991. That is, *state enterprise output* has increased impressively during the period of Chinese reforms. We will not recount the grim record of Russian industrial output since the Gaidar reforms began there. As Naughton observes, "That Chinese SOEs, despite their numerous failings, were able to support a transitional process without serious disruption is significant."[204]

"The real question," Sachs and Woo ask, is "why gradualism failed" in the EEFSU countries.[205] Key factors in the answer for Russia revolve around Yeltsin's actions against Gorbachev and the USSR that Gorbachev headed. Gradualism failed there partially because Yeltsin's multi-pronged attack on the Soviet Union thwarted it in a campaign that undercut Gorbachev's reforms on both the economic and the political fronts. The Union economy was purposefully undermined by Russian leadership through the deliberate withholding of taxes, and other measures, and Union authority was challenged by Yeltsin and other Russian leaders through a variety of clearly provocative actions. In Yeltsin, Russia got a champion of radical reform whose priorities seemed to be consistent with those of Western approach advocates; and in the Russian ministries that took over the functions of their Union counterparts, Russia got a number of people who were inexperienced at the job of running a country.[206] From the time that the Gaidar reforms began through the end of voucher privatization, the small but thriving entrepreneurial class that had emerged under Gorbachev was held back, at the same time that organized crime penetrated deeply into all aspects of both private and state business. What was proclaimed as a program to free the invisible hand of the market became a program whose most important achievements arguably were to unshackle the all-too-visible fist of the mafia and the long-familiar reach of the state bureaucracy.

Several Western approach proponents had voiced strong displeasure with Gorbachev's gradual, and often halting, approach to reform before the Soviet Union's dissolution.[207] The reform path has been crooked in China, also. Woo recognizes this fact but treats it as evidence *against* a situation-specific approach to reform. In a 1994 paper, Woo points out that "gradualism in China is the result of the political deadlock between the Stalinists and the reformers, and not the result of a particular theory of reform."[208] This is not unlike the political situation in the Soviet Union in the late 1980s, when opposition to Gorbachev's initiatives frequently caused reversals in the momentum of change and prevented the systematic promulgation of a coherent reform strategy.

"There is no theory behind Chinese gradualism," Woo objects. Thus he follows his monetarist colleagues in failing to appreciate the practical value of not being bound by the dictates of a rigid theory, when the question is how to transform a specific economy in a particular period of its development. This "no theory" option had brought China's macroeconomic performance to a point of rivaling that of Japan and Korea in 1994.[209] China's transformation has not been guided by an overarching theory of *what* should be done *when*, certainly, and that has been its strength. Rather than being guided by a prefabricated theory, Chinese reforms have been realized according to a clearly identifiable perspective about *process*—"a step at a time," as Shahid Yusuf, research administrator at the World Bank, characterizes the Chinese way. By "always ensuring that each economic initiative passed the test of socio-political acceptability before it was widely implemented," China has "maintained the momentum of change while minimizing the risk of instability," Yusuf notes.[210]

The choice between shock therapy and a situation-specific approach is not a choice between two competing theoretical templates, each with its own set of inflexible forms, but rather a choice between a rigid formula, with overriding emphasis on speed, on the one hand, and a preferred process on the other—the latter involving, at its heart, coalition building, compromise, and reassessment. It has often been characteristic of Russian reform plans, including Yavlinskii and Shatalin's 500 Days program, for predictions to be made with too much confidence that particular "stages" of reform could be reached in predetermined time periods. But we see in the 500 Days program, and also in the subsequent proposal outlined by Allison and Yavlinskii,[211] recognition that reform planning and implementation are dynamic processes, which necessarily involve active response to initiatives that are introduced and openness to modification as demanded by circumstances. This orientation is not a part of the Western approach. It is arguable that deep-seated cultural factors may be implicated in China's choice of gradualism and Yeltsin's preference for a "big bang" approach. This would not explain, however, the decision of Western advisers and financial institutions to push Russia in the "big bang" direction.

Woo argues, rightly, that "gradualism is not like a person putting on his pants one leg at a time," because "the main reason behind gradualism is absence of social consensus over what the final state of affairs should be."[212] It is clear that the situation under Gorbachev was similar. If the 500 Days program suggests the crystallization of a plan, its failure to win approval underscores the absence of social consensus in the economic sphere.

And Woo believes that the strength of "big bang" is that, in contrast to gradualism, it "means a person who, while putting in his first leg, cannot wait to put in his second one."[213] Unfortunately, the evidence suggests, with the "big bang" approach advocated by Sachs and Woo, in his haste to get the job completed, the person is all too likely to pull his pants on over his head.

5

Coordination Issues in Russia's Privatization Program

To get to the point where restructuring is seriously contemplated, Russia needs to be privatized. It is therefore essential to push for this, and to grease the wheels when they are slow-turning.

—Andrei Shleifer and Maxim Boycko,
"The Politics of Russian Privatization"[1]

In October 1991, when Boris Yeltsin asked the RSFSR Congress of People's Deputies to give him special emergency powers to carry out economic reform, he stated his reasons for the request. First, he said, economic reform would be hard, and he needed extraordinary authority to maintain the reform course during the months when life would be more difficult for nearly everyone. Further, he insisted, it was important to preclude the possibility that local governments in Russia might interfere with decisions at the state level. At the same time that Yeltsin was calling for strengthened executive power with a resolutely vertical authority structure, he also emphasized that the work of the parliament and the executive branch would be closely coordinated.[2] After four days of intense discussion, the Congress voted to grant Yeltsin the emergency powers he had requested.

It was not long, however, before clear signs appeared that the expected cooperation among the executive and legislative branches would prove to be elusive. Only eleven days after price liberalization was introduced at the beginning of 1992, Supreme Soviet chairman Ruslan Khasbulatov, speaking to a delegation of Italian senators, said that Yeltsin's government ministers were proving to be unqualified and might have to be replaced. Already, Khasbulatov was having second thoughts about the parliament's decision to grant Yeltsin the emergency powers he had requested ten weeks earlier. What had caused the rapid turnaround in Khasbulatov's perspective? Most prices had been freed, and after only a few days many citizens were already questioning Yeltsin's October promise that people's lives would begin to improve by the next autumn. The initial jolt had been too severe, and the objections of prominent Russian economists to the "shock therapy" idea too urgent, to sustain the level of unqualified public support for Yeltsin that was manifest after the August putsch. Khasbulatov's rapid reversal in January may have been connected to a visit he had just made to workers in the city of Riazan'. Speaking of this visit, and a similar change of perspective by Aleksandr Rutskoi after meeting with workers in Siberia, correspondent Nikolai Bodnaruk described the emerging new mood as "populism."[3] Whatever its source, this conspicuous crack in the wall of support for Yeltsin's reform policy was a warning for the future.

In this chapter, we will review key coordination issues that were important to the Russian voucher privatization initiative that was concluded at the end of June 1994. In chapter six, we will offer an overall assessment of the program. We will suggest below that the complex issues of coordination that necessarily attended such an ambitious effort were magnified by the attempt to carry out rapid privatization without adequate consideration of divergent interests in Russian society. Centralization of the privatization decision-making process, under the supervision of the State Property Management Committee (GKI), facilitated the rapid privatization pace that Yeltsin's reformers wanted, but it did not produce outcomes that were consistent with the stated objectives of the privatization program. In reality, the actual priorities of the reformers were not clarified in the program's announced objectives. Both below and in chapter six we will examine implications of this divergence.

We include here a number of excerpts from our interviews with privatization officials, officials in local administrations and soviets, and directors of privatizing and privatized enterprises. (Our methodological procedure for selecting these excerpts is described in Appendix A.) In selecting this illustrative material, we consistently attempted to choose statements that represented the *characteristic* viewpoints and positions that a particular subset of respondents voiced about the particular issue being discussed. This approach has the disadvantage of failing to highlight the full range of positions and views among our respondents, but if it is consistently followed it offers the advantage of reflecting the overall trends in our data.

Interest Groups and Privatization Policy

The mixed messages sent by Russian leaders and the public during the first days of Yeltsin's reforms highlight the most fundamental coordination issue that has faced Russia's economic reformers. Whose interests, and whose visions for the future, should be most closely heeded as the reform program unfolded? Public opinion studies showed strong public support for transition to a market economy, if not for some key features of the reform strategy, as we will see in chapter seven. But no one knew how to achieve the overriding goal. The public and the parliament had accepted Yeltsin's proposal largely on faith. Inevitably, however, outside pressures on both the parliament and Yeltsin's planners were soon felt, as we indicated in chapter two. The lawmakers were lobbied heavily by enterprise directors, labor unions, and members of the central planning apparatus. They increasingly responded to pressure from these groups, as well as from growing dissatisfaction among the population with the first results of reform. And the executive branch was being urged by foreign advisers to follow the economic strategy that *they* favored.

These diverse groups did not speak with unified voices. Especially among enterprise directors, interests often diverged sharply. "The directors' corps have the most complicated assortment of motives among all of those whose interests are affected by privatization," Dmitrii Vasil'ev told us in May 1992, at a time that the privatization of large enterprises was under intensive discussion. Vasil'ev was a deputy chair of GKI. "That is because some directors think that they would benefit more by preservation of the command system, while others see greater opportunities in a market environment," he added. "One group of directors wants to become the *de facto* owners of their enterprises, while another group fears negative effects from losing state patronage and Central Bank credits. Some favor ownership among workers' collectives, and others anticipate benefits from outside investment."

At that time, Vasil'ev estimated that about half of all directors favored the privatization of their enterprises, and about half opposed it. Because Russian privatization began with the kinds of enterprises that would, in general, be the ones where ownership could be transformed with the least difficulty, directors of those enterprises that were privatized early in the program were likely to be drawn primarily from that group of directors who saw privatization as serving their interests. "The other group realizes that privatization cannot be stopped," Vasil'ev added, "and they are calling for collective ownership among enterprise personnel. That is the way to insure that the director stays in control." Vasil'ev had already seen how persuasive the argument for worker ownership could be, and that lobbying for employee control had already, in May 1992, led to a restructuring of the privatization program, which would be approved by the Supreme Soviet the following month. The new privatization variant that emerged from these discussions was to become the most popular privatization method among directors, and it would undercut one of the principal objectives of privatization: to promote enterprise restructuring through an influx of outside owners.

That same week in 1992, we spoke with Petr Filippov about the new proposal to allow workers to buy their enterprises. Because of strong and effective pressure from a group of directors and the Supreme Soviet, by that time Anatolii Chubais's planners had already incorporated into their privatization program the new variant, which would permit 51 percent worker ownership of privatizing enterprises. Filippov was still chairman of the Subcommittee on Privatization of the Russian Supreme Soviet at that time. (He later became a close Yeltsin adviser.) "It is obvious to any economist," he argued, "that the most important need now is to bring in outside owners, who are interested in new opportunities and can make enterprise operations more efficient. If we permit workers to keep 51 percent of the shares of their enterprises, then those enterprises will have no chance of outside investment—either foreign or domestic. Who would want to invest their money under those conditions?" But Filippov recognized, too, that pressure from those directors who wanted to retain control of their enterprises could not be ignored. "The interests of different layers of the population became transparent during the first stage of privatization," he noted, "and the battle to satisfy these different groups quickly became more severe." In early 1994, Filippov reflected on that critical revision in the privatization program. "We agreed to this new privatization variant because the alternative was to give up on privatization entirely," he stated. "This was our concession to the Supreme Soviet."[4]

Filippov believed in 1992 that the privatization planners had themselves extracted a concession by insisting that all privatizing enterprises to be transformed into joint stock companies would be open rather than closed—thus allowing the sale of enterprise shares on the market. The privatization planners hoped in that way to leave open the possibility that outsiders who wanted to invest in an enterprise could persuade enterprise personnel to sell a substantial proportion of their shares. As privatization proceeded after 1992, however, it became clear that directors were typically maintaining tight control over their enterprises—either by actually withholding the possession of shares from workers, even though workers legally own the shares, or by buying shares from workers or through voucher auction purchases.

The Structure of Coordination and Authority in the Privatization Program

Political cross-currents were nothing new to Russian leaders in the waning days of the Soviet era, of course, and when the RSFSR Supreme Soviet drafted its early privatization legislation in 1991, it built into the structure being created a division of powers to prevent the interests of either the executive or the legislature from becoming dominant. The lawmakers were experienced in the pitfalls of a system where deputies were empowered by law but thoroughly dominated by the executive branch, as had been the case under Soviet communism before Gorbachev's political reforms. Thus, as the overall scheme of privatization decision making was conceived, *property management committees* were structured to represent the interests of the executive branch at each administrative level, from federal to municipal; and *property funds*,[5] also to be established at each level of administration, were to represent the interests of the legislature.[6]

Initially, the interests of the executive and legislative branches were thought of as being complementary in terms of the two criteria for reform that were widely regarded as being the most critical—that privatization should proceed rapidly and that it should be carried out in a way that would improve the country's economic performance. We will return to these points later in this chapter, where we will outline the considerations that led the executive and legislative branches to diverge and ultimately sharply disagree about the importance of both of these criteria.

Stakeholding among Local Officials

Our interviews with local privatization officials indicated that there were a large number of coordination problems involving various units linked together in privatization decision making, and that frequently those problems interfered significantly with the privatization process (Table B–5.1). But there is a qualitative difference between the kinds of coordination problems that result from micro-level organizational inadequacies and those that stem from the larger strategies and objectives of the various stakeholders in Russian privatization. Below, we will focus on this second set of problems.

One of the most frequently voiced complaints among our respondents in property management committees, property funds, and administrations and soviets of local governments was that voucher privatization impeded the task of coordinating the transition from state to nonstate ownership. These officials preferred other forms of privatization by a large margin (Table B–5.2).

Local soviets and administrations in several regions attempted to stop voucher auctions. This effort was based, they insisted, on the need to serve the interests of people in their cities and oblasts. A property fund official in Smolensk told us, "Our city soviet made several decisions that contradict Yeltsin's decree [authorizing voucher auctions]. One was that they decided not to put some of the designated enterprises up for auction. They sometimes thought that the pace of privatization was too fast to ensure that necessary products would still be available locally. The privatization of a bread factory was stopped, for example, because the deputies believed that, after privatization, there wouldn't be any bread." But a property management committee member in Smolensk explained the outcome of that conflict. "We have a major dispute with the local soviet about the list of enterprises to be privatized. They wanted to shorten it. But we are going to proceed with the original list." A Voronezh property management committee official said that her committee disagreed with the local soviet about several aspects of privatization. "They think privatization is too fast, too encompassing, and harmful to the enterprises," she noted. "But we will not deviate from our plan."

We found evidence that resistance to privatization among local administrations was not a desire to retain their long-standing control over enterprises. An official in the Voronezh city property fund whose job was to prepare enterprises for auctioning observed, "We are experiencing very serious conflict with the local administration. They want to keep the most efficient enterprises under their supervision by slowing privatization. At the same time they are pressuring workers to change their decision about which variant of privatization to choose, how to distribute shares, and who will manage the enterprise. The main theme here is that the administration wants to retain as much control as possible." A member of the Voronezh oblast property fund stated this point emphatically: "Local soviets and the local administration often try to prevent large enterprises from privatizing in order to preserve 'the state property' from being lost." A Smolensk oblast property management committee member told us, "The chairman of our committee is too subservient to the oblast soviet. He reports to them. And they don't actually understand the privatization process. In their minds, by slowing privatization they are preserving state property from being plundered."

This was the problem that Yeltsin highlighted most pointedly in requesting emergency powers in October 1991. Subsequent developments indicated that this concern was justified—and not just in Voronezh. In all of our research cities and oblasts, we found evidence of attempts by local administrations and soviets to delay privatization or to change privatization procedures in order to retain control. This problem was made even more thorny as issues arose over whether a particular property was under federal, oblast, or city control as privatization began. Discussing this situation in Moscow during the summer of 1993, for example, Moscow's public prosecutor, Gennadii Ponomarev, observed that these conflicting claims were creating "constant conflict between the Russian government and Moscow's government, between city power structures and district soviets." Since 1990, when work on this question began, Ponomarev continued, the problem of authority for managing real estate located on Moscow territory has not been resolved. "As a result, there is continual bargaining about the privatization of property, the ownership of which is uncertain. Because of this there have been a large number of disagreements, and many privatization decisions have had to be changed." Local administrations, at both the city and okrug levels, often want to keep the decision-making power themselves, Ponomarev added, "not taking into account the legal prerogatives of the appropriate property fund and property management committee."[9]

This problem persisted through the end of the voucher privatization program. In May 1994, Oleg Tolkachev, the fourth person to chair the Moscow Property Management Committee in two years, continued to emphasize, "Now, the most important thing to decide is . . . what belongs to whom in Moscow?"[10]

We also found substantial evidence that the resistance among local stakeholders that Yeltsin had feared was often related to the breakdown of constructive deliberation between his planners and Russian lawmakers. As the Supreme Soviet turned increasingly negative about the way GKI was directing the privatization campaign, independently of legislative efforts at oversight, local soviets tended to take the side of the Supreme Soviet. "The uncertainty about who is in charge 'at the top' makes it possible for local soviets to make decisions that contradict privatization regulations and presidential decrees," an Ekaterinburg property management committee member charged. And a number of other respondents in both property management committees and property funds pinpointed the inadequacy of attempts at coordination among federal branches as a critical source of local disputes.

The Issue of Inflexibility

Our research indicated that the property management committee structure was characterized by a high level of compliance with federal-level directives. Outside Moscow, exceptions to this generalization were rare in our experience and according to the reports of respondents both within and outside the privatization decision making structure. (Several Yeltsin decrees authorized Moscow officials to develop their own privatization procedure.) This administrative hierarchy in the executive branch repeatedly produced conflicts between local soviets of people's deputies and local property management committees.

The disadvantage most frequently noted by our respondents to the rigidity of privatization decision making was that, by enforcing compliance at the local level with directives from the center, variations among regions and enterprises were not being adequately taken into account, and this flaw was working against effective privatization. A Smolensk property management official complained to us that "the center should not plan the percentage of enterprises in each sector that are to be privatized in local areas. The mix of enterprises is too different from place to place." An Ekaterinburg (Sverdlovsk oblast) privatization official went further. "There isn't any meaningful coordination between the State Property Management Committee and local authorities," he charged. Another concurred, stating, "They [GKI] are eager to decide everything by themselves. They are not considering local interests."

The State Committee's unwillingness to allow a large measure of discretion in privatization decision making below the federal level probably accelerated the pace of privatization among smaller, nonfederal enterprises; and rapid privatization was the most important objective of privatization planners. But about 60 percent of the large production enterprises that were undergoing privatization in 1993 were federal property, and according to the privatization program, the State Committee was required to directly oversee the privatization of federal-level enterprises. Economist Larisa Piiasheva, commenting on this situation in May 1994, said, "They physically are not able to manage such a huge job."[11] Even Yeltsin aide Petr Filippov, who strongly supported the privatization program, faulted this approach. He was concerned that not enough enterprises were offering shares for voucher auction. "The reason for that is excessive centralization of the procedure" for privatizing large enterprises, he insisted.[12]

Privatization Pace and Concern
with Economic Improvement

The rapid pace of privatization was a major issue in all four of our research cities. As privatization head Chubais saw the situation, if privatization were to be accomplished at all, it would have to be made "irreversible" before the legislature had the opportunity to derail the process. Clearly, a guiding principle of the privatization planners was to move quickly to take advantage of what has been judged to be a short-term opportunity, and thereby to so emphatically dismember the command system that it could never be reconstituted.

"Rapid privatization creates problems," Chubais told us in August 1993, "but a slower pace would create more problems." This position reflected the prioritization that had been articulated by the Yeltsin government's "Economic Policy Memorandum" in February 1992, which had included a pointed assurance to the International Monetary Fund that the privatization process would be "considerably speeded up."[13] The reformers' view, that Russian privatization could succeed only if it were rapid, meshed fully with their perceptions about how to meet the IMF's expectations as the Yeltsin reforms were beginning, and thereby increase the likelihood of IMF membership and the opportunity to use Fund-provided resources.[14]

This tension between concern with privatization efficiency and the overriding concern about pace of privatization among government planners created inevitable conflict. Demands that privatization be carried out through procedures that would stabilize and improve the faltering production system came from many sources. In addition to many Russian economists, members of the Congress of People's Deputies, local soviets, and local property funds, industrial ministries and a large number of enterprise directors also held that reform should proceed deliberately. Surgery was urgently needed, they argued, to save the Russian economy from further decline, but the operation should not kill the patient.

Many federal-level executives, however, saw privatization as the *starting point* for economic reform. Eliminating state control over the production system was a necessary precondition, they maintained, for healthy economic development. The "Economic Strategy of the Russian Government," which was issued a month after the "Economic Policy Memorandum," underscored this strategy. "We are striving to create a market economy based on private property," the report stated.[15] Once ownership of enterprises was transferred into private hands, they believed, real economic reform could begin.

Our respondents tended to be less willing than the reform strategists to see enterprises suddenly thrust into an economic environment for which they were not prepared. Their concerns typically centered around the ability of enterprises to adapt to changing economic circumstances and the necessity, with rapid privatization, for enterprise executives to make administrative decisions for which they were not trained. A number of officials decried the State Committee's inattention to adequate preparation of enterprises and their personnel for the economic conditions that privatization was quickly creating. According to a property fund official in Ekaterinburg, "The pace of privatization is impeding the development of a business environment that can sustain the privatizing enterprises." Even among the property management committee members we interviewed in 1993—officials who were directly subordinate to Chubais's State Committee—a higher percentage judged the pace of privatization to be too rapid (29 percent) than thought that it should be speeded up (25 percent). Among our property fund respondents, the differential was markedly greater. Fourteen percent of those privatization officials believed that the pace should be accelerated, but 33 percent believed that the pace should be slowed.

Our results indicate substantial support, however, for the then-current pace of privatization. Thirty-nine percent of property management committee officials thought that no change of pace was needed,[16] and among property fund officials the corresponding percentage was 44.[17] We repeatedly found divergent perspectives about this issue among members of the same committees and funds, and in our interviews we probed in a variety of ways for information that would help us to understand these different points of view. In studying the officials' responses to a large number of queries during our interviews, we identified one characteristic that clearly differentiated a large number of those who wanted the pace of privatization to be slowed from many who gave other answers. Overall, the responses of those who wanted privatization to be slowed tended to reflect more concern with enterprise efficiency after privatization than was characteristic of many who would have preferred that privatization be speeded up.

A Voronezh official who believed that privatization's pace was too rapid argued, "Privatization needs to be slowed down because the old economic mechanisms are being destroyed too quickly, and replacements are not being developed." Another suggested, "People are not psychologically prepared for privatization now. Thus, as it is being carried out now, it is nothing but a formal act." A Smolensk property management committee member said, "Privatization needs to be slower, so that the business environment of each enterprise can be evaluated, and privatization carried out in light of each firm's particular situation." And a Moscow official worried that "the legal basis for privatized enterprises is not being provided with the current rate of privatization."

"The vehicle to carry out economic reform has turned out to be a squanderer of state property," a Moscow property fund member insisted. And several officials leveled the charge made by a Moscow district property management committee member: "Today, people are being pushed into privatization the same way they were pushed into collective farms in another time." An administrator in a Moscow prefecture stated the point emphatically: "We are having serious conflicts with territorial agencies of the Moscow property management committee. They are trying to privatize enterprises as quickly as they can, and we are trying to preserve the infrastructure. Services and goods are needed *after* privatization, and that is our concern." An official in a different Moscow okrug prefecture concurred. "Our people are members of several privatization commissions," she stated, "and they often complain about experiencing very strong pressure from privatization agencies to make quick decisions—not thoughtful, but quick. Such decisions can't help but lead to negative results." Such concerns were voiced repeatedly among officials we interviewed in local administrations.

A property fund member in Voronezh told us that the local property management committee was accepting assessments of enterprises' value that were too low, for the purpose of speeding up privatization. As the economics chairman of the fund, he was concerned that these low assessments were having negative consequences. "With this strategy they increase the likelihood that privatization will proceed quickly," he noted, "and they pave the way for either enterprise workers or an outsider to acquire shares at bargain prices. But in the process the state is deprived of needed revenue and the enterprise loses the chance for a more deliberate property transfer that could improve its efficiency."

The Role of Branch Ministries and Departments

During the Soviet period, ministries were at the heart of the economic bureaucracy. Some were eliminated, and some were consolidated and restructured. A number of ministries and departments remained important to supervision and coordination in the production system at every administrative level during the period of voucher privatization. The stakeholder interests of these ministries and departments became an increasingly important factor in privatization negotiations as the privatization of production enterprises replaced "small privatization" as the main focus of the privatization effort.

Branch ministries and departments were often particularly reluctant to relinquish their control and planning functions, when, as a property management committee official in Smolensk told us, "privatization breaks up production chains." In a similar vein, branch ministries tended to object to the provision in the state privatization program that permitted departments within an enterprise to privatize separately from the larger enterprise. In early 1994, Filippov admitted that the government's provision allow departments of enterprises to privatize separately had not been very successful. "All of our attempts to break up enterprises into smaller units ... have not produced the desired result yet. We will probably have to make some hard decisions, and to establish progressive taxation on enterprise income according to the number of workers," he added.[18]

Several officials told us that a strategy of branch ministries was that, if they failed to prevent the transformation of enterprises under their authority into joint stock companies, they then attempted to acquire enough shares to be able to control the firms after privatization. Holding companies provided a means of achieving that purpose, and branch ministries often supported the proposal to create these umbrella organizations. Opponents of the idea saw holding companies as vehicles for preventing competition and reduction of unnecessary production.[19] Proponents of the idea argued, however, that holding companies would facilitate better coordination and thus improve economic performance.

The State Property Management Committee recognized the potential of branch ministries to modify the Committee's privatization plans. According to the 1992 privatization program, ministry approval was required for the privatization of some enterprises. But it was thought within GKI that, as Vasil'ev phrased it, ministries wanted "to restore a command economy."[20] A Yeltsin decree on May 8, 1993 authorized GKI to circumvent the ministries' authority in many situations,[21] but the Supreme Soviet attempted to prevent the implementation of this decree by appealing its legality to the Constitutional Court. Their basis was that Yeltsin's emergency powers had expired in December 1992, and the Congress of People's Deputies had not renewed them. Yeltsin now had no legal right to continue ruling by decrees that contradicted Russian laws. On July 22, 1993, the Supreme Soviet decided that the authority to supervise the privatization of federal property would be transferred from GKI to the Council of Ministers. The Supreme Soviet had given GKI its supervisory authority in December 1991, but increasing dissatisfaction with the course and results of privatization caused the lawmakers to reconsider and change that arrangement. This decision directly overrode Yeltsin's May 8 decree, which was intended to strengthen GKI's hand over the ministries.[22]

Chubais's reaction was immediate. His was a populist appeal to retain the authority that GKI enjoyed. "The interests of tens of millions of people have been squandered in secret—behind their backs—for the political aims of the leaders of the Supreme Soviet and the intransigent, frenzied opposition forces who back them,"[23] Chubais insisted. He was attempting to deflect attention from the important practical and legal issues that had been highlighted in the discussion. Then chairman of the Commission on Economic Reform of the Russian Supreme Soviet, Vladimir Mazaev, responded unequivocally. The Supreme Soviet is not trying to stop privatization, he replied. Yeltsin's decree contradicts the law, and the Supreme Soviet is correct to question the results of privatization as it is now being carried out.[24] Yeltsin was away from Moscow at that time. Four days later, just after Yeltsin's return, Chubais called a press conference to announce a new Yeltsin decree. This decree repeated the message of Yeltsin's May 8 decree that the Supreme Soviet had overturned. Informing those present that the May 8 decree had already been sent to property management committees throughout Russia, Chubais added, "The only change that we have made . . . [is that], whereas the first one stated, 'In accordance with Presidential Decree No. 640,' it now reads 'In accordance with Presidential Decree No. 1108. . . .' "[25]

A Coordination Crisis Within the Executive Branch

Chubais's defiant public stance could not contain the internal discord that was building within the executive branch, also, during the summer of 1993. And by the end of August, even Yeltsin had been persuaded to consider major changes in the privatization program. Oleg Lobov, who then headed the Ministry of Economics, discussed problems that he and his staff in the Ministry of Economics saw with voucher privatization. Lobov outlined a different approach, which he believed would overcome some of the disadvantages of the voucher program. Yeltsin wrote in response, "I support this submitted proposal in principle. I ask that the draft for a decree be submitted within 10 days."[26]

On September 3, Lobov held a press conference to discuss his ideas. He suggested that the continuing decline in production necessitated a change in Russia's privatization program. He was unhappy that such a high percentage of state property was being privatized with vouchers, which provided neither enterprises nor the state with needed money. It is important for privatization to be not only a mechanism for changing ownership, he argued, but also a means to reduce the federal budget deficit and provide enterprises with needed capital. Remembering the 500 Days proposal, Lobov noted that the idea of selling state property rather than giving a large proportion of it away at no charge had a solid basis in Russian economic reform planning.[27]

Lobov's press conference came at a critical time in the unfolding of Russia's voucher privatization effort. Many of Russia's most valuable and productive assets, including major oil and gas enterprises, had not yet been privatized. But now, the time was near for some of Russia's biggest prizes to be transferred out of state hands. Further, a number of large production enterprises that badly needed modernization were about to lose state subsidies, as they were privatized subsidies that had allowed them to continue operating. Lobov's idea would either forestall privatization for those companies, if investors were unwilling to pay for shares with cash as opposed to vouchers, or at least bring in needed capital, if they should be sold according to his plan. As Lobov well knew, the Supreme Soviet had never approved voucher privatization—a critical point which we addressed in chapter two—Yeltsin's authority to continue operating the program by decree had expired.

Two days later Chubais appeared on "Ostankino" television. His back was against the wall, and he knew it. We had met with him only a few days earlier, and had been obviously worried. It was being widely rumored in Moscow that his office might soon be vacant. We thought that his chances for survival this time were not good; he seemed to concur. It had not helped his cause that a variety of other opinion leaders had quickly rallied behind Lobov. A number of prominent and influential Russian economists supported Lobov's proposal. And Moscow's mayor, Yurii Luzhkov, declared, "Chubais's privatization qualifies as a crime against city management."[28]

Chubais responded to Luzhkov on Russian television by accusing him and his administration of corruption. He answered Lobov uncompromisingly, insisting that the proposal Lobov had presented was "unacceptable from beginning to end."[29] But it seemed that Chubais had lost in this power struggle. On September 7, a draft document was published in *Nezavisimaia gazeta* that called for radical changes in the privatization process, along the lines that Lobov had outlined in his press conference.[30] Yet, by September 11 Yeltsin was hedging on the

Lobov proposal. He charged Chernomyrdin with the task of meeting with Lobov and Chubais and creating "a common position regarding the proposal of the Economics Ministry directed to implement changes in the current privatization procedure."[31] Chernomyrdin had just returned from Washington, D.C., where he was trying to secure an agreement to postpone payment on Russia's debts.

Washington pressure on this issue was soon in plain evidence. On September 13, U.S. treasury secretary Lloyd Bentsen cautioned, "There has been slowing down in some areas. That is certainly a concern."[32] That day, the Senate Foreign Relations Committee approved a $2.5 billion foreign aid bill for the former Soviet Union, most of which was for Russia. The next day, an under secretary for international affairs at the U.S. Treasury Department, Lawrence Summers, arrived in Moscow. The previous week, Summers had told the U.S. Foreign Relations Committee, "The battle for economic reform in Russia has now entered a new and critical phase in which many of Russia's accomplishments on the economic front are being put at risk. The momentum for Russian reform must be reinvigorated and intensified *to ensure sustained multilateral support*."[33] And Jeffrey Sachs, Harvard professor and then-adviser to the Russian government, warned on September 15 that the drift in the Russian government was "dreadful," and added, "Things are dead in the water."[34] They were not for long. The next day Yeltsin announced that Gaidar would return, replacing Lobov in the Ministry of Economics. Five days later Yeltsin disbanded Russia's Congress of People's Deputies.

6

An Assessment of the Voucher Privatization Program

In the aftermath [of voucher privatization], we can see that the task of creating a new structure of ownership—which was the main goal of privatization—is still ahead.

—Aleksandr Radygin, "Delo Chubaisa zavershit tol´ko vtorichnyi rynok" (Only a Secondary Market Will Complete Chubais's Task)[1]

According to the Russian government's 1993 privatization program, which was approved by Yeltsin's ministers on November 30, 1992, the priority for 1993 was to be "people's privatization" (*narodnaia privatizatsiia*)—the distribution of state property for vouchers to all citizens. Of all the property to be privatized in 1993, about 23 percent was expected to be sold for money at auctions. The other 77 percent would be redeemed with vouchers. The State Property Management Committee (GKI) considered 1993 to be the most critical year for "building a fair people's capitalism." As many people as possible would be involved in voucher auctions for state property.[2]

Voucher privatization officially ended on June 30, 1994.[3] Of the 148 million vouchers that had been issued, 144 million (97 percent) had been traded for shares of privatizing enterprises or exchanged for investment fund shares, according to GKI's preliminary estimate.[4]

As we noted in chapter one, in early July, GKI reported that among large and medium-sized enterprises, 21,000 had been transformed into joint stock companies by June 30 in the voucher privatization (*bol'shaia privatizatsiia*) program. Although 70 percent of large and medium-sized Russian industries had been thus "privatized," accounting for more than half of Russia's total production, the state retained controlling interest in most "privatized" production enterprises through its ownership of joint stock company shares. On average, the state owned 35 percent of joint stock company shares around the country. [5] (We will discuss below what "joint stock company" status means in the overall scheme of Russian privatization.) More than 40 million citizens owned shares in enterprises or investment funds. Further, data from GKI also indicated that over a million people could claim ownership in the more than 84,000 small enterprises that had been privatized by that time in the "small privatization" (*malaia privatizatsiia*) program.[6]

But Russian privatization statistics mask several less positive qualitative features of voucher privatization. Our task in this chapter is to look behind the numbers.

A Hard Sell Among Enterprise Directors

Throughout Russia, among those enterprises that had been transformed into joint stock companies by the end of the voucher privatization period, about three-fourths had chosen the variant of privatization that allowed workers to own 51 percent of a company's shares from the start, with an opportunity to buy additional shares—thus diminishing the possibility that outside investors could have a strong voice in the operation of those enterprises. Although this outcome was not what the government had wanted, it was consistent with the usual preferences of the directors we interviewed in 1993.[7]

In a December 1993 press conference, Chubais had been asked by a reporter to comment on the common perception that, "There is opposition among the directors' corps to the current approach to privatization." Chubias's response was unequivocal: "All of the directors today are on our side," he insisted.[8] Our data point to a different conclusion, however.

Chubais was not as incorrect in the abstract as when the subject was the actual privatization of real enterprises through the methods adopted by GKI. When asked whether they believed voucher privatization to be "a good idea or a bad idea," 38 percent of the directors in our 164 enterprises that had distributed shares answered that it was a good idea.

Of course, even with that theoretical wording, 38 percent support hardly justifies Chubais's claim that "all of the directors today" agreed with the GKI approach. And when we rephrased the question to focus specifically on privatization through voucher auctions, the directors' initially modest level of support dropped precipitously.

"Several ideas have been proposed for the privatization of large production enterprises," we began. "Of the following proposals, which one do you think has the most merit?" "Privatization through voucher auctions" was the choice of only 6.5 percent. Forty-two percent favored "privatization by turning ownership over to the personnel in an enterprise," and 16 percent preferred "selling shares of enterprises to anyone who wants to buy them." Directors were four times more likely to respond that "large enterprises should not be privatized" (27 percent) than to say that they favored voucher auctions.[9]

These findings suggest that our directors wanted enterprise personnel either to own their enterprises, if they were to be privatized at all, or to be able to sell shares to acquire needed capital. What they opposed was what the privatization plan had attempted to realize—a giveaway of shares, at no cost, to new outside owners. One might argue that voucher privatization was successful, in spite of the lack of support for this approach among enterprise personnel, *if* the government's objective of improving enterprise efficiency through the strong presence of outside investors had nevertheless been realized. But the government program failed to prevent most enterprises from acquiring controlling interest among their personnel, also. Most of them said, in essence, "We don't care much for your privatization scheme, but since it's the one we have, we'll get as much out of it as we can."

The Unsatisfied Need for Restructuring

A second inadequacy of the voucher program is that it did not clearly promote fundamental restructuring within enterprises. The most obvious internal transformation that was effected through privatization was to change the formal ownership of privatizing enterprises. Most management teams remained intact. Most workers kept their old jobs. At most plants, long-overdue modernization did not begin. Most privatized production enterprises attracted no foreign investment, and most did not sell shares for much-needed working capital. State ownership declined, but because of marked inattention to such critical factors for economic development as the maintenance of supply and distribution networks during the transition, severe disruptions resulted. The burden of coping with skyrocketing inflation produced a nonpayment-for-goods epidemic and a severe shortage of working capital.

Voucher auctioning did not ensure that outside owners would be brought in, because personnel were themselves free to purchase shares of their enterprises with vouchers. Among the thirty-three enterprises in our 1993 study that had been involved in voucher auctions, the utilization of vouchers for employee purchase of shares was the trend. Workers were majority shareholders in 76 percent of the cases where shares had been distributed through voucher auctions (n = 25).

Writing about this trend, Sergei Mikhailov, chair of the department for voucher utilization of the Property Fund of the Russian Federation, observes, "The majority of joint stock companies that are being formed count on purchasing as large a percentage of the shares of their own enterprises as possible. The reason is their unwillingness to give away a substantial proportion of their firm's profits, through dividends, to a number of small shareholders. They are also fearful of losing their jobs if any large investors should be interested in restructuring the enterprise."[10] Underscoring Mikhailov's assessment, the head of the Federation of Russia Stock Exchanges' information center, Lev Makarevich, notes that, in the process of distributing enterprise shares through voucher auctioning, most enterprises "very skillfully eject outsiders—ordinary citizens—from the stage."[11]

The exclusion of outside investors might be seen as self-defeating for enterprises if outsiders were offering money in exchange for ownership of shares, but voucher auctions did not bring money to enterprises. Voucher privatization substituted "worthless paper," as Nizhnii Novgorod's governor Boris Nemtsov put it, for real money in the purchase of enterprise shares. In the production sphere, the need for extensive modernization was acute at the time of voucher privatization, and investment capital was in short supply.

When we asked directors in our study about the most serious obstacles to increasing productivity and profits, the enormity of this problem became obvious. Directors' most pressing concerns centered not around supply questions or work force deficiencies but money. The director of a Voronezh firm that manufactured electrical supplies, told us, "I don't have any money to replace our obsolete and worn-out production equipment. When machines break down, if we can't repair them with parts that are on hand, we just have to stop using them. And selling what we make doesn't bring in much money, because our buyers often can't pay."

Life goes on with a shortage of electrical supplies, but not without food. The director of a plant in Voronezh that produced canned goods complained that his buyers (retail stores) had reduced their orders to a trickle. "Many aren't able to pay for even basic food items now," he said. And at a Moscow factory where more than one thousand workers made clothing for children and adults, the director noted, "We are working as well as we ever have, and our workers have always been capable, but most of what we make goes to pay taxes. We have no money to upgrade our old equipment or even to repair our buildings, and we can't afford the high interest for loans."

Ekaterinburg is known for its heavy machinery production, and we interviewed the general director of one of the largest of these enterprises. A substantial percentage of the firm's output was used for raw materials extraction. The director told us that he had originally supported voucher privatization, but he had learned, he said, that voucher distribution had done nothing to make his enterprise more effective. Nearly 30 percent of the company's shares had been claimed through voucher auction, mostly by outsiders. "But my most acute problem is lack of working capital," the director said, "and vouchers haven't helped me at all in solving that problem, or in dealing with any of my company's other barriers to improved productivity." Although outside investors who acquired enterprise shares for vouchers brought nothing to an enterprise that it needed, their investment represented a claim on the enterprise's profits. It should not be surprising, then, that enterprises resisted such "investment," which they often predictably saw as only unjustified intrusion.

The director of Ekaterinburg's mammoth heavy machinery enterprise Uralmash, Viktor Korovkin, was interviewed in mid-1993 by a *Moskovskie novosti* correspondent. "I am in no hurry to sell [through vouchers] the 20 percent of my company's shares that are owned by the state," Korovkin stated.[12] Correspondent Andrei Borodenkov summarized this point of view, which has been widely expressed among the directors of production enterprises. "We have nothing against the arrival of private capital, but we do not favor the arrival of owners who get their shares for a song" ("*vauchernyi bestsenok*").[13]

Sometimes, money did change hands through voucher auctioning. But ironically, the exchange did not benefit the enterprises whose shares were being acquired in the process. Uralmash is an apt example. More than 18 percent of its shares were bought early in the privatization process by Kakha Bendukidze, whose firm Bioprotsess paid the U.S. dollar equivalent of about a million dollars for 130,000 vouchers. (By the end of 1993, Bendukidze owned 25 percent of Uralmash's shares.)

Bendukidze acknowledged that his expenditure was small relative to the value of the shares he bought. "Why shouldn't I buy," he asked, "if it is being offered for, actually, 'a ruble.' "[14] But none of Bendukidze's modest investment went to Uralmash. It was paid to individual Russian citizens, who sold vouchers for enough to buy perhaps a bottle of vodka or three kilograms of butter, and to speculators, who traded in vouchers. The main beneficiaries in these exchanges were not the individual citizens, certainly. They had exchanged their share from Soviet collectivization for *another* "song." Those who gained the most in this activity were the voucher speculators and, if the investment should achieve what Bendukidze hoped, Bioprotsess—which acquired, in this case, a substantial percentage of a solid enterprise's shares for a very small price. (Raw materials extraction is one of Russia's most notable growth areas for investment—one that attracts a lion's share of the foreign investment in Russia today.)

The Uralmash situation is actually an example of a favorable outcome for an enterprise, in the context of other possible voucher privatization scenarios. Although Uralmash received no benefit in exchange for the shares it turned over to Bioprotsess, at least Bioprotsess developed a significant interest in the corporate well-being of Uralmash. In December 1993 Bendukidze stated that Bioprotsess was helping Uralmash in a variety of ways—by working to help expand the firm's markets and investing in modernization.[15]

The Equity Issue

Voucher privatization also failed to deliver on its promise of equity. For most Russian citizens, an amount of investment in Russian enterprises that could be meaningful in even a symbolic sense—prominently hailed by Yeltsin and his ministers as voucher privatization's chief feature—remained as elusive in 1994 as it was under Communist rule. With the realization of voucher privatization, there was no credible pretense of broad social equity.

Back when voucher privatization was still an idea being discussed by Gaidar's planning team, it was first met with skepticism. Finally, though, the reformers decided that a substantial part, at least, of "the people's property" should be distributed to citizens free of charge. This was a critical development, which had broad implications for the way the privatization effort evolved in 1992 and early 1993. There was also a practical consideration here. With the liberalization of prices in January 1992, savings were largely wiped out, and most people did not have enough money to buy property while at the same time adjusting to rapidly rising prices for necessary expenses. Thus, the Russian reformers ultimately incorporated the concept of free distribution of property to citizens as a keystone of their program,[16] and equity considerations were showcased as one of voucher privatization's key strengths.[17]

In this way, the architects of Russian privatization took the side of those radical democrats whose chief objective was relatively equal distribution of property, and against those who believed that the primary goal of privatization should be to increase productivity and efficiency. The radical democrats did not often speak about efficiency. They instead assumed that productivity would not suffer if owners were able to acquire enterprises without competition from other would-be buyers and if they were not required to invest real, preexisting assets into their enterprises.

But public confidence in the voucher program was seriously weakened by special regulations that benefited enterprise personnel more than other citizens—especially those who worked in the relatively small number of enterprises that were seen as particularly desirable. People who were not employees of those unusually successful firms were disadvantaged in some conspicuous ways. Securing useful information about the financial prospects of privatizing enterprises proved to be virtually impossible for the average person, and that problem nagged potential investors throughout the voucher privatization period.

Yeltsin proclaimed that the principal objective of the voucher program was to divide state property among the citizens, and in this way to give all people an opportunity to be active participants in the transformation to a market economy.[18] "We don't need a few millionaires," he maintained at the outset of the voucher privatization initiative. "We need millions of owners."[19]

Yet many citizens concluded, not without cause, that they were being given the unenviable opportunity to own enterprises that were often unprofitable, and many of which were on the brink of bankruptcy. When asked about this problem in August 1992, Chubais responded, "We are dealing here with a closed circle. Of course, *before* privatization would be the best time to revitalize our industries, but it is clear already that without the first step, privatization, the second won't happen."[20] But what Chubais neglected to emphasize in public was that many of those industries would never be revitalized, and as we note below, he was fully aware of that undesirable feature of voucher privatization.

Information about the competitive potential of privatizing enterprises was not completely lacking during the voucher privatization period. Rather, much of the information that investors have found useful was not made public. And a large number of citizens were keenly aware that they knew too little about how to successfully navigate the uncharted waters of Russian privatization. Nor did the opportunity to exchange personal vouchers for shares in investment funds offer a promising solution for most of the millions who chose that option. By the time that voucher privatization ended, more than six hundred voucher investment funds were registered in Russia, and surveys indicated that about 30 percent of citizens interviewed throughout the country had exchanged their vouchers for investment fund shares. Most were not paying significant dividends, however, because of the difficulties faced by the enterprises where funds had invested the vouchers they had collected.[21] Large numbers of private investors in these funds became impatient with the funds' inability to pay the expected dividends. By mid-1994, many funds had either stopped functioning or were selling large numbers of vouchers at stock exchanges in the hope of being able to make at least a one-time payment to investors. And the widely publicized "pyramid" scheme of MMM was another way of attempting to satisfy investors without having to depend on the performance of privatized enterprises. Such disappointing outcomes were not what voucher recipients had anticipated.[22]

The State Program for Privatization for 1992 stated that "enterprises whose activity is not efficient" were expressly targeted, among others, for "obligatory privatization."[23] The State Property Management Committee complied with this instruction in developing a list of large and middle-sized enterprises slated for obligatory privatization.[24] Speaking about this list in late 1992, Dmitrii Vasil'ev, GKI deputy chair, predicted that, "the properties of the 4,500 enterprises that are to be privatized in the 'obligatory' category are enough to bring in all the vouchers that have been allocated."[25] (This estimate turned out to be incorrect. GKI had to auction many more enterprises than had been anticipated in order to meet the demand for voucher utilization.)

Not all enterprises on the 'obligatory' list were bad investments, of course. A number of enterprises in several categories were promising by any measure. Also, enterprises were allowed to voluntarily opt for privatization, except for those in categories that were explicitly or implicitly excluded,[26] and many did. But the machine building sector turned out to be the overall voucher privatization leader by the end of the voucher privatization period, and this sector was experiencing a steep production decline.[27]

A further disadvantage accrued to those who were not employed by the more successful enterprises when they invested their voucher. Because of the manner through which vouchers were distributed at auction, in firms where shares were in high demand among outside investors, a voucher bought less because the purchasing power of vouchers was dependent on demand. But workers in a privatizing enterprise did not have to cope with the fluctuating value of vouchers experienced by other investors, many of whom worked at jobs that precluded their participating in "insider" privatization. Enterprise assessments that determined the price of shares to enterprise personnel were based on January 1992 prices.[28] The result was that outside investors who wanted to purchase shares of an attractive privatizing enterprise had to pay the much higher market prices—even as much as one thousand times more—for shares that were in high demand. "To each according to his employment," thus became an operative principle in the new Russia. But only 12 percent of the population worked in large industrial enterprises, and only a few of those were considered good investments—perhaps only about one-tenth.[29]

Even those enterprises that survived privatization and the difficulties of establishing market relations in a chaotic economic environment would not, for the most part, soon be paying dividends to outside shareholders. Privatized Russian enterprises did not face the constraint of shareholder discontent that typifies public companies in the West. Because voucher privatization gave no working capital to enterprises, privatized firms had neither a financial obligation to shareholders nor an incentive to provide dividends to stimulate further investment.

Politics in the Name of Economic Reform

A fourth flaw of the voucher program should have been obvious, and its inevitably negative effects anticipated, from its inception. There is a fundamental contradiction between the program's underlying political objectives and its stated economic ones. It was only a matter of time until this contradiction created both a crisis of production and a crisis of political legitimacy.

Although the second aim listed in the 1992 State Program for Privatization was "to increase the productivity of enterprises,"[30] it was clear by the time the Congress approved the program that the primary focus of privatization had changed. The government's chief concern had shifted to dismantling the state control system as quickly as possible. Along the way, and in spite of a chorus of warnings and cautions by analysts outside the Yeltsin government's circle of privatization planners, questions about efficiency were largely ignored. The possibility of disruptions during the rapid shift to decentralized planning was now seen as less sinister than the fear that opposition forces might halt the process entirely if given enough time.

In nearly every important detail, the voucher privatization program was intended to promote the realization of political more than economic goals. On that point Chubais is clear. When we interviewed him in August 1993, he told us unhesitatingly, "This is not an economics program; it is a political program. It is 5 percent economics and 95 percent politics." He did not hesitate, in addressing colleagues, to make gloomy long-range predictions for the prospects of a very large number of privatizing enterprises. In a July 1993 speech he warned, "The biggest price that we will pay will come tomorrow. The main danger to the whole privatization program is the risk that it will face when some of the privatized enterprises, or probably most of them, become bankrupt."[31] Before 1993 ended, Chubais's State Property Management Committee was estimating that more than half of all federal property was on the brink of bankruptcy.[32]

Russia's privatization planners inherited a faltering production system, certainly. Their mistake was in not seriously addressing problems of industrial performance and misplaced incentives. The voucher privatization program established a process for divesting the state of property without first developing procedures for facilitating the survival of those newly privatized enterprises in an alien economic environment. Divestment was the simpler of the two tasks, by far. And the second need was not adequately, or even seriously, addressed by the privatization planners during the voucher privatization period. This was the privatization program's most costly defect, whose negative consequences had already been enormous by the time the program ended in mid-1994.

Who Are the Owners?

"Arguably, the most successful part of the Russian transformation has been privatization," Anders Åslund stated at an April 1994 Congressional hearing. "At present," he continued, "more than half of the Russian labor force works in the private sector and it produces more than half of the GDP."[33] But what Åslund characterized as "the private sector" hardly qualifies as private, according to standard meanings for the term. Åslund's statement ends with this upbeat interpretation: "All management power has been transferred to the enterprise level, and no authorities in Moscow [that is, federal authorities] hold any sway at privatized enterprises any longer."[34]

If Åslund's conclusion were correct, Russian privatization would have accomplished something notable, in spite of its inadequacies. But the conclusion is wrong. In March 1994, about three weeks before Åslund's testimony, the first vice president of Stanislav Shatalin's Reforma Foundation, Stanislav Assekritov, addressed Åslund's subject. "Chubais's thesis that the state must leave the management sphere turned out to be untenable," Assekritov writes. "The transformation into joint stock companies [what Åslund calls "privatization"] changed the form of ownership, of course, but this does not at all mean the complete independence of enterprises from those who own controlling shares. Upon opening the Goskomstat [State Statistics Committee] report [for 1993], one can see that in 81 percent of the joint stock companies at the federal level, a controlling share is in state hands." (We have already spoken about the percentage of *production* enterprises that remained under state control in late 1994.) Assekritov continues, "If budget money continues to come [from the state] and these enterprises continue to receive special privileges, . . . *what have we been struggling for?*"[35]

Economist Larisa Piiasheva contends that, "If the directors [of a large number of privatized enterprises] had been given both a controlling share and the juridical right to manage their enterprises, they would have immediately begun improving them. But they were not. Now it is not clear who the owners are." She concludes, "What kind of privatization is that?"[36]

Post-Voucher Privatization

In April 1994, GKI released a paper describing the committee's "Conception of Post-Voucher Privatization," which would begin after the voucher stage ended on June 30.[37] The principal shift in emphasis signaled by GKI's new strategy was now to focus more on the improvement of enterprise operation. The overriding goal would be to attract "efficient owners"[38] willing to invest money in order to acquire enterprise shares.

Thirty percent of Russia's large and medium-sized enterprises were still state owned at the end of June, according to GKI. It was expected that two-thirds of these enterprises would be privatized, and that the other one-third would remain in the state sector. Of the enterprises remaining to be privatized after the end of voucher privatization, a large number were in the military-industrial complex, transportation, and energy. Many other enterprises that were not privatized earlier for a variety of reasons were now slated for privatization.

Enterprises that were already joint stock companies after June 1994 were also to be objects of ongoing attention from GKI. Privatization planners hoped that workers who owned enterprise shares but needed money would sell their shares in the secondary market. Investors would be eager to buy, they believed, if the state would, at the same time, sell a substantial proportion of joint stock company shares that were still in *its* hands—thus making it possible for an investor to acquire enough shares in a particular firm to influence the enterprise's operation. GKI anticipated that this opportunity would draw in both Russian and foreign investors. GKI also hoped to attract outside investors with the promise that they could purchase both buildings and the land on which enterprises were located.

On July 21, 1994, the post-voucher privatization bill was defeated by twelve votes in the State Duma, but the next day Yeltsin issued a decree that promulgated basic features (although not all) of the bill that had been submitted to the Duma.

During the time that the bill was being considered, Chubais's posture was described by a number of analysts as "provocative" and "defiant." Analyst Irina Demchenko, for example, reports that, "Evidently, the chair of the State Property Management Committee intended to anger deputies with the tone and manner of his remarks—provoking them to vote against the program and then to plead 'Duma conservatism' and the impossibility of delaying" the proposal. That would be Chubais's case for a presidential decree, Demchenko adds, thus "avoiding the introduction of changes in the program—including those that would limit the absolute power of the State Property Committee and its independence from other state bodies."[39] On May 30 Chubais had announced that GKI's post-voucher privatization program would be submitted to the Duma by June 15, and he added that if the parliament did not adopt the program by July 1, the new program would be implemented by presidential decree.[40] This demand was a continuation of a familiar Chubais strategy to gain political advantage by deliberately offending his opponents. It seems clear that Chubais never wanted the proposal to be submitted for legislative consideration.[41] He had strongly approved Yeltsin's earlier refusal to allow Supreme Soviet deliberations to interfere with executive branch policy plans, and this preference for ignoring the legislature continued in 1994. As analyst Boris Boiko describes the circumstances surrounding the post-voucher proposal, "The State Property Management Committee, from the very beginning, insisted on implementing the program through presidential decree, worrying about unavoidable corrections [in the proposal] if it should be submitted to the State Duma."[42]

Chubais has never made a secret of his desire for unchecked power in privatization planning. In a July 1993 address, whose written text he gave us a month later, he described several dilemmas that, he said, "we faced regarding privatization." One of these dilemmas "concerned the status of the GKI: Should it be a normal ministry or its own master holding all property rights *and able to make any kind of decision*, with its own network all over the country?" "The only right answer is the second answer," Chubais concluded.[43]

And in July 1994, during the time that post-voucher privatization was being considered by Russia's lawmakers, Sergei Filatov, head of the presidential administration, warned that a draft of the presidential decree was already prepared, and "in case the State Duma does not approve the program for the second stage of privatization, the president can issue the decree to initiate the program."[44] Chubais repeatedly voiced the same threat.[45]

It is too early, as we write, to evaluate post-voucher privatization. But it is already obvious that planning mistakes that impeded the effectiveness of "*malaia*" and "*bol'shaia*" privatization are being repeated. Rather than seeking input and ideas from groups that will be affected by GKI initiatives and attempting to build a broad-based political constituency, GKI's strategy continues to be one of working behind closed doors as much as possible and then provoking their opponents in order to secure presidential intervention that will prevent modifications of their ideas. The State Investment Corporation was established in February 1993 by a Yeltsin decree with the objective of insuring foreign investments against political instability, and other initiatives followed later. We pointed out in chapter four that the results of these initiatives were disappointing.

The principal justification for the GKI stance is that these planners ostensibly know what should be done. But GKI's record since 1992 is not encouraging in that regard. Chubais believes, for example, that his post-voucher program, with its incentives for land acquisition and the purchase of large quantities of state-owned stocks, will bring in foreign investment—a theme he has continued to emphasize in his new post as first deputy prime minister in charge of the economy.[46] The foreign investment component of their program is a critical factor, the reformers recognize, because they acknowledge that there is inadequate available investment money in Russia to provide strong demand in the secondary market for the volume of shares that will be available.[47] But back in 1992, Chubais also thought that his original privatization program would attract foreign capital. "Particular attention should be paid to foreign investment," Chubais and Maria Vishnevskaia wrote that June. "The government is supplying the legal structure, know-how, and practical mechanisms for receiving foreign investments."[48]

In June 1994, Prime Minister Viktor Chernomyrdin launched a new government initiative to attract foreign capital, promising a five-year income tax "holiday" for foreign companies, the removal of restrictions on capital flows in and out of the country, the right to keep all hard currency earnings from exports, relief from import tax on materials to be used for production, and a three-year exemption for foreign investors from changes in tax legislation (seven years, if the foreign investment was more than $100,000).[49]

With the conclusion of voucher privatization, the process of comprehensively implementing policies to sustain the course of reforms was clearly just beginning. Aleksandr Radygin, head of the privatization department in Egor Gaidar's Institute for the Economy in Transition and one of the authors of the Russian privatization program, observed in May 1994 that the administrative elite still controlled the levers of Russian enterprise.[50] In a like vein, Evgenii Yasin, then head of the Analytic Center of the administration, wrote in June 1994, "There is no so-called 'effective' owner yet, and in this sense privatization has not achieved its aims."[51] And Boris Fedorov, former minister of finance, cautioned in July, "The danger now is that . . . local powers—communists and other interest groups—will start the last battle to stop privatization. There are signs of that in the parliament, in the regions, and in the government."[52] Gaidar describes the current situation in similar terms, especially emphasizing the importance of regional politics. "Capitalism cannot, in reality, be stopped," he maintains. "But the dilemma is bureaucratic (nomenklatura, state) capitalism or democratic (civic, open) capitalism." The potential of bureaucratic elites to derail the reforms is especially strong in the regions, where they "retain absolute power," he continues.[53]

Russia's reform results through late 1994 underscore Merilee Grindle and John Thomas's point that "however difficult and politically risky it is to decide to introduce a reformist initiative, the process of implementing and sustaining that decision is likely to be even more fraught with difficulty and risk."[54] As Stephan Haggard and Robert Kaufman point out, the "politics of initiation," in the first phase of a reform program, may allow for the insulation of "politicians and their technocratic allies from particular interest group constraints." But in the second phase, the "politics of consolidation" demand "a somewhat different balance between state autonomy and the representation of interests"—one that requires studied constituency building and the crystallization of alliances among affected interest groups.[55] It is at this point that the fit of state initiatives with interest group concerns that are effectively voiced becomes critical to maintaining the direction and momentum of reforms, John Waterbury argues, because "top-down change without the support of organized constituencies probably cannot be sustained."[56] The end of voucher privatization, then, also signaled the necessity for more effective political work than Russia's reformers had carried out until that time.

7

In the Balance

People no longer want an abstract government in the Kremlin. The person who has taken upon himself the title of "leader" must be comprehensible, controllable, and dependent upon public opinion. He must listen.
                    —Boris Yeltsin, *The Struggle for Russia*[1]

We are now living through the trough of the economic crisis. In the next few months we can make a break from the basic negative tendencies which have held back our development in the past two or three years. I am certain that we will make the break. Russia has only one path to tread—that of reform—and it will not depart from it.
                    —Viktor Chernomyrdin, "No Exits on the Road to Market"[2]

Václav Klaus, prime minister of the Czech Republic and himself an economist, argues that "the leading role in transforming a society and its economy belongs not to economists but to politicians."[3] Broad popular support for reforms is vital, Klaus insists, and "that means that there must be politicians who are trusted." In a democracy such trust comes, he continues, through citizen approval of policies enacted by the politicians. A further consideration, in addition to the desirability of democratic decision making, is that the magnitude of change that results from reform in formerly socialist countries is too great for reform programs to be successful without effective constituency building. And the enduring public support necessary to carry out ambitious programs cannot be realized just on the basis of "negation—saying, 'We don't want to return to the past.'" Public approval will be forthcoming, Klaus adds, only when leaders clearly state the objectives of reform and pursue those objectives effectively.[4] Thus, Klaus applies to the post-Soviet context the requirements for governability in democracies that have been highlighted by Ralf Dahrendorf which we discussed in chapter two.

The Public Verdict on Yeltsin's Reforms

June 1991–December 1993

When Yeltsin announced his radical reform initiative in late 1991, the Russian electorate were primed for a sharp break with the Soviet past.[5] A national survey by the Russian Center for Public Opinion Research (VTsIOM) found that 70 percent of respondents at that time favored a market economy. Yet most of the population wanted the transition to be gradual.[6] Indeed, Yeltsin's earliest problem with the electorate seems to have been directly tied to the price liberalization policy that was implemented in January 1992. According to a nationwide VTsIOM survey that was conducted at the end of 1991, only 26 percent of the respondents said they supported price liberalization; another 18 percent said they didn't know; and 56 percent stated that they definitely opposed the idea.[7]

The skeptics never formed an organized opposition, but another VTsIOM study found in February 1992 that 45 percent of respondents would support a general strike against the price increases that had been instituted the previous month,[8] and three months later, in May, 70 percent of the respondents in a nationwide survey continued to believe that price liberalization would not help to lead the country out of its economic crisis.[9]

Both Yeltsin and Gaidar had been promising the public an economic turnaround during 1992, and clear signs that the "upturn" they had heralded was nowhere in sight only underscored the reluctance of most people to accept the logic of price liberalization. By June 1992, Yeltsin's approval rating had dropped to an unenviable 32 percent[10] (down sharply from his ratings in 1991), and his support among the public continued to decline until the time of his December clash with the Seventh Congress of People's Deputies that created the conditions for a head-to-head appeal to voters in April 1993.[11] Yeltsin's strongest public support had always come when he was in conflict with his adversaries—first with Gorbachev, in mid-1991; then with the putsch forces that August; and finally, with Russia's lawmakers on the issue of economic reform. Consistent with this overall pattern, support for Yeltsin rose sharply in March 1993 when the Congress nearly impeached him, and it continued to improve until the time of the controversial April 25 referendum. In this most direct confrontation with the opponents of his reform program to that point, he achieved a notable victory—winning a confidence vote among 59 percent of the voters and support from 53 percent for his economic reforms. But his ratings fell again after the referendum, until his September offensive against the parliament, when they peaked for the second time in the year.[12] Until October 4, each decisive action in his struggles with enemies strengthened his hand with voters, but his approval ratings dropped sharply after the shelling of the Russian White House.[13] By the time of the December 12 elections, support for Yeltsin had declined to its lowest level ever,[14] in spite of his vigorous attempt to justify his September–October actions in the December election campaign. And in the elections, Yeltsin and the Gaidar bloc, Russia's Choice, paid the high price of not only the October conflict but also of having disregarded the electorate in two key areas. First, these leaders were deeply implicated in the unilateral actions that led to the demise of the USSR—an act overwhelmingly opposed by Russia's citizens. (Seventy-two percent of our four-city respondents believed that "the decision to break up the Soviet Union at the end of 1991" was "the wrong decision" [Table B–7.1].[15])

Further, basic features of the economic program they had created continued to be opposed by most citizens, and the effects of those features were being widely felt. By a large majority, most of our four-city respondents continued to believe in 1993 that price liberalization had been unnecessary, and a majority thought it to have been a mistake (Table B–7.1). Only about a third had gained more hope for the future (Table B–7.2), and fewer than one in eight were more optimistic about the political situation than they had been a year earlier (Table B–7.1). There were fundamental issues here of whether or not political strategies were furthering economic goals, as our analysis of questions about the dissolution of the USSR and the January 1992 price liberalization initiative illustrate.

Voting Patterns in Four Cities:
April and December 1993

Our research cities span a broad spectrum of Russian public opinion regarding Yeltsin's reform at the time of the April 1993 referendum, and they illustrate the public opinion turnaround in Russia after that time. In April, Yeltsin and his reforms had received an impressive vote of confidence in large cities. His showing in his home city of Ekaterinburg was especially strong, with 88 percent expressing confidence in him and 81 percent favoring his reforms. In Moscow, the favorable percentages were 75 and 70, respectively. He did less well in some smaller cities, and his support was even weaker in rural areas. In Smolensk (city), for example, a bare 40 percent had voiced confidence in Yeltsin, and 37 percent had endorsed his reforms. The usual rural-urban divergence can be seen in the Voronezh oblast, where in the city of Voronezh 65 percent voted for Yeltsin and 58 percent favored his reforms, but in the more rural areas of the oblast, where nearly two-thirds of the people live, the corresponding percentages were 42 percent and 38 percent.[16]

Defeat for Reformer in Smolensk

In April, voters in the Smolensk oblast were also electing a governor. The sitting governor at the time, Valerii Fateev, was a committed Yeltsin reformer who had worked for radical economic transformation throughout the oblast. By the end of 1992, there were no collective farms remaining in the oblast and privatization was strongly under way. The pace of privatization had bested the state's goal for the oblast. Smolensk was the site of one of the first voucher auctions in Russia, at the beginning of the "large privatization" effort. But production in the oblast declined 42 percent during 1992, and by year's end 60 percent of the population had incomes below the poverty level. From a field of seven candidates, Smolensk voters picked Anatolii Glushenkov, an enterprise director who was a member of the Smolensk oblast soviet. In his campaign, Glushenkov promised to slow the pace of economic reform. Defeated governor Fateev took a job in the Ministry of Economics in Moscow and began working with Gaidar's Association of Privatized and Private Enterprises. "The results of this election mean that there will be a turnaround in all spheres in the life of Smolensk," Fateev stated in an *Izvestiia* interview, and added, "I hope that the people of Smolensk will find the courage within themselves to recognize this mistake and correct it."[17] But contrary to Fateev's hope, in December only 43 percent of Smolensk oblast voters supported the Yeltsin constitution. Thirty-three percent voted for Zhirinovsky's LDP, compared with 11 percent for Russia's Choice (thirteen parties/blocs were on the ballot).[18]

Fateev's interpretation of the April results in Smolensk was repeated by a number of Yeltsin team members when the vote did not go their way in December, either. The people were to blame—not the government program, they believed. And if the people could not be convinced, they should simply be ignored. Just after the first results became known in the December elections, Gaidar held a press conference. "The government's economic course will be corrected," Gaidar stated—but added that "the corrections" would be entirely in the direction of solidifying and deepening the reform course that was "interrupted" in the spring of 1992. Any kind of compromise would be rejected, he emphasized.[19] And Western leaders did not shrink from advising Yeltsin to "stay the course," even after the December 1993 elections—although the people's voice had been clearly heard.

Conservative Ascendancy in Voronezh

Voronezh's governor, Andrei Kovalev, had been appointed by Yeltsin in the summer of 1992, but he did not become a strong advocate of the Yeltsin government's reform program. Ivan Shabanov, who had formerly served as first secretary of the Voronezh *obkom* (oblast party committee), organized a local campaign in opposition to the reforms. Both the executive and the legislative branches in Voronezh worked during 1993 to ease the pain of economic hardship among Voronezh residents—keeping the prices for consumer goods more in line with salaries than they were in most regions, as Russia's galloping inflation remained unchecked during much of the year. And voters in the Voronezh oblast, who had barely failed to give Yeltsin majority support in April (49.7 percent favorable), gave their greatest support in December to Zhirinovsky's LDP (31 percent), Gennadii Zuganov's Communist Party of the Russian Federation (15 percent), and the Agrarian Party (12 percent). Only 45 percent of Voronezh oblast voters favored the new constitution.[20]

Economic Uprising in Ekaterinburg

The Urals region posed privatization dilemmas; and the Ekaterinburg voting pattern in 1993 highlights, on the one hand, the area's obvious pride in its native son and, on the other, the muting effect of economic concerns on Yeltsin's appeal even in his home territory. The Urals boasts many huge enterprises that were undoubtedly undervalued, such as the heavy machinery giant Uralmash which we discussed in chapter six. Many huge firms in the Urals badly need modernization, however, and a number are undoubtedly doomed to fail in a market environment. Our Ekaterinburg respondents were markedly less satisfied than Muscovites with the results of "small privatization," and only one in five believed that privatization would soon bring any improvement in people's lives (Table B–7.3). And with the advent of privatization in the Sverdlovsk oblast had come a particularly severe crime problem.[21] So in April 1993, while backing Yeltsin by a one-sided margin of nearly nine to one, the Sverdlovsk electorate voted to take economic matters into their own hands by wresting themselves free of control from Moscow in the economic sphere. More than 80 percent of voters approved a proposal to create a Urals Republic within the Russian Federation. Its constitution was approved on October 27 by the Sverdlovsk soviet, but this action was declared void by the Kremlin. And in the December elections, most of the electorate stayed home. Yet among the 49 percent of Sverdlovsk oblast residents who voted, Russia's Choice did much better than in many other regions of Russia, garnering 25 percent of the vote. Zhirinovsky's LDP, in comparison, received 18 percent.[22]

National Verdict in December

Our four-city results indicate that well into the summer of 1993 general support for market reforms and endorsement of the government's price liberalization initiative and privatization program continued to be stronger in Moscow than in the smaller cities—both among employed respondents and retired individuals (Tables B–7.1 and B–7.3). Already, Ekaterinburg was showing clear signs of departure from the Yeltsin fold, with a pattern of responses to some questions that more closely resembled Voronezh and Smolensk than Moscow.

Eight months later, Russia's Choice garnered only 15 percent of the votes for the 225 "party" seats in the State Duma. Zhirinovsky's LDP received an impressive 23 percent, and Zyuganov's Communist party 12 percent. Eight parties/blocs gained party seats in the Duma, and by any account, reformers were outnumbered by opposition deputies. The remaining 225 Duma seats went to deputies elected from local single-mandate (single-member) constituencies, and it is difficult to categorize some of these deputies in terms of parties and blocs. Overall, however, it can be said that in the State Duma "reform" deputies were in the minority. Deputies favorable to Russia's Choice initially held about 94 of the 450 seats (21 percent). By May 1994, however, about 20 of the elected Russia's Choice deputies had left the bloc and aligned themselves with other factions. (Members of the 176-member Federation Council, the upper house, could not be neatly categorized according to political affiliation.)

There was apparently another sharp drop in the appeal of Yeltsin and his reforms right before the December 12 elections. Because the Central Electoral Commission had ruled that no public opinion data could be published within ten days of the elections, the last survey data available within Russia were released on December 1. At that time, according to a nationwide VTsIOM poll, only 43 percent of eligible voters had decided to take part in the elections. Russia's Choice was clearly ahead of any other party or bloc at that time, with backing from 30 percent of voters. Second place went to the Yavlinskii-Boldyrev-Lukin bloc, with 14 percent.[23] Polling continued after December 1, however, and later results were available in the West. A VTsIOM survey on December 8 found that, by that time, Zhirinovsky's party had climbed "from nowhere" to second place.[24]

VTsIOM analyst Leonid Sedov attributes a substantial proportion of Zhirinovsky's last-minute strength to the choices of previously undecided voters.[25] And two other VTsIOM researchers, Vladimir Shokarev and Aleksei Levinson, after studying a large volume of survey data collected in the weeks before the December elections, concluded that about 40 percent of those who voted for Zhirinovsky decided which candidate to support during "the very last days."[26] They attribute Zhirinovsky's unexpectedly strong showing to effective television campaigning right before the elections.[27]

A significant reason that a large number of voters were undecided on the eve of the December elections seems to be that political involvement, in general, ebbed substantially in Russia from the end of the Soviet period until December—dropping notably after the September–October crisis. A VTsIOM national survey in early November found that 60 percent said they were "only slightly" or "not at all" interested in politics—up from 36 percent who expressed those views in the fall of 1991.[28] This represented the lowest level of political interest among the population that had ever been recorded by VTsIOM. Consistent with this attitudinal change, December's voting turnout of 46 percent was down 18 percent from the April referendum.[29] (This final voting percentage was several points lower than the turnout originally claimed by the Central Electoral Commission—and means, if the review board's finding is accurate, that the constitutional referendum actually failed to pass, since the vote on the constitution required a turnout of 50 percent to be valid. On May 5, however, Vladimir Mezhenkov, a spokesman for the presidential administration, stated that there would be no new referendum on the constitution.)[30]

The VTsIOM study found that the December turnout was particularly low among key constituencies where support for Yeltsin had traditionally been strong—geographically, in Moscow, St. Petersburg, and the Urals region; and sociodemographically, among the young and among entrepreneurs and other private-sector personnel. A notably higher turnout, on the other hand, was found among rural and small-city residents, older respondents, and state enterprise personnel—in short, among those who were customarily more likely than many others to oppose Yeltsin's reforms.[31]

Another factor in the December elections was growing sentiment that "authoritarian power or a dictatorship is the only possible way to lead the country out of the crisis." When VTsIOM posed the question after the April 1993 referendum, only 20 percent of respondents agreed.[32] But by November, 29 percent agreed with this statement, and 44 percent disagreed.[33] The shift at both ends of this question was toward an authoritarian resolution.

The December election results, then, and the success of forces opposed to Yeltsin, can be accounted for by both disaffection with Yeltsin's policies in his usual strongholds of support and the ability of his foes to mobilize voters from traditional pockets of resistance to his reforms. These trends were fed by the failure of Yeltsin's strategists to build, over time, a solid basis of support for their economic reforms among voters, and actions of both the executive and the legislative branches in September and October 1993, which alienated large numbers of people and inevitably hastened the Yeltsin government's day of reckoning with Russia's electorate.

"Economic stabilization is like successful chess strategy," Jeffrey Sachs suggested in the wake of Yeltsin's preemptive strike against the Russian parliament. "As in chess, speed is decisive. And now, the reformers can take the offensive."[34] But Sachs had it wrong. The reformers' neglect of the fundamental political requirements for negotiation and constituency building in a democratic context would soon place them in the awkward position of having to answer directly to Russia's electorate for the failures of their hastily implemented policies.

Voucher Privatization and the Public

Political issues come and go, but the effects of enterprise restructuring would be a continuing measure, of the achievements of radical reform, both in the larger economy and in people's private lives. Privatization needed a solid base of public approval deriving from its achievements if the reforms were to have long-term viability. Maxim Boycko, and others, present, as evidence for the success of Russian privatization, survey data from Russia's State Property Management Committee (GKI), which suggest that more than 60 percent of the Russian population supported privatization.[35] In our four-city study, 63 percent of working Muscovites and 51 percent of retired Moscow residents held that position; and in the four cities overall, 50 percent of working respondents and 33 percent of retired respondents favored it (Table B–7.3). Among those who supported privatizatization in our four cities, nearly two-thirds wanted it to proceed more rapidly.

But support for privatization in general tells little about orientations regarding specific privatization initiatives, such as voucher privatization, which enjoyed little public support when compared with other privatization alternatives.[36] Whereas nearly half of our sample thought that voucher privatization had been "a good idea" when we posed that question by itself (Table B–7.3), very few favored voucher privatization when it was considered along with several other possibilities for bringing about the privatization of large enterprises (Table B–7.4). We did not need to probe far to learn why. Fewer than ine quarter found much benefit for the general population in voucher privatization (Table B–7.5), whereas more than three-fourths believed that enterprise directors, current officials, and crime groups were benefiting from the program. Only 34 percent of these respondents were even "somewhat satisfied" with the results of privatization in the retail and consumer services spheres, which, at that time, were more than 50 percent privatized. The privatization of retail and consumer services enterprises had made more goods, and a better selection of merchandise, available in all of our research cities, but neither the quality of goods nor the ability of people to buy them were seen as having improved (Table B–7.2).[37]

Yet several groups inside Russia did benefit from the voucher phase of Russian privatization. A number of powerful financial groups acquired enterprise shares at rock-bottom prices through voucher speculation. Those relatively few individuals who had liquid assets available for investment following price liberalization in January 1992 were presented with extraordinary opportunities. Many members of the old Communist party nomenklatura took advantage of their positions and power in that time of economic disorder to secure valuable assets for themselves and their associates, and many local officials also broadened their power in privatization decision making. A number of enterprise directors found themselves strategically placed to transfer the control of state property into their own hands. Russians with an entrepreneurial spirit but lacking nomenklatura connections or large sums of money, however, had less success.

In retrospect, it is evident that voucher privatization's most fundamental stated objectives were not achieved. An important reason, we have concluded, was the unrealistically rapid pace of privatization. The objectives stated in the privatization program were neglected in the rush to privatize as quickly as possible. Further, privatization's rapid pace exacerbated coordination problems among agencies and organizations involved in privatization. These problems would be challenging under the best of circumstances, but there is strong evidence that critical coordination questions were neglected by the reformers. There is a chance, in post-voucher privatization, to learn from these mistakes.

The Trend in 1994

Yeltsin's political strength continued to wane in early 1994, when for the first time since his rise to unparalleled prominence in Russian politics, other leaders were rated more highly than he was in major surveys.[38] And the view of Yeltsin remained dim among the electorate after mid-1994. A July VTsIOM study in cities throughout Russia found that only 11 percent of respondents said that they would vote for Yeltsin in the next presidential election.[39] Other public opinion studies carried out during this time both verify Yeltsin's striking loss of support among the electorate and document a continuing decline in his public approval ratings after the December elections. One study found, for example, a twelve-point drop in Yeltsin's approval rating from January through September.[40] With the old parliament eliminated and a new constitution written to Yeltsin's specifications, there was now no obvious stage for the confrontational dramas that had elevated his standing in the past. And the economic slump continued to deepen.[41] As voucher privatization ended, Russia's GDP was still tumbling, production still declining precipitously, and consumer prices still soaring.[42] Short-term interest rates were 392 percent.[43] At that time, the research arm of *The Economist* was predicting that, whereas China's economy was expected to grow 10 percent in 1994 and 6.5 percent in 1995, the Russian economy would decline 8 percent in 1994 and another 3 percent in 1995.[44]

Conclusion

"This Is the Only Way . . ."

Sociologist Tat'iana Zaslavskaia summarizes the reversal of both people's fortunes and the priorities of economic planners after Gorbachev was stripped of his authority. Reflecting on the days of Gorbachev's *perestroika*, she observes that the initial idea of perestroika was to improve people's lives—"to create a system that would stimulate work, allowing people to make good money and live better and better. . . . Now, no one talks about that." Instead, she observes, government planners today measure "the success of reforms" by the increasing number of goods whose prices have been freed, the growing number of privatized enterprises, and perceived progress in stabilizing the exchange rate. "They speak about everything *except* the quality of people's lives. The reformers prefer not to notice what is going on with people now, what price they are paying for the transformations, and what they will pay in the future. These problems do not occupy the reformers," who consider the "human factor" to be an impediment to the realization of their depersonalized ideas. "Only if there is a threat of social explosion can they be persuaded to make corrections in their strategy. . . . Not only are reformers not listening to the voices from below, but they do not want to hear them," Zaslavskaia maintains.[45]

It is clear from our data that what most Russian people meant by privatization and economic reform more generally was quite different from the neoliberal positions held by Gaidar and members of his team. But issues important to the building of solid constituencies and the development of workable reform initiatives were brushed aside as the reformers worked to put their plans in place with the utmost haste.

The carte blanche freedom that Yeltsin was afforded at the end of 1991 to follow an economic reform path that broke sharply with the wishes of most citizens derived from his broad-based popularity, on the one hand, and the people's already-seasoned rejection of the familiar command system, on the other. The uncritical support provided to Yeltsin by Western leaders during this time added valuable camouflage to the plainly undemocratic actions of Yeltsin's planners. Thus democratic development was sacrificed in the name of economic reform, at the same time that major elements of the economic reform program were acknowledged even by privatization head Anatolii Chubais to be, at their core, political in intent and little concerned with economics, as we noted in earlier chapters.

It would have been a daunting task for any reform team to have persuaded a largely skeptical electorate to support a reform program whose specifics were not only unpopular with most people from the start, but whose objectives appeared further from realization the longer the program continued. The task became impossible, the way Yeltsin's reformers approached the problem, "refusing," as even Yeltsin admits, "to 'dirty their hands with politics.'" In his 1994 autobiography, *The Struggle for Russia*, Yeltsin complains that "Gaidar and his people never traveled around the country to take the pulse of the nation."[46] Yet Yeltsin himself did not hesitate to issue a torrent of decrees that carried his government's reforms increasingly off the course that was favored by most voters. Yeltsin blames Gaidar for these developments, which resulted in economic turmoil and sapped his public support. "Yegor Gaidar kept giving assurances that stabilization was just around the corner," Yeltsin states in *The Struggle for Russia*, adding, "I was in turn forced to mimic his confidence."[47]

The Russian electorate, on the other hand, was forced into a position of having to judge the reforms almost entirely by their post-implementation results, since opportunities for careful public deliberation and debate were notably limited. This was partially due to the fact that Yeltsin's reformers themselves had only a sketchy outline at the beginning of reforms, and they made major changes in the program during its first few months—introducing the voucher privatization scheme, for example, when both Gaidar and Chubais had originally opposed such a plan. But with unchecked authority to devise a reform strategy, they pushed ahead with implementation of their ideas and asked voters to trust their judgment. And the voters did—during months in which economic promises were unkept and the very economic, political, and social fabric of the country was being severely strained.

The reformers defended these developments by insisting that the Yeltsin government's approach was the only available alternative to a return to the discredited command economy. Yeltsin, Gaidar, and other government reformers repeatedly made this claim in justifying their position.[48] Key Western advisers and government officials also delivered the same message. As Yavlinskii puts it, "Your experts came in and said, 'This is the only way to do it. This is *absolutely* the *only* way.' "[49]

But reflecting the dramatic shift in public opinion that was underscored by the December 1993 election results, the national priorities being articulated by officials in the Russian government had changed markedly by the end of 1993. This new emphasis would highlight social protection more than macroeconomic stabilization, at least in words, and in broader policy strokes it would seek to focus more on Russian national interests than it had earlier. These corrective measures by the executive branch, necessitated by the poor showing of Russia's Choice and the unexpected success of Zhirinovsky in the December elections, signaled, in the foreign relations arena, the beginning of a more wary approach to Western prescriptions for economic reform. As Foreign Minister Andrei Kozyrev highlights the problem, "A mature strategic partnership has yet to emerge" between Russia and the United States—partially because, he implies, it is not clear that the West's recent "supportive policies" toward Russia have not been "motivated by paternalism or an assumed inequality."[50] Kozyrev emphasizes the importance of public opinion in mandating reformulations of both Russian reforms and Russia's foreign policy objectives. "For the first time, the policies of Russian reformers and their friends abroad must be pursued taking into account how these policies are perceived inside," he observes, because "public opinion is decisive in democracies."[51] But at the end of 1994, it remains to be seen how decisive public opinion will be in Russia's ongoing struggle to restructure its economic and political systems.

The Political Failure of Shock Therapy

David Lipton, writing about the course of Russian reform, complains that after Gaidar "started Russia swiftly down the [monetarist] road at the beginning of 1992 . . . , an intense political backlash began almost immediately: In six months," Lipton laments, "the reform effort was hamstrung by its opponents."[52] This course of events should have come as no surprise. The Eastern European and Russian experiences with shock therapy illustrate why, as students of politics have long known, there is no adequate substitute for open deliberation and political coalition building in a society that encourages open public expression of ideas.

In his foreword to Sachs's 1993 work, *Poland's Jump to the Market Economy*, another former adviser to the Russian government, Richard Layard, notes that Sachs had already decided by 1989 that "action should be as rapid as possible on all fronts" in reforming post-Soviet economies. "Since then," Layard continues, "he has applied his strong mind and tenacious powers of persuasion to developing appropriate plans of action in one country after another, as it abandoned communism. Rarely does an academic economist have such an immediate effect on world events."[53]

Layard's interpretation of the Western advisers' influence is supported by our research. Sachs's persuasive skills succeeded in giving his shock therapy approach an extraordinary opportunity for implementation in the post-Communist world. But this chance was, of course, a double-edged sword.

Ongoing inquiry into economic policy making under conditions of massive societal change is benefiting immeasurably from data now pouring in about the course and implications of reforms in Russia and Eastern Europe. Several of these countries, which for decades had sought to realize the Marxist vision of an economic utopia, understandably responded to the demise of the command system by reflexively embracing Marxism's economic antithesis when they acquired a measure of political freedom not yet enjoyed in China. But after several attempts at reform through shock therapy, proponents of this approach cannot claim a single success in maintaining an orthodox shock therapy program while nourishing democratic processes.

The Neglect of Political Reform

For decades, the USSR Party Congresses unanimously approved, without debate, every initiative of Communist party bosses. Western observers deplored this situation, and Soviet citizens grew disdainful of their unchallengeable power structure. Then in 1989, Gorbachev brought to life a democratic alternative in the form of the Congress of People's Deputies and a newly constituted Supreme Soviet with real legislative power. At every administrative level—from national to local—Gorbachev's initiatives during the late 1980s were designed to further democratization and facilitate open debate on important public issues. Gorbachev's political reforms were arguably deeper and more extensive than his economic reforms, but with Yeltsin at Russia's helm, democratic institution building ground to a halt. As Yavlinskii characterized this shift in February 1994, Yeltsin "did not make a single step to continue the process of political transformation."[54] Rather, capitalizing on the public support he had won to press forward his own reform agenda, Yeltsin tried to reestablish a vertical executive structure throughout Russia—thus reversing the democratizing process that Gorbachev had initiated.[55]

Yeltsin's attack on USSR structures, which we highlighted in chapter one, was part of a consistent pattern in which he took advantage of opportunities to consolidate personal power both before the breakup of the Soviet Union and during the course of economic reform implementation. From the time he won election to the newly formed USSR Congress of People's Deputies in 1989, riding a wave of popular sentiment against the Kremlin Old Guard, through his February 1991 denunciation of "presidential rule" and call for Gorbachev's resignation,[56] and including his blistering attacks against a Russian parliament determined to restrain his uncompromising approach to decision making, Yeltsin had always found, until October 1993, that confrontation could serve to galvanize public support for his political agenda.

The ultimately disbanded parliament's increasing restiveness from 1992 onward had been occasioned by unmistakable evidence that

Yeltsin's economic program was faltering badly, and also by spreading alarm among lawmakers about the high degree of autonomy enjoyed by administrators of the government's privatization program. Both concerns were justified, as we have shown elsewhere.[57] Yeltsin's combative stance toward the parliament did uncover mean spiritedness in many Russian lawmakers, and a substantial proportion of them merited the label "obstructionist" at the end. The historical record is unambiguous, however, in showing that Yeltsin's authoritarian approach to economic reform was deeply implicated in this outcome.

The rapid erosion of Yeltsin's power base among the Russian electorate following the shelling of the White House was accompanied by growing regional distrust of his increasingly urgent moves to promote executive power at the expense of elected regional representatives. And with the end of voucher privatization in Russia, the domain for local discretion in the implementation and consolidation of reforms was notably expanded. This development, combined with the centrifugal tendencies that had already strengthened regional autonomy, meant that the potential among local officials and interest groups for influencing the course of economic reforms had increased substantially.[58]

In late 1994, there seemed to be little likelihood that Yeltsin and his chief advisers would soon begin earnestly shoring up the fragile democratic structures that had been imperiled by their drive for power. Mikhail Poltoranin, formerly a close Yeltsin adviser and information minister, voiced the conclusion of many political leaders and close observers in November when he charged, in decrying Yeltsin's veto of amendments to the Russian media law, "There is no true democrat in him."[59]

And by 1994, according to the head of the Russian Public Opinion Foundation Igor' Kliamkin, Yeltsin had noticeably lost ground in the public eye as a representative of democratization. After October 1993, Kliamkin concludes from his foundation's surveys, the electorate tended to classify Yeltsin and his entourage as "so-called democrats" rather than "true democrats." During the same period, democracy itself seemed to be losing its appeal among many voters, and, as RFE/RL Research Institute analyst Julia Wishnevsky describes one facet of this trend, there was a "rather unexpected reemergence of the Stalinist variety of communism as a significant political force." Some observers attributed this development to disappointment with the Yeltsin regime. As Elena Bonner, the widow of Andrei Sakharov and a former Yeltsin admirer, summarized this position, "We have never lived under democracy, but we have managed to discredit democracy in the past three years."[60]

In the Balance

With the appointment of Viktor Chernomyrdin to replace Egor Gaidar in December 1992, Russia got a new prime minister who often seemed to be adept at both redirecting the country's economic course away from key neoliberal priorities that had prevailed under Gaidar and reassuring the West that Russia's reforms were still on "the right track." He employed this strategy throughout his first year in office. And after the December 1993 elections, he lost little time in reacting to the electorate's voice. In an interview six days later, Chernomyrdin issued a sharply worded warning that Russia's reforms would now follow a different course. Accusing reformers in his own cabinet of having implemented "poorly thought-out experiments," Chernomyrdin criticized Gaidar and Chubais by name, arguing that the election results were their personal defeat. "They have a lot to think about now," he added.[61]

And Chernomyrdin then seemed to signal that Russia's reformers would now heed the people's voice. "It was a correct decision to reform," he continued, "but it is also true that serious miscalculations were made and that no one thought about the near future and the people, for the sake of whom the reforms were started."[62]

In the days following the election, Western leaders seemed to also have gotten the Russian people's message. U.S. vice president Al Gore criticized the International Monetary Fund and its member nations for failure to consider the hardship brought on during the reforms,[63] and the administration's Russia specialist, Strobe Talbott, suggested that the Russian people needed "less shock and more therapy." Secretary of State Warren Christopher underscored this view, suggesting that the reformers should take the December vote as a "wake-up call" to "be very conscious of the pain that takes place in the transition" away from communism.[64]

But U.S. president Bill Clinton was in Moscow in mid-January, and the idea that the Russian reforms might be slowed was clearly not on his mind. Clinton's overriding theme, which was described in the *New York Times* as having been "sugarcoated in a number of ways, with many bear hugs and vodka toasts," stood out sharply amid the public pleasantries: "'More money for Russia, more quickly, but only after more reform.'"[65] Yeltsin vowed in response that he would, indeed, "speed up" and "strengthen" his reforms, and that key reformers would remain in the government.[66] Clinton promised in return "to use U.S. influence to intensify financial support for Russian reform," as Talbott put it a few days later.[67]

Policy making surrounding the reforms was clearly in flux. Gaidar resigned as first deputy prime minister the day after Clinton left Moscow, and Finance Minister Boris Fedorov, who was widely viewed as the ablest remaining pro-market reformer in the government, resigned four days later. Economic advisers Sachs and Åslund also quit, charging that Chernomyrdin did not understand basic principles of monetarism and that Central Bank chair Viktor Gerashchenko was inept.[68] On January 20, Yeltsin named a new cabinet that Fedorov quickly characterized as "incompetent" to carry out reforms. Chernomyrdin stated in a press conference following Fedorov's announcement that while he and Yeltsin would not retreat from reforms, the era of "market romanticism" had ended, and that the new cabinet would "move from primarily monetaristic tactics to non-monetaristic ones," including the imposition of price and wage controls.[69]

In the West, however, pressure was intensifying to get Russian reforms back on their pre-December course. Testifying in January before the House Foreign Affairs Committee, Deputy Secretary of State–Elect Strobe Talbott, while acknowledging that reform "needs to be redefined in a way that takes more account of the social and, indeed, the political consequences of reform," emphasized, ". . . there should be no serious discussion of slowing it down." Talbott was now insisting, "Slowing the pace of reform will not ease the social pain of economic transition—in fact, quite the contrary. Gradual reform is a prescription for hyperinflation and economic collapse."[70]

In mid-February, Jean-Michel Camdessus, managing director of the IMF, was urging that Russia needed to follow a stable course for lowering inflation, and that nothing would be achieved if the reforms were made less harsh.[71] And at the end of the month, a high-level Russian delegation meeting in Frankfurt with G-7 finance ministers and national bank heads tried to reassure the West that Russian reforms would continue to proceed largely along monetarist lines.[72] Additional meetings followed.[73] And when the G-7 finance ministers met in April, they praised Russia's economic reforms, which had led to a new $1.5 billion loan from the IMF the week before. U.S. treasury secretary Lloyd Bentsen noted that the commitment Russia had by then made to reduce the budget deficit and bring down inflation had prompted the G-7 to urge that the World Bank accelerate the process of granting new loans to Russia.[74]

Writing in *Financial Times* during May 1994, Chernomyrdin displayed his diplomatic skill in seeming to simultaneously be endorsing two divergent reform paths: the stabilization course being advocated in the West, and the reorientation of reforms that he had promised after the December elections. Nodding to neoliberals while rejecting their claim that economic principles are applicable without modification in all situations, Chernomyrdin wrote that "while economic laws work the same in all countries, the possibility of a government responding to them depends on the historic particularities of that country's economy." Charting a hazardous course between Western demands for rapid economic restructuring and the Russian reality that massive dislocations would bring human suffering and quite possibly further conflict, Chernomyrdin noted that some enterprises were "beyond salvation and should be closed down"—also emphasizing, "We do not, however, want to throw the baby out with the bathwater; and we cannot ignore the social consequences of each step on this road."[75]

"What should be done?" Chernomyrdin asks. "We have no choice," he continues, "but to study carefully each case and patiently find a solution."[76]

The Russian government's policies in mid-1994 are less difficult to assess than is the meaning of Chernomyrdin's words. His overall approach in practice was aimed, as the West insisted that it should be, primarily toward reducing the deficit and inflation, while his statements suggest that he intended to temper those measures by working to ease the pain of transition among the citizenry.

Gaidar labels this strategy "a hidden anti-inflation policy" in an April interview, noting that "in principle they [the government] continue on the same course" that he himself had followed after rejoining the government the previous September—one of sharply reducing state subsidies to promote macroeconomic stabilization.[77] Åslund's assessment is similar. "Quietly and mostly in private," he observes, "Chernomyrdin refused requests for new expenditures. . . . The financial and monetary stabilization initiated by Fedorov in the fall of 1993 continued." And he adds, "Chernomyrdin rid himself of the most conspicuous liberals for political reasons, but he maintained both their policies and their aides."[78]

Yet Gaidar was no supporter of Chernomyrdin's approach in 1994. He agreed with Chernomyrdin's emphasis on stabilization but faulted his tendency to respond to interest group pressure with ad hoc promises of government support—promises that he had no intention of keeping. Such a strategy, he insisted, destroys public confidence in government. Gaidar wanted to see more government accountability and less political maneuvering. He also deplored the government's inattention to creative planning that would transcend the "macroeconomic dead-end" in which the reforms were stuck.[79]

In July, Prime Minister Chernomyrdin reported on the state of the economy at a meeting of the Council of Ministers. "The most important lesson of . . . the past two and a half years is that Russian reforms have achieved their goals," he began. Then he highlighted, as a welcome effect of the reforms, the fact that long lines to buy products had disappeared, without noting that the cost of food had skyrocketed and a large proportion of the population had been left without the ability to buy much besides food. He emphasized that the pace of inflation had dropped, without mentioning that an important factor in producing this improvement had been nonpayment by the state to enterprises and by enterprises to their employees.[80] He argued that the production decline was slowing, but others using the same evidence saw a different picture.[81] He stressed that the first stage of privatization had been completed, without referring to any of the failures of the privatization program.[82]

Reporters Tat'iana Romanenkova and Aleksei Vorob'ev observed at the time that "Far from all the participants in the meeting shared the optimism of the head of the government. 'Who are we fooling, Viktor Stepanovich?' asked Pavel Balakshin, the head of administration of the Arkhangel'sk oblast." And correspondent Irina Demina observed, "The signs of stabilization that the prime minister mentioned were not obvious to many ministers and regional representatives."[83] Nikolai Gonchar, a deputy of the Federation Council (the parliament's upper house), reflects the assessment of a large number of Russian analysts, and, survey results suggest, also of citizens: "How can such a paradoxical situation exist? When the volume of production is declining, unemployment growing, and the rate of inflation falling—under these conditions, we are told that salaries are catching up with the increase in prices. Such a thing never happens."[84]

And while Chernomyrdin was boasting inflation figures that were pleasing to the IMF, Yavlinskii was one of many prominent Russian leaders who had a very different view of this accomplishment, arguing that the main foe now was not inflation but rather disintegration of the economy, which works against progress toward economic improvement and invites social unrest.[85] An economy can have very low inflation and be dying, Yavlinskii argued. Low inflation can be a *sign* that it is dying.[86] But it soon became clear that the government had been more active than many wanted to admit in issuing credits to prop up failing enterprises and to support agriculture, and the IMF and G-7 were soon insisting on more austerity as a condition for further assistance. The IMF began pressing for a monthly inflation rate of 1 percent by the beginning of 1996, and at the IMF Madrid summit in October, Russia was denied an increase in its borrowing limit.[87] Further complicating the increasing resistance of G-7 nations to Chernomyrdin's balancing act, finance ministers from developing countries were demanding a larger share of IMF allocations.[88]

On October 27, a no-confidence vote in the Chernomyrdin government fell just 32 votes short of passage in the State Duma. Only 54 of the 450 deputies voted against the initiative. (Fifty-five abstained, and 146 did not vote.) A number of deputies who were sharply critical of government policies abstained from the voting, maintaining that Russia's best hope now was not to replace one set of ministers with others who might be no better. And to approve a "no confidence initiative" could spell the dissolution of the State Duma itself, according to the new constitution.[89]

In the wake of voucher privatization, Russian reforms were at a critical juncture. Russia's economic slide had been markedly steeper and more rapid than the reformers had predicted, and economic conditions continued to worsen. Yet the structure of Russian industry had not been improved, and public support for Russia's post–USSR leaders was at an all-time low. Yeltsin remained Russia's most durable symbol of reform, but his ability to galvanize public opinion seemed to be exhausted. Wishnevsky suggested in November 1994 that Gaidar appeared at that time "to be the only prominent independent politician" who continued to support Yeltsin.[90]

Three years after Yeltsin had announced his radical reform campaign, Russia's economic crisis was decidedly more acute and the society more fragmented than before. As the West continued to press for economic policies that the Russian electorate had shown they did not favor, Russia's government was faced with the unwanted choice of either inviting a reduction in the Western aid upon which the reforms had come to depend or risking widespread social unrest. The promise of radical reform seemed ever more elusive, as the possiblity of pursuing feasible alternatives to the Russian government's course grew increasingly uncertain.

There is a sense in which Economics Minister Evegnii Yasin is correct in arguing, "Unlike socialism, you don't have to 'build' capitalism. It builds itself."[91] But during the first three years of post-Gorbachev reforms, independent entrepreneurship in Russia was stymied by a hardy bureaucracy and a rapidly expanding network of organized crime. Democratic institution building had again been impeded in the name of a higher good. Now, the ongoing effort to realize normal economic development in Russia and finally to transcend the oppressive traditions of an authoritarian past had also become a struggle against the negative effects of the Yeltsin reforms.

Appendix A

Data Collection in 1993

In 1992 we began studying the privatization decision-making process in Moscow, Ekaterinburg, Voronezh, and Smolensk, working with about seventy full-time researchers in the four cities to collect 5,782 interviews with government privatization officials, enterprise directors (state, privatized, and private), and nonmanagerial enterprise personnel.

We chose Moscow because of its political importance as a large capital city and center of intellectual and cultural activity, and because it was the locus of many early privatization efforts. Ekaterinburg (population 1,372,000) is the largest city in the Urals region and is a major manufacturing center.[1] Chemical equipment, electric turbines, and heavy machinery account for half of the city's industrial production; but there are also a large number of other enterprises there as well. Ekaterinburg was a closed city until recently. It has long been a major military production center. The military-industrial complex is prominently represented in Voronezh. Voronezh (population 895,000) is in south-central Russia near the Don River. Heavy machinery, electronics equipment, chemicals, construction materials, processed food, and clothing are among Voronezh's principal products. Smolensk is one of Russia's oldest cities and with a population of 346,000 was the smallest city in our study. Located on the Dnepr River in western Russia, its industries include automation equipment, electronics equipment, clothing, aircraft, and household appliances.

We continued working in the same four cities during 1993, interviewing 5,019 people from late June until early August following a pretest (n = 140) in Moscow and Voronezh. There were four interview schedules. All schedules were pretested, and we received detailed comments from the pretest interviewers which were utilized in revising the schedules. The schedules were back translated.

Our 1993 interviews were conducted among four subsamples in each city: (1) general population subsamples; (2) directors of enterprises; (3) administrators in the government's privatization program; and (4) city, oblast, and federal-level officials.

General Population Samples

The general population subsamples in each of the four cities were full probability samples. Names were randomly selected from address bureau lists in Moscow and Ekaterinburg, and from voucher lists in Voronezh and Smolensk. We interviewed 1,000 people in each city from these lists, for a total of 4,000 respondents. All respondents were interviewed in person, and all interviews were conducted during the evening. No substitutions were permitted within a household for the individual named on address bureau and voucher lists, and interviewers made two follow-up attempts, if needed, to contact not-at-home individuals. (Ten percent of the interviews in each city were verified either in person or by telephone.)

In our analysis with the four-city general population sample, students, military personnel, and individuals under fifty years of age without employment outside the home were excluded. The resulting sample size is 3,294. The overall response rate was 93 percent. (Among the 2,720 respondents who were employed, 1,344 worked in state enterprises; 1,048 worked in privatized or privatizing firms; and 328 worked in private start-up businesses. City-by-city totals for employed respondents and those who were retired or were homemakers older than fifty are as follows: Moscow, 746 employed and 82 retired/homemaker; Ekaterinburg, 695 and 124; Voronezh, 684 and 167; and Smolensk, 595 and 201.) Both because retired individuals are disproportionately represented in our overall sample and because retired people often have life situations that diverge markedly from those of employed individuals, we separated these two respondent categories in several tables. Our response rate in the general population sample was 93 percent.

Enterprise Directors/Administrators

Our central focus in 1993 was on the privatization of *production* (not sales and service) enterprises. We were especially interested in large production enterprises. Our goal was to interview at least 100 enterprise directors (or enterprise executives) in Ekaterinburg, Voronezh, and Smolensk and twice that number or more in Moscow. Our subsamples in each city were selected according to the following hierarchy of priorities:

(1) to interview all enterprise directors that we interviewed in 1992 whose enterprises were privatized or in the process of being privatized by the summer of 1993;

(2) to interview as many directors of large production enterprises as possible, using lists furnished by local property management committees;

(3) to interview as many directors of other production enterprises (not large) as possible (using lists from the same source);

(4) to interview directors of other kinds of privatized enterprises who had not been previously interviewed.

Overall, 59 percent of our respondents in this category were enterprise directors; 27 percent were vice-directors; and 14 percent were privatization specialists.

Our totals for each city are as follows:

- Moscow (n = 273; response rate = 88 percent)
- Ekaterinburg (n = 100; response rate = 81 percent)
- Voronezh (n = 110; response rate = 78 percent)
- Smolensk (n = 100; response rate = 92 percent)

Our 1993 sample of enterprise directors/executives includes all production enterprises that had begun or completed privatization by June 1993 in Voronezh and Smolensk, most in Ekaterinburg,[2] and about half of the Moscow total.[3]

Privatization Decision Makers

Each city and oblast has its own property management committee, which acts under the supervision of the State Property Management Committee. Each city and oblast also has its own property fund. Our objective was to interview the most influential members of these committees and funds.

During 1993 we interviewed 105 property management committee members and 41 property fund personnel in our four research locations who served at the okrug, city, oblast, and federal levels. We also interviewed 171 privatization officials in these locations during 1992,[4] as well as observing selected privatization committee meetings. In this respondent category, response rates are not meaningful. We sometimes chose to terminate an interview because the respondent did not have the kind of information we wanted. By design, this was not a probability sample.

Officials, Specialists, and Opinion Leaders

We interviewed leaders in the city and oblast governments of our target sites who were especially influential, and in Moscow we interviewed a number of additional opinion leaders and specialists who were not officials but were key participants in political and economic decision making at the national level. We also took into account diversity of views, trying to gather data from as broad a spectrum of positions as possible. Both the executive and the legislative branches are represented among officials. We interviewed 127 officials, specialists, and opinion leaders in Moscow; 41 officials in Ekaterinburg; 39 officials in Voronezh; and 36 officials in Smolensk.

Our subsample of officials includes members of executive and legislative branches at the federal, oblast, municipal, and okrug levels, as well as members of the Constitutional Court, Procuracy officials, heads of local administrations, and State Antimonopoly Committee members.

Other Types of Data Collected

In each city, we gathered information about the number of enterprises privatized each year since the beginning of the government's reform program, by sector. We also collected information about changes in the privatization processes of each city during the past year, and we chronicled political changes in city and oblast executive and legislative branches. Additionally, we collected and utilized secondary material from a large number of published and unpublished sources.

Analysis and Interpretation

Quantitative Analysis

In part of our analysis, we were interested in the "pure" effects of independent variables. (Considerations in the decision of whether to include control variables are discussed in *Property to the People*.)[6]

Several tables present our results with controls introduced. For several control variables, we utilized the typological regression standardization (TRS) procedure, which is discussed elsewhere.[7] All tables cited in the narrative are included in this appendix.

Qualitative Analysis

In selecting illustrative material from interviews of *unnamed* respondents for the narrative, we consistently attempted to choose statements that represented the characteristic viewpoints and positions that a particular subset of respondents voiced about the issue being discussed. This approach has the disadvantage of failing to highlight the full range of positions and views among our respondents, but if it is consistently followed, it offers the advantage of reflecting the overall trends in our data.

Some details have been changed in the narrative to protect confidentiality of interviews with respondents whose names are not given.

Appendix B
Tables

Table B–5.1

Perceived Seriousness of Coordination Problems between Agencies and Organizations Involved in Privatization (%)

Other Agency/Organization with which Coordination was Necessary	Respondent's Agency	
	Property Management Committees	Property Funds
Privatization Agencies		
(1) Problems were significant	55.9	59.5
(2) Problems interfered with privatization[a]	75.0	90.5
Branch Ministries and Departments		
(1) Problems were significant	50.6	40.7
(2) Problems interfered with privatization	78.0	61.5
Privatizing Enterprises		
(1) Problems were significant	71.6	55.3
(2) Problems interfered with privatization	69.7	65.0

[a]This question was asked only of respondents who stated that coordination problems were significant.

Table B–5.2

Preferred Method for Privatizing Large Production Enterprises, by Respondent Type (column percentages)

Preferred Method	Officials Involved in Privatization					
	Property Management Committees	Property Funds	Anti-monopoly Committees	Okrug Prefectures	Local Executives	Local Soviets
Voucher auctions	22.2	12.1	28.6	20.0	17.0	22.5
Transfer of ownership to enterprise personnel	13.1	9.1	0.0	40.0	21.3	7.5
Sale of shares to interested buyers	40.4	66.7	50.0	33.3	17.0	37.5
Opposed to privatization	11.1	9.1	21.4	6.7	29.8	25.0
Uncertain	13.1	3.0	0.0	0.0	14.9	7.5
(Column *n*)	(99)	(33)	(14)	(15)	(40)	(47)

Table B–7.1

Political and Economic Attitudes, by City and Employment Status
(Percentages in Parentheses for Employed Respondents Are Standardized on Moscow, with Controls for Age, Sex, Education, and Enterprise Type [State, Privatized, Private].[a] Students, Military Personnel, and Individuals under 50 Years of Age without Employment Outside the Home Are Excluded.)

Attitudes and Employment Status	City				Sig.?[b]
	Moscow	Ekaterinburg	Voronezh	Smolensk	
Percent who believed that the decision to break up the Soviet Union at the end of 1991 was the right decision					
Employed respondents[c]	23.9	24.4 (27.9)	16.9 (19.8)	16.3 (18.6)	yes
Retired/homemaker, 50+	21.0	14.2	10.2	9.1	yes[d]
Percent who favored stronger political ties among the CIS countries					
Employed respondents	71.7	62.2 (61.6)	66.5 (66.8)	78.1 (78.9)	yes
Retired/homemaker, 50+	75.3	71.8	64.7	78.5	yes
Percent who favored a market economy for Russia					
Employed respondents	71.5	63.9 (67.5)	62.0 (65.4)	65.2 (67.8)	yes
Retired/homemaker, 50+	62.5	53.8	40.1	40.5	yes
Percent who believed that price liberalization in January 1992 was "a necessary action for the Russian economy"					
Employed respondents	41.6	30.7 (33.8)	27.7 (30.9)	25.0 (28.1)	yes
Retired/homemaker, 50+	28.8	30.3	15.6	14.4	yes

Percent who believed that price liberalization January 1992 "was a mistake"[e]

Employed respondents	45.4	43.1 (41.1)	55.9 (53.5)	60.4 (58.5)	yes
Retired/homemaker, 50+	55.0	47.1	59.9	74.6	yes

Percent who were more optimistic about the political situation than they had been a year earlier[f]

Employed respondents	17.9	9.2	13.7	12.1	yes
Retired/homemaker, 50+	11.3	8.8	16.5	13.0	yes

Percent who were less optimistic about the political situation than they had been a year earlier[g]

Employed respondents	48.5	59.9 (58.0)	58.5 (57.7)	56.1 (56.2)	yes
Retired/homemaker, 50+	62.5	57.0	61.6	59.5	yes

[a]For a discussion of this typological regression standardization (TRS) procedure and citation of related literature, see Lynn D. Nelson and Irina Y. Kuzes, Property to the People: The Struggle for Radical Economic Reform in Russia (Armonk, NY: M.E. Sharpe, 1994), 202–4.

[b]Chi-square $p < .05$.

[c]Overall, among employed respondents, 69.7 percent thought that the decision was wrong, and 9.7 were uncertain. In the retired/homemaker category, 81.8 percent believed that the decision was wrong, and 6.0 percent were uncertain.

[d]In 2 x 4 table.

[e]The third choice was "Uncertain."

[f]Dependent variable split is too extreme for TRS analysis.

[g]Other choices, in addition to "More optimistic" and "Less optimistic," were "No change" and "Uncertain." "No change" was chosen by 24.1 percent of employed respondents and by 16.3 percent of those in the retired/homemaker category.

Table B–7.2

Percent Who Believed That There Had "Definitely" or "Probably" Been a Positive Change during the Past Year on the Dimensions Listed, by City and Employment Status (Percentages in Parentheses for Employed Respondents Are Standardized on Moscow, with Controls for Age, Sex, Education, and Enterprise Type [State, Privatized, Private].) Students, Military Personnel, and Individuals under 50 Years of Age without Employment Outside the Home Are Excluded.

Dimension	City				Sig.?[a]
	Moscow	Ekaterinburg	Voronezh	Smolensk	
"The availability of more goods in stores"					
Employed respondents	84.5	80.3 (81.2)	69.6 (70.4)	74.8 (75.2)	yes
Retired/homemaker, 50+	75.6	83.6	67.1	67.2	no
"A better selection of goods"					
Employed respondents	78.3	72.6 (73.9)	66.2 (67.4)	72.8 (73.6)	yes
Retired/homemaker, 50+	69.5	74.6	63.5	62.7	no
"Better quality goods"					
Employed respondents	31.8	17.1 (18.0)	19.9 (20.5)	26.4 (26.7)	yes
Retired/homemaker, 50+	28.0	17.5	21.6	20.9	no
"More money for most people to purchase the goods they need"					
Employed respondents	31.7	25.9 (27.9)	27.4 (29.0)	26.7 (28.1)	no
Retired/homemaker, 50+	20.7	22.3	26.3	22.7	no

"Higher paying jobs for people in privatized enterprises"				
Employed respondents	44.5	40.7	42.0	41.1	no
		(40.3)	(41.8)	(39.8)	
Retired/homemaker, 50+	34.1	45.0	40.0	35.2	no
"A higher crime rate"[b]				
Employed respondents	94.5	98.1	94.6	94.1	yes
Retired/homemaker, 50+	89.0	91.8	91.6	94.0	no
"A general sense that there are better job opportunities now"				
Employed respondents	39.7	10.3	13.7	8.8	yes
		(12.1)	(14.8)	(9.5)	
Retired/homemaker, 50+	24.4	7.4	13.2	10.5	yes
"More hope for the future in the society overall"				
Employed respondents	45.1	22.6	33.0	34.1	yes
		(23.6)	(33.1)	(33.3)	
Retired/homemaker, 50+	35.4	30.3	35.9	30.5	no

[a]Chi-square p $< .05$.
[b]Dependent variable split is too extreme for TRS analysis.

Table B–7.3

Privatization Attitudes and Assessments, by City and Employment Status (Percentages in Parentheses for Employed Respondents Are Standardized on Moscow, with Controls for Age, Sex, Education and Enterprise Type [State, Privatized, Private].) Students, Military Personnel, and Individuals under 50 Years of Age without Employment Outside the Home Are Excluded.

Attitudes/Assessments and Employment Status	City					Sig.?[a]
	Moscow	Ekaterinburg	Voronezh	Smolensk		
Percent who were supportive of the government's privatization program						
Employed respondents	62.6	49.2 (51.3)	44.0 (45.8)	41.5 (42.5)		yes
Retired/homemaker, 50+	51.3	34.5	32.7	25.8		yes
Percent who believed that voucher privatization was "a good idea"						
Employed respondents	52.0	48.0 (48.8)	46.6 (47.5)	40.6 (41.6)		yes
Retired/homemaker, 50+	47.5	51.7	45.7	36.7		yes
Percent who would prefer voucher auctions to alternative proposals[b]						
Employed respondents	5.9	8.8	6.9	5.5		no
Retired/homemaker, 50+	5.2	7.7	1.2	4.1		no

Percent who were "not at all satisfied" with the results, "so far," of the privatization of retail and consumer services enterprises in their city, or who had not seen any change as a result of "small privatization"[c]					
Employed respondents	53.6	62.7 (60.6)	64.9 (63.4)	63.9 (64.2)	yes
Retired/homemaker, 50+	67.5	69.0	70.1	79.4	no
Percent who believed that privatization would make people's lives *better* within the next 5 years[d]					
Employed respondents	34.4	20.5 (22.1)	25.3 (26.5)	23.1 (23.6)	yes
Retired/homemaker, 50+	32.5	17.5	22.9	20.1	yes
Percent who believed that privatization would make people's lives *worse* within the next 5 years					
Employed respondents	21.0	18.9 (16.9)	25.3 (23.8)	30.7 (29.8)	yes
Retired/homemaker, 50+	21.3	16.7	25.3	38.2	yes

[a]Chi-square p < .05.
[b]See Table B–5.2 for additional choices. Dependent variable split too extreme for TRS analysis.
[c]The other stated choices were "Fully satisfied" (9.2 percent) and "Not quite satisfied" (24.1 percent).
[d]Other choices, besides "It will make life worse," were "There will not be much change," and "Uncertain."

Table B–7.4

Preferred Method for Privatizing Large Production Enterprises, by City and Employment Status (Column Percentages within Each Employment Status Category) Students, Military Personnel, and Individuals under 50 Years of Age without Employment Outside the Home Are Excluded

	City					
Employment Status and Answer	Moscow	Ekaterinburg	Voronezh	Smolensk	Sig.?[a]
Employed respondents					
Voucher auctions	5.9	8.8	6.9	5.5	
Transfer of ownership to enterprise personnel	27.2	43.3	46.6	45.7	
Sale of shares to interested buyers	19.1	11.6	10.7	13.1	
Opposes privatizing large production enterprises	35.2	20.4	28.2	29.1	
Uncertain	12.6	15.9	7.6	6.6	yes
Retired/homemaker, 50+					
Voucher auctions	5.2	7.7	1.2	4.1	
Transfer of ownership to enterprise personnel	26.0	35.9	36.6	31.0	
Sale of shares to interested buyers	11.7	3.4	5.6	3.6	
Opposes privatizing large production enterprises	27.3	25.6	30.4	37.1	
Uncertain	29.9	27.4	26.1	24.4	yes

[a]Chi-square p < .05.

Table B–7.5

Percent Who Believed That Selected Groups Were Benefiting "A Great Deal" or "Somewhat" from the Voucher Program,[a] **by City and Employment Status** (Percentages in Parentheses for Employed Respondents Are Standardized on Moscow, with Controls for Age, Sex, Education, and Enterprise Type [State, Privatized, Private] Students, military personnel, and individuals under 50 years of age without employment outside the home are excluded)

	City				
Group Benefiting	Moscow	Ekaterin-burg	Voronezh	Smolensk	Sig.?[b]
The general population					
Employed respondents	29.3	12.4	18.9	16.3	yes
		(12.5)	(18.8)	(16.1)	
Retired/homemaker, 50+	28.2	20.0	29.5	20.4	no
Enterprise directors					
Employed respondents	79.0	78.3	76.7	77.4	no
		(76.6)	(75.2)	(75.5)	
Retired/homemaker, 50+	68.8	81.6	76.8	75.3	no
Former nomenklatura					
Employed respondents	70.5	73.7	64.3	59.6	yes
		(73.4)	(64.4)	(60.1)	
Retired/homemaker, 50+	66.7	81.1	58.8	55.2	yes
Mafia and crime groups					
Employed respondents	79.3	84.3	82.0	86.9	yes
		(83.1)	(81.0)	(86.1)	
Retired/homemaker, 50+	77.8	86.6	79.0	79.5	no
Current officials					
Employed respondents	81.1	78.6	75.8	75.0	yes
		(77.8)	(75.2)	(74.4)	
Retired/homemaker, 50+	77.2	82.9	68.9	68.3	no

[a]Other choices were "Not much," "Not at all," and "Uncertain."
[b]Chi-square $p < .05$.

Notes

Introduction

1. Aleksandr Borisov, ". . . plius sploshnaia vaucherizatsiia vsei strany," *Megapolis-Express*, no. 35 (2 September 1992), 3.

2. See Lynn D. Nelson and Irina Y. Kuzes, *Property to the People: The Struggle for Radical Economic Reform in Russia* (Armonk, NY: M.E. Sharpe, 1994).

3. Philip Roeder provides a useful characterization of these two approaches in Philip G. Roeder, *Red Sunset: The Failure of Soviet Politics* (Princeton: Princeton University Press, 1993), 13–14. See also Paul Boreham, Stewart Clegg, and Geoff Dow, "Political Organisation and Economic Policy," in *Democracy and the Capitalist State*, ed. Graeme Duncan (New York: Cambridge University Press, 1989), 253–76; and Peter B. Evans, Dietrich Rueschemeyer, and Theda Skocpol, eds., *Bringing the State Back In* (New York: Cambridge University Press, 1985).

4. Robert Gilpin, *The Political Economy of International Relations* (Princeton: Princeton University Press, 1987), 8–9.

5. Theda Skocpol, *States and Social Revolutions: A Comparative Analysis of France, Russia, and China* (New York: Cambridge University Press, 1979), 293.

6. Dietrich Rueschemeyer, Evelyne Huber Stephens, and John D. Stephens, *Capitalist Development and Democracy* (Chicago: University of Chicago Press, 1992), 63. See also Leslie Sklar, *Sociology of the Global System* (Baltimore: Johns Hopkins University Press, 1991), 2–5.

7. Rueschemeyer et al., *Capitalist Development*, 65.

8. Ibid.

9. Gilpin, *The Political Economy of International Relations*, 12.

10. "Society and Enterprise between Hierarchy and Market," in *Societal Change between Market and Organization* (Aldershot: Avebury, 1993), 203.

11. Dietrich Rueschemeyer and Peter B. Evans, "The State and Economic Transformation: Toward an Analysis of the Conditions Underlying Effective Intervention," in *Bringing the State Back In*, 47.

Chapter 1. The Twentieth-Century Russian Dialectic

1. Quoted in Mikhail Heller and Aleksandr M. Nekrich, *Utopia in Power: The History of the Soviet Union from 1917 to the Present* (New York: Summit Books, 1986), 59.

2. *The Current Digest of the Soviet Press* (hereafter, *CDSP*), 43 (27 November 1991), 2; from *Izvestiia* (28 October 1991), 1–2. Emphasis added.

3. Theodore H. Von Laue, *Why Lenin? Why Stalin? Why Gorbachev? The Rise and Fall of the Soviet System*, 3rd ed. (New York: Harper-Collins, 1993), 3; James Billington, *The Icon and the Axe: An Interpretive History of Russian Culture* (New York: Random House, 1966), 114–50; and Stephen White, *After Gorbachev* (New York: Cambridge University Press, 1993), 261–85.

4. Robert V. Daniels, *Russia: The Roots of Confrontation* (Cambridge: Harvard University Press, 1985), 89, 106.

5. See Loren R. Graham, *Science in Russia and the Soviet Union: A Short History* (New York: Cambridge University Press, 1993).

6. See, for example, Billington, *The Icon and the Axe*, 148–51.

7. Quoted in Vladlen Sirotkin, "Novoe u nas—eto vsegda khorosho zabytoe staroe," *Nezavisimaia gazeta*, no. 29 (15 February 1994), 5.

8. Billington, *The Icon and the Axe*, 114.

9. See Teodor Shanin, *Russia as a "Developing Society"* (New Haven: Yale University Press, 1985), 110.

10. David Lane, *Soviet Economy and Society* (New York: New York University Press, 1985), 51.

11. Alec Nove, *An Economic History of the U.S.S.R.* (New York: Penguin Books, 1989), 3.

12. Ibid., 60.

13. *CDSP* 43 (27 November 1991), 1; from *Izvestiia* (28 October 1991), 1–2.

14. *CDSP* 43 (20 November 1991), 5; from *Rossiiskaia gazeta* (22 October 1991), 2.

15. *CDSP* 43 (27 November 1991), 2; from *Izvestiia* (28 October 1991), 1–2. Yeltsin nodded to the other republics, stating, "We are prepared to cooperate closely with the friendly states in achieving transformations," but cooperation and coordination were clearly not in his plan. Yeltsin emphasized, for example, "The preparation of a package of measures to reform the banking system is nearing completion" (ibid.), whereas ten days earlier he had agreed to "participate in coordinated actions [among the signatories of the treaty] in the field of monetary and credit policy" (*CDSP* 43 [20 November 1991], 5; from *Rossiiskaia gazeta* [22 October 1991], 2).

16. *CDSP* 43 (18 December 1991), 1; from *Komsomol'skaia pravda* (19 November 1991), 1.

17. Ibid. On October 28, Yeltsin announced, "Russia will stop financing Union ministries and other central institutions ... whose existence is not stipulated by the Treaty on an Economic Community" (*CDSP* 43 [27 November 1991], 2; from *Izvestiia* [28 October 1991], 1–2). Subsequently, the State Council adopted a decision providing for the abolition of thirty-six all-Union ministries and thirty-seven departments (*CDSP* 43 [4 December 1991], 4; from *Izvestiia* [5

November 1991], 1).Yeltsin's action in this situation was also clearly preemptive.

18. World Bank, *Russian Economic Reform: Crossing the Threshold of Structural Change* (Washington, DC: World Bank, 1992), 5.

19. The other signatories (besides Gorbachev) were representatives of Armenia, Belarus, Kazakhstan, Uzbekistan, Turkmenistan, Kyrgyzstan, and Tajikistan. Ukraine was expected to join later, and also possibly Moldova, which (along with Ukraine) had sent a delegation of observers to the signing ceremony. See *CDSP* 43 (20 November 1991), 1–2; from *Izvestiia* (19 October 1991), 1. 27. See also *CDSP* 43 (20 November 1991), 5; from *Rossiiskaia gazeta* (22 October 1991).

20. See *CDSP* 43 (8 January 1992), 1–2; from *Komsomol'skaia pravda* (10 December 1991), 1. Inexplicably, analyst Dimitri Simes describes Yeltsin as having been practically a bystander as the USSR crumbled, demonstrating a "response to the collapse" that "was probably as restrained as was politically feasible." A few sentences later, Simes characterizes Yeltsin's "overall approach to the end of the empire" as having "been fairly flexible, benign and pragmatic" (Dimitri K. Simes, "America and the Post-Soviet Republics," *Foreign Affairs* 72 [Summer 1992], 80–81).

21. *The Struggle for Russia*, written and produced by Sherry Jones, directed by Foster Wiley, 89 min. (Boston: WGBH Educational Foundation, 1994), videocassette.

22. On December 1—a week before the Minsk (Belovezhskaia pushcha) meeting—more than 80 percent of Ukraine's voters endorsed the Act on the Independence of Ukraine that had been adopted by the Ukrainian Supreme Soviet shortly after the failed August putsch. (Eighty-four percent of the electorate participated in the referendum.) The evening before the referendum, Yeltsin had appeared on Ukrainian television to proclaim that Russia would not sign the Union Treaty without Ukrainian participation, a move *Izvestiia* characterized as "pour[ing] oil on the flames" that had been ignited earlier in the day in a televised speech by Kravchuk (*CDSP* 43 [1 January 1992], 1; from *Izvestiia* [2 December 1991], 1).

Prophetically, an analysis published in *Rossiiskaia gazeta* the next week concluded, "If Yeltsin and Kravchuk pool their efforts, the Union center cannot withstand a struggle for its survival" (*CDSP* 43 [1 January 1992], 5; from *Rossiiskaia gazeta* [5 December 1991], 1). Yeltsin was apparently not eager to give up on the Union Treaty, however. With his October and November actions, which put Russia in an even more aggressively dominant position over the other republics than it had been earlier, in both the political and economic spheres, he was in a no-lose position in insisting, as discussions about the Union continued, that Russia should not initiate the breakup of the USSR. However that question would be decided, now *Yeltsin*, and not Gorbachev, would be the leader to be reckoned with. It may be true, as Kravchuk has indicated, that Yeltsin brought to the Belovezhskaia pushcha meeting (December 7–8) a final appeal from Gorbachev to Kravchuk that urged that the Union Treaty not be abandoned (see Roman Solchanyk, "Russia, Ukraine, and the Imperial Legacy," *Post-Soviet Affairs*, 9 [October–December 1993], 354). Yeltsin could have lived with a "yes" from Kravchuk. Indeed, that outcome would have provided an attractive opportunity for Yeltsin to further extend his power in the FSU. But Yeltsin was riding too high on his own wave of conquests to begin coaxing Kravchuk to join the Union negotiations at this point. And Russia would be fine on its own, advisers Burbulis and Gaidar were insisting. So Yeltsin quickly abandoned Gorbachev at Belovezhskaia pushcha.

23. The circle would be closed, minus the Baltic states, on March 1, 1994, when the Georgian parliament voted 121 to 47 in favor of ratifying membership in the CIS. See Liz Fuller, "Georgian Parliament Ratifies CIS Membership," *RFE/RL Daily Report*, no. 42 (2 March 1994). Available from listserv@ubvm.cc.buffalo.edu, Internet.

24. *CDSP* 43 (22 January 1992), 10; from *Rossiiskaia gazeta* (25 December 1991), 3.

25. And as Gorbachev pointed out in a prepared statement, "This happened at a time when the republic parliaments [were] discussing the draft Treaty on the Union of Sovereign States that was worked out by the USSR State Council" (*CDSP* 43 [8 January 1992], 4; from *Izvestiia* [10 December 1991], 2).

26. Irina Demchenko, "Epokha 'reformatorstva sverkhu' v Rossii zakonchilas'," *Nezavisimaia gazeta*, no. 20 (4 February 1993), 5; quoting *Moskovskie novosti* (26 April 1992).

27. Egor Gaidar, "Rossiia i reformy," *Izvestiia*, no. 187 (19 August 1992), 3.

28. Demchenko, "Epokha 'reformatorstva sverkhu'."

29. Yurii Sorokin, "Parlament, pravitel'stvo i prezident nikuda ne denutsia drug ot druga," *Novaia ezhednevnaia gazeta*, no. 67 (1 December 1993), 2.

30. Demchenko, "Epokha 'reformatorstva sverkhu'."

31. Ibid.; quoting *Komsomol'skaia pravda* (6 June 1992).

32. Ibid.

33. Then in March 1991, Georgian voters overwhelmingly supported a referendum initiative to seek full independence from the Soviet Union.

34. Kazakhstan voted in favor of independence on December 16.

35. *CDSP* 43 (20 November 1991), 4; from *Rossiiskaia gazeta* (22 October 1991), 2.

36. *CDSP* 43 (18 December 1991), 11; from *Nezavisimaia gazeta* (16 November 1991), 1–2.

37. Significantly, Ukraine had called for a referendum on the question of independence, and Kravchuk had decided, with the recommendation of the Ukraine Supreme Soviet that he chaired, not to participate in the work of Union bodies until the referendum results in Ukraine were known (*CDSP* 43 [18 December 1991], 11; from *Nezavisimaia gazeta* [16 November 1991], 1). Kravchuk also made public his personal resistance to the November treaty negotiations (see Solchanyk, "Russia, Ukraine, and the Imperial Legacy," 353).

38. *CDSP* 43 (25 December 1991), 7; from *Rossiiskaia gazeta* (28 November 1991), 1.

39. Simon Johnson and Oleg Ustenko, "The Road to Hyperinflation: Economic Independence in Ukraine, 1991–93," paper presented at the Conference on First Steps toward Economic Independence at the Stockholm Institute of East European Economics, Stockholm, Sweden (23–24 August 1993), 2–7.

40. Constantine Michalopoulos and David Tarr, *Trade and Payments Arrangements for States of the Former USSR* (Washington, DC: World Bank, 1992), 4–5. See also Constantine Michalopoulos, *Trade Issues in the New Independent States* (Washington, DC: World Bank, 1993).

41. Grigorii Yavlinskii, "Zapadnaia pomoshch': Rossii neobkhodim ne narkotik, a lekarstvo," *Literaturnaia gazeta*, no. 32 (11 August 1993), 10.

42. Grigorii Selianinov and Konstantin Smirnov, "Za geopolitiku Rossiia zaplatila po maksimumu," *Kommersant-daily*, no. 66 (13 April 1994), 1. See also "Predvaritel'nye itogi razvitiia promyshlennosti Rossii v 1993 godu," *Biznes, banki, birzha*, no. 40 (25 November–1 December 1993), 2.

43. Grigorii Tsitriniak, "Pogranichnaia situatsiia," *Literaturnaia gazeta*, no. 44 (28 October 1992), 11.

44. Quoted in Tony Cliff, *Lenin*, vol. 2: *All Power to the Soviets* (London: Pluto Press, 1976), 379.

45. Alexis de Tocqueville, *The Old Régime and the French Revolution*, trans. Stuart Gilbert (Garden City, NY: Doubleday Anchor Books, 1955), 211.

46. Ibid., 209.

47. David S. Landes, *The Unbound Prometheus: Technological Change and Industrial Development in Western Europe from 1750 to the Present* (Cambridge: Cambridge University Press, 1969), 142–43.

48. Theda Skocpol, *States and Social Revolutions: A Comparative Analysis of France, Russia, and China* (New York: Cambridge University Press, 1979), 177.

49. J.M. Roberts, *The French Revolution* (New York: Oxford University Press, 1978), 101.

50. *CDSP* 43 (27 November 1991), 3; from *Izvestiia* (28 October 1991), 1–2.

51. "Ob uskorenii privatizatsii gosudarstvennykh i munitsipal'nykh predpriiatii," in *Vse o privatizatsii v torgovle* (Moscow: Torgovlia, 1992), 47–60. The program authorized by this decree deviated on several points from the one that had been outlined in the July 3 legislation of the RSFSR Supreme Soviet. See Lynn D. Nelson and Irina Y. Kuzes, *Property to the People: The Struggle for Radical Economic Reform in Russia* (Armonk, NY: M.E. Sharpe, 1994), 44.

52. Vladimir Orlov, "Gosudarstvo idet s molotka," *Moskovskie novosti*, no. 2 (12 January 1992), 14.

53. Boris Boiko, "Gosduma podygrala GKI," *Kommersant-daily*, no. 125 (8 July 1994), 2.

54. "Goskomstat RF o khode privatizatsii," *Segodnia*, no. 191 (6 October 1994), 2.

55. Lev Makarevich, "Nereshitel'nost' v reformakh dorogo obkhoditsia ekonomike," *Finansovye izvestiia*, no. 47 (11 October 1994), 2.

56. Boiko, "Gosduma podygrala GKI." These figures are discussed more in chapter six.

57. Anders Åslund, "Russia's Success Story," *Foreign Affairs* 73 (September/October 1994), 68.

58. Paul R. Gregory and Robert C. Stuart, *Soviet Economic Structure and Performance*, 3rd ed. (New York: Harper and Row, 1986), 58.

59. 1See Pitirim A. Sorokin, *Hunger as a Factor in Human Affairs*, trans. Elena P. Sorokin (Gainesville: University of Florida Press, 1975), 109–17, 209–15.

60. Angelica Balabanoff, *My Life as a Rebel* (Bloomington: Indiana University Press, 1938), 204. Parts of the above are quoted in Alan M. Ball, *Russia's Last Capitalists: The Nepmen, 1921–1929* (Berkeley: University of California Press, 1987), 9. Nicholas Riasanovsky estimates that about twenty million people

had died by 1921, in the wake of the October Revolution, because of "epidemics, starvation, fighting, executions, and the general breakdown of the economy and society" (Nicholas V. Riasanovsky, *A History of Russia*, 2nd ed. [New York: Oxford University Press, 1969], 540).

61. Leon Trotsky, *The Defense of Terrorism: Terrorism and Communism; A Reply to Karl Kautsky* (London: George Allen and Unwin, 1935), 94–95. Quoted in Nove, *An Economic History of the U.S.S.R.*, 71. Emphasis in original.

62. Gaidar, "Rossiia i reformy."

63. *CDSP* 43 (27 November 1991), 1; from *Izvestiia* (28 October 1991), 1–2.

64. See Tsitriniak, "Pogranichnaia situatsiia"; and *CDSP* 43 (11 December 1991), 11; from *Izvestiia* (11 November 1991), 1–2. The price liberalization idea was *not* a result of Gaidar's influence, after Burbulis met him and brought him into the Yeltsin camp. Yeltsin had proposed "a completely freeing and stabilizing process for basic groups of commodities within a short period" in the spring of 1991. See *CDSP* 43 (1 May 1991), 8; from *Izvestiia* (2 April 1991), 2.

65. Marek Dabrowski, "The First Half-Year of Russian Transformation," in *Changing the Economic System in Russia,* ed. Anders Åslund and Richard Layard (New York: St. Martin's Press, 1993), 7. Åslund's description of these developments is more oblique. One could readily infer from it, for example, that Gaidar had been chosen by Yeltsin and was working for him, along with Gaidar's team of economists, for two months before Yeltsin's October 28 speech; but even Yeltsin's own statements contradict such an interpretation (see below, n. 67). See Anders Åslund, "Russia's Road from Communism," *Daedalus* 121 (Spring 1992), 88.

66. Nikolai Fedorov, "Bor'ba pod kremlevskimi kovrami," *Megapolis-Express*, no. 48 (8 December 1993), 16.

67. Boris Yeltsin, *The Struggle for Russia*, trans. Catherine A. Fitzpatrick (New York: Times Books, 1994), 155. Yeltsin's description of that situation is somewhat different: "Burbulis became acquainted with Yegor Gaidar in the fall of 1991. . . . When he met Gaidar's team at a dacha outside Moscow, he couldn't help but like them. . . . Once I had grasped Gaidar's concept of economic reform and then met the author himself, I had to agree with Burbulis. Several days later, I signed a decree appointing Gaidar deputy prime minister and economics minister. Several of Gaidar's close colleagues were appointed along with him to key economic posts in the government" (155–56).

68. *The Struggle for Russia*, written and produced by Sherry Jones.

69. Alexei V. Mozhin, "Russia's Negotiations with the IMF," in *Changing the Economic System in Russia*, 65, 71.

70. See Nelson and Kuzes, *Property to the People*, 38–44.

71. *CDSP* 42 (27 June 1990), 1; from *Pravda* (23 May 1990), 4.

72. At the time, Allison was dean of Harvard's Kennedy School of Government.

73. Graham Allison, preface to Graham Allison and Grigory Yavlinsky, *Window of Opportunity: The Grand Bargain for Democracy in the Soviet Union* (New York: Pantheon Books, 1991), vii.

74. Ibid., ix.

75. Allison and Yavlinsky, *Window of Opportunity*, 39–66. The primary responsibility of Allison and his team was for the parts of the proposal that discussed Western perspectives and possible Western initiatives and responses.

76. Ibid., 12–13. Emphasis added.

77. Ibid., 97.

78. Allison, preface to *Window of Opportunity*, xii.

79. Tsitriniak, "Pogranichnaia situatsiia."

80. Ibid.

81. Demchenko, "Epokha 'reformatorstva sverzku'."

82. International Monetary Fund, World Bank, Organisation for Economic Co-operation and Development, and European Bank for Reconstruction and Development, *A Study of the Soviet Economy*, vol. 3 (Paris: Organisation for Economic Co-operation and Development, 1991), 362. See also *A Study of the Soviet Economy*, vol. 1, 38–47. The last quotation is from vol. 1, p. 40.

83. See World Bank, *Russian Economic Reform*, 4–5.

84. Ibid., 7.

85. Allison and Yavlinsky, *Window of Opportunity*.

86. Graham Allison and Robert Blackwill, "America's Stake in the Soviet Future," *Foreign Affairs* 70 (Summer 1991), 94.

87. Allison, preface *Window of Opportunity*, xi.

88. Jeffrey Sachs, "The Grand Bargain," in *The Post-Soviet Economy: Soviet and Western Perspectives*, ed. Anders Åslund (New York: St. Martin's Press, 1992), 213, 215.

89. Marshall I. Goldman, *Lost Opportunity: Why Economic Reforms in Russia Have Not Worked* (New York: W.W. Norton, 1994), 82–83.

90. Vladimir P. Lukin, "Russia and Its Interests," in *Rethinking Russia's National Interests*, ed. Stephen Sestanovich (Washington, DC: Center for Strategic and International Studies, 1994), 112.

91. International Monetary Fund, *Economic Review: Russian Federation* (Washington, DC: IMF, 1992), 11.

92. Ibid., 32.

93. We find Peter Schweizer's alternative argument in *Victory* to be an inadequate interpretation of these events. That subject, however, is outside the scope of this book; see Peter Schweizer, *Victory: The Reagan Administration's Secret Strategy that Hastened the Collapse of the Soviet Union* (New York: Atlantic Monthly Press, 1994).

94. Viktor Kremeniuk, "V nachale dlinnogo puti," *Nezavisimaia gazeta*, no. 95 (24 May 1994), 5.

95. Sergei Viktorov and Elena Kotel'nikova, "Zapadnye finansisty gotovy priostanovit' pomoshch'," *Kommersant-daily*, no. 166 (1 September 1993), 3.

96. Georgii Bovt, "Kreditov pod obeshchaniia bol'she ne budet," *Kommersant-daily*, no. 175 (14 September 1993), 3.

97. Steven Greenhouse, "I.M.F. Delays $1.5 Billion Loan to Russia Because Reform is Stalled," *New York Times* (20 September 1993), A3. Available from "NEWS" library, "NYT" file, in Mead Data Central, Inc., LEXIS/NEXIS (database online). See also "Korotko," *Nezavisimaia gazeta*, no. 180 (22 September 1993), 2. See also Vladimir Nadein, "Zaimy zamorozheny iz-za spada reform," *Izvestiia*, no. 180 (22 September 1993), 3.

98. World Bank, *Russian Economic Reform*, 7–8; and Vladimir Prokhvatilov, "Mezhdu Stsilloi infliatsii i Kharibdoi spada," *Literaturnaia gazeta*, no. 10 (9 March 1994), 10.

99. Egor Gaidar, "A Tunnel Two Years Long," *Delovie lyudi*, no. 22 (April 1992), 19.

100. Quoted in *Delovie lyudi*, no. 29 (December 1992), 33.

101. Tsitriniak, "Pogranichnaia situatsiia"; and "Sotsial'no-ekonomicheskoe polozhenie i razvitie ekonomicheskikh reform v Rossiiskoi Federatsii v 1992 godu," *Ekonomika i zhizn'*, no. 4 (January 1993), 13–15.

102. Penny Morvant, "New Figures on Russian-Soviet Debt," *RFE/RL Daily Report*, no. 222 (23 November 1994).

103. John Lloyd, "Pay Gaps Threaten to Split Russia," *Financial Times*, (14 October 1993), 3.

104. Boris Boiko, "Parlamentskie slushaniia vymiraiut kak dinozavry," *Kommersant-daily*, no. 123 (6 July 1994), 3; and Leonid Lopatnikov, "Spros poluchaet brazdy pravleniia," *Delovoi mir*, no. 141 (4–10 July 1994), 1.

105. "Economica Weekly Press Summary: Electronic Mail Version," (8–14 October 1994), 1–2; from *Vek*, no. 38 (1994). Available from dwestman@ccs.carleton.ca, Internet.

106. Evgenii Vasil'chuk, "Prodolzhenie reform trebuet peresmotra roli gosudarstva," *Finansovye izvestiia*, no. 45 (4 October 1994), 1–2.

107. David Lipton and Jeffrey Sachs, "Prospects for Russia's Economic Reforms," paper prepared for the Brookings Panel on Economic Activity, Washington, DC, (17–28 September 1992), 2, 44. This paper is also available in *Brookings Papers on Economic Activity*, no. 2 (1992), 213–83.

108. Åslund, "Russia's Success Story," 70, 71.

109. Jeffrey D. Sachs, "Russia's Struggle with Stabilization: Conceptual Issues and Evidence," paper presented at the Annual Bank Conference on Development Economics. World Bank, Washington, DC, 28–29 April 1994.

110. Jeffrey Sachs, "Betrayal: How Clinton Failed Russia," *The New Republic* (31 January 1994), 14–18.

111. Sachs, "Russia's Struggle with Stabilization"; and Jeffrey Sachs, "Testimony to the Committee on Banking, Housing, and Urban Affairs: United States Senate" (5 February 1994; photocopy), 8.

112. Michael Mandelbaum, "By a Thread," *The New Republic* (5 April 1993), 20.

113. Claudia Rosett, "Figures Never Lie, but They Seldom Tell the Truth about Russian Economy," *Wall Street Journal* 224 (1 July 1994), A10.

114. Liudmila Biriukova, "Spasti sittsevuiu Rus'," *Delovoi mir*, no. 203 ("Region," no. 1; 15 September 1994), 12; Lidiia Malash, "Vse khorosho, prekrasnaia markiza," *Megapolis-Express*, no. 26 (21 September 1994), 14; Goskomstat Rossii, "Sotsial'no-ekonomicheskoe polozhenie i razvitie ekonomicheskikh reform v Rossiiskoi Federatsii v 1992 godu," 14; and Goskomstat Rossii, "O sotsial'no-ekonomicheskom polozhenii Rossii v 1993 godu," *Ekonomika i zhizn'*, no. 6 (February 1994), 7.

115. Åslund, "Russia's Success Story," 66.

116. Vladimir Gurevich, "Legkie resheniia—samye opasnye," *Moskovskie novosti*, no. 28 (10–17 July 1994), 27.

117. Åslund, "Russia's Success Story," 66.

118. Malash, "Vse khorosho, prekrasnaia markiza."

119. Oleg Moroz, "Aleksandr Livshits: 'Nizkaia infliatsiia tozhe opasna,' " *Literaturnaia gazeta*, no. 28 (13 July 1994), 10; and Grigorii Tsitriniak, " 'Mne detiam svoim v glaza smotret' . . .' " *Literaturnaia gazeta* (5 October 1994), 11;

and Gleb Cherkasov, "Sergei Glaz'ev nazval privatizatsiiu 'raznovidnost'iu kaznokradstva,' " *Segodnia*, no. 185 (25 September 1994), 2.

120. Åslund, "Russia's Success Story," 66.

121. Judith Thornton, "Soviet Electric Power in the Wake of the Chernobyl Accident," *Gorbachev's Economic Plans: Study Papers Submitted to the Joint Economic Committee of the Congress of the United States*, vol. 1 (Washington, DC: U.S. Government Printing Office, 1987), 520.

122. See, for example, Masaaki Kuboniwa, "Microeconomics of the Russian Economy," paper presented at the annual meeting of the American Association for the Advancement of Slavic Studies, Philadelphia, PA (17–20 November 1994).

123. Vincent Koen and Evgeny Gavrilenkov, "How Large Was the Output Collapse in Russia? Alternative Estimates and Welfare Implications," paper presented to the Research Department, International Monetary Fund, Washington, DC (17 November 1994), 6.

124. Rosett, "Figures Never Lie. . . ."

125. Tat'iana Zaslavskaia, "Dokhody rabotaiushchego naseleniia Rossii," *Ekonomicheskie i sotsial'nye peremeny*, no. 1 (January 1994), 5, 10.

126. Liudmila Khakhulina, Natal'ia Kovaleva, and Larisa Zubova, "Bednost' v novykh ekonomicheskikh usloviiakh," *Ekonomicheskie i sotsial'nye peremeny*, no. 4 (July–August 1994), 25–26. See also Miroslav Buzhkevich, "Na puti k stabilizatsii urovnia zhizni naseleniia," *Delovoi mir*, no. 210 (23 September 1994), 1, 4.

127. Lopatnikov, "Spros poluchaet brazdy pravleniia."

128. See Andrei Orlov, "Uzh plakat' nevterpezh," *Nezavisimaia gazeta*, no. 92 (20 May 1993), 4.

129. "Informatsiia," *Ekonomicheskie i sotsial'nye peremeny*," no. 4 (July–August 1994), 43.

130. Viacheslav Bobkov, "Denezhnye dokhody rastut, no daleko ne u vsekh," *Izvestiia*, no. 141 (27 July 1994), 9.

131. Åslund, "Russia's Success Story," 66.

132. *Economic Newsletter*, Russian Research Center, Harvard University, vol. 29 (25 March 1994), 1.

133. Formerly a deputy minister—then minister—under both Gaidar and Chernomyrdin.

134. Sergei Glaz'ev, "Nesostoiavsheesia vystuplenie na rasshirennom Sovmine," *Nezavisimaia gazeta*, no. 154 (16 August 1994), 4.

135. Natal'ia Kovaleva, "Potrebitel'skie ustanovki i otsenki naseleniia," *Ekonomicheskie i sotsial'nye peremeny*, no. 5 (September–October 1994), 48; and "Informatsiia," *Ekonomicheskie i sotsial'nye peremeny*, no. 5 (September–October 1994), 56.

136. Radek Sikorski, "Mirage of Numbers," *Wall Street Journal* 223 (18 May 1994), A14.

137. Daniel Yergin and Thane Gustafson, "Let's Get Down to Business, Comrade," *Financial Times* (9 July 1994), 1. Available from "NEWS" library, "FINTME" file, in Mead Data Central, Inc., LEXIS/NEXIS (database online).

138. Herbert J. Ellison, "A Journey from Moscow to St. Petersburg," *News-Net: Newsletter of the American Association for the Advancement of Slavic Studies* 34 (September 1994), 1.

139. See, for example, Adam B. Ulam, *Stalin: The Man and His Era* (New York: Viking Press, 1973), 358–78.

140. Åslund, "Russia's Success Story," 65.

141. Nikita Gololobov, "Osen'–94. Vremia kadrovykh perestanovok," *Nezavisimaia gazeta*, no. 169 (6 September 1994), 3.

142. Igor' Karpenko, "Anatolii Chubais preduprezhdaet rossiian . . . ," *Izvestiia* (23 September 1994), 4.

143. Åslund, "Russia's Success Story," 70.

144. Koen and Gavrilenkov, "How Large Was the Output Collapse in Russia?" 15.

145. See Glaz'ev, "Nesostoiavsheesia vystuplenie na rasshirennom Sovmine," 1, 4; and Koen and Gavrilenkov, "How Large Was the Output Collapse in Russia?" 9–10.

146. Graham, *Science in Russia and the Soviet Union*, 200.

Chapter 2. The Political Dimension of Economic Reform

1. "Talking to Gaidar," *The Economist* 323 (25 April 1992), 18.

2. John Williamson, "What Washington Means by Policy Reform," in John Williamson, ed., *Latin American Adjustment: How Much Has Happened?* (Washington, DC: Institute for International Economics, 1990), 7–20. Williamson also highlights tax reform, market determination of interest rates, deregulation, and security of property rights.

3. Ibid., 18.

4. See, for example, Jeffrey D. Sachs, "Russia's Struggle with Stabilization: Conceptual Issues and Evidence," paper prepared for the Annual Conference on Development Economics, World Bank, Washington, DC (28–29 April 1994), 3.

5. Seymour Martin Lipset, *Political Man: The Social Bases of Politics* (Garden City, NY: Anchor Books, 1960), 64ff.

6. Ralf Dahrendorf, "Effectiveness and Legitimacy: On the 'Governability' of Democracies," *The Political Quarterly* 51 (October–December 1980), 396–97.

7. Peter Hall, "Patterns of Economic Policy: An Organizational Approach," in *States and Societies*, ed. David Held, et al. (Oxford: Martin Robertson, 1983), 369–70.

8. Lipset, *Political Man*, 64.

9. Ibid., 65.

10. Hall, "Patterns of Economic Policy," 370. See also Robert A. Dahl, "Governments and Political Oppositions," in *Macropolitical Theory*, ed. Fred I. Greenstein and Nelson W. Polsby (Reading, MA: Addison-Wesley), 115–74.

11. Adam Przeworski, "Some Problems in the Study of the Transition to Democracy," in *Transitions from Authoritarian Rule: Prospects for Democracy, Part III: Comparative Perspectives*, ed. Guillermo O'Donnel, Philippe C. Schmitter, and Laurence Whitehead (Baltimore: The Johns Hopkins University Press, 1986), 57.

12. Lipset, *Political Man*, 80.

13. Robert A. Dahl, *Dilemmas of Pluralist Democracy: Autonomy vs. Control* (New Haven: Yale University Press, 1982), 47.

14. Anders Åslund, "Principles of Privatisation for Formerly Socialist Countries," working paper no. 18, Stockholm Institute of [Soviet and] East European Economics, Stockholm, Sweden (1991), 8.

15. Anders Åslund, "A Critique of Soviet Reform Plans," in *The Post-Soviet Economy: Soviet and Western Perspectives* ed. Anders Åslund (New York: St. Martin's Press, 1992), 169.

16. Anders Åslund, *Post-Communist Economic Revolutions: How Big a Bang?* (Washington, DC: Center for Strategic and International Studies, 1992), 12, 14.

17. Ibid., 29.

18. Ibid., 29–30.

19. Ibid., 30.

20. Ibid., 32. Emphasis added.

21. Sachs, "Russia's Struggle with Stabilization," 26. Emphasis added.

22. Jeffrey Sachs, "The Reformers' Tragedy," *New York Times*, (23 January 1994), E17.

23. Leonid Lopatnikov, "Al'ternativa" (interview with Anders Åslund), *Delovoi mir*, no. 154 (14 August 1993), 2.

24. Anders Åslund, "Prospects for a Successful Change of Economic System in Russia," working paper no. 60, Stockholm Institute of East European Economics, Stockholm, Sweden (November 1992), 3.

25. Anders Åslund, "Runaway Rubles," *New York Times* (24 November 1993), A25. Available from "NEWS" library, "NYT" file, in Mead Data Central, Inc., LEXIS/NEXIS (database online). See also Jeffrey Sachs, "Varianty finansovoi politiki dlia Rossii," *Izvestiia*, no. 179 (21 September 1993), 4; Anders Åslund, "Goskredity sel'skomu khoziaistvu—eto podarok monopoliiam," *Izvestiia*, no. 179 (21 September 1993), 4; Lopatnikov, "Al'ternativa"; Andrei Shleifer, "Nastuplenie na reformy—poslednii boi kommunistov," *Izvestiia*, no. 149 (10 August 1993), 4; and Jeffrey Sachs, "Kak pokonchit' s infliatsiei," *Izvestiia*, no. 202 (22 October 1993), 4.

26. Sachs, "Russia's Struggle with Stabilization," 3.

27. Anders Åslund, "Russia's Success Story," *Foreign Affairs* 73 (September–October 1994), 60.

28. On the eve of the December 1993 elections, Åslund was decrying the dilution of state power "even before the demise of Communism" and maintaining that "One reason President Gorbachev failed to reform the Soviet Union was that *so few obeyed him.* The state as a policy-making center had simply withered away. . . . The critical difference between failure and success is the *re-creation of a state policy apparatus*" (see Åslund, "Runaway Rubles"; emphasis added).

29. Kennan Institute for Advanced Russian Studies, "New Round of Russian Constitutional Reform Begins," *Meeting Report* 21, no. 11 (1994). Sharlet goes on to hope that "workable politics" will be possible in Russia, in spite of the constitution's deficiencies, and in a subsequent analysis he suggests that Yeltsin was using prudence in taking advantage of his new constitutional powers. That conclusion does not, however, mitigate the opportunities for authoritarianism that were opened up by the constitution. See Robert Sharlet, "Constitutional Politics in the Second Russian Republic," paper presented at the annual meeting of the American Association for the Advancement of Slavic Studies, Philadelphia, PA (17–20 November 1994).

30. Grigorii Tsitriniak, "Pogranichnaia situatsiia," *Literaturnaia gazeta*, no. 44 (28 October 1992), 11.

31. Irina Demchenko, "Kratkii kurs poiska soglasiia," *Moskovskie novosti*, no. 11 (13–20 March 1994), A14.

32. Ibid.

33. Egor Gaidar, "Rossiia i reformy," *Izvestiia*, no. 187 (19 August 1992), 3.

34. Åslund, "A Critique of Soviet Reform Plans," 172.

35. Åslund, "Principles of Privatisation for Formerly Socialist Countries," 9.

36. Åslund, "A Critique of Soviet Reform Plans," 172–73. In another work he states, "Galbraith's resistance to quick privatization may be discarded as social democratic nostalgia based on poor understanding of socialist economies" (Åslund, *Post-Communist Economic Revolutions*, 75). The only qualification Åslund offers that could check the pace of privatization is that "true property rights must obtain" (ibid., 74). Of course, establishing a sound legal basis for property rights is not the only prerequisite to effective privatization in a highly centralized system. Other factors, such as training executive personnel in principles of economic management, establishing dependable supply networks, and creating a competitive economic environment are also critical. Yet for most analysts, Åslund's attention to this one precondition, the establishment of property rights, might seem to be a formidable obstacle to a rapid privatization pace in a country such as Russia with a weak legal system—but not for Åslund. After mentioning questions of restoring former property rights, establishing a "rule of law," and developing procedures to "sanctify" property rights at the outset of privatization, he continues, "These questions must be solved fast, and legal procedures should be facilitated by unequivocal and irrevocable political decisions" (ibid.).

37. David Lipton and Jeffrey D. Sachs, "Prospects for Russia's Economic Reforms," *Brookings Papers on Economic Activity*, no. 2 (1992), 213.

38. "O kommertsializatsii deiatel'nosti predpriiatii torgovli v RSFSR," *Vse o privatizatsii v torgovle* (Moscow: Torgovlia, 1992), 44–45.

39. Aleksandr Bykov (ed. Ol'ga Osetrova), "Bol'shaia, malaia, kriminal'naia," *Delovoi mir*, no. 26 (7–13 February 1994), 18.

40. Lora Velikanova, "Larisa Piiasheva: 'Vaucher—eto eshche ne sobstvennost'," *Literaturnaia gazeta*, no. 20 (18 May 1994), 10.

41. "Osnovnye polozheniia programmy privatizatsii gosudarstvennykh i munitsipal'nykh predpriiatii v Rossiiskoi Federatsii na 1992 god," *Vse o privatizatsii v torgovle* (Moscow: Torgovlia, 1992), 48.

42. Introductory summary to "Ob uskorenii privatizatsii gosudarstvennykh i munitsipal'nykh predpriiatii," *Vse o privatizatsii v torgovle* (Moscow: Torgovlia, 1992), 47.

43. Åslund, "Principles of Privatisation of Formerly Socialist Countries," 14.

44. Mikhail Malei, "Tri perioda privatizatsii," *Nezavisimaia gazeta*, no. 172 (10 September 1993), 2.

45. "Annotatsiia osnovnykh zakonodatel'nykh i normativnykh aktov, reguliruiushchikh otnosheniia sobstvennosti i privatizatsiiu gosudarstvennykh i munitsipal'nykh predpriiatii v Rossiiskoi Federatsii," *Delovoi mir*, no. 131 (10 July 1992), 7. This was the same day that the Russian Supreme Soviet approved the law On Privatization of State and Municipal Enterprises.

46. Malei, "Tri perioda privatizatsii."

47. Vladimir Orlov, "Gosudarstvo idet s molotka," *Moskovskie novosti*, no. 2 (12 January 1992), 14.

48. Petr Filippov (ed. Ol'ga Osetrova), "Kuda poshel protsess?" *Delovoi mir*, no. 26 (7–13 February, 1994), 19.

49. Åslund, "Principles of Privatisation for Formerly Socialist Countries," 20.

50. Oleg Bogomolov, "Razdaetsia nicheinoe bogatstvo," *Nezavisimaia gazeta*, no. 13 (23 January 1993), 4.

51. Åslund, *Post-Communist Economic Revolutions*, 87–88.

52. Olivier Blanchard, Rudiger Dornbusch, Paul Krugman, Richard Layard and Lawrence Summers, *Reform in Eastern Europe* (Cambridge, MA: The MIT Press, 1991), 37.

53. "Talking to Gaidar," 20.

54. Maxim Boycko and Andrei Shleifer, "The Voucher Program for Russia," in *Changing the Economic System in Russia*, eds. Anders Åslund and Richard Layard (New York: St. Martin's Press, 1993), 100.

55. "Gosudarstvennaia programma privatizatsii gosudarstvennykh i munitsipal'nykh predpriiatii v Rossiiskoi Federatsii na 1992 god," 17.

56. *The Oxford Russian-English Dictionary*, 2nd ed., s.v. *"imennoi."* The reformers added the paranthetical phrase (*privatizatsionnye cheki*) after *"imennye privatizatsionnye scheta,"* but that phrase could not reasonably have been taken to alter the meaning of the nonparenthetical part of the description. The stated intent of the reformers in adding *"privatizatsionnye cheki"* was to simplify the privatization procedure by taking banks out of the process. There was no suggestion at this point that the checks would not have been issued in people's names, or that they would become negotiable.

57. Gaidar became acting prime minister on June 15.

58. Introductory commentary to "O vvedenii v deistvie sistemy privatizatsionnykh chekov v Rossiiskoi Federatsii," *Kommersant*, no. 34 (17–24 August 1992), 24.

59. Pavel Sorokin, "Kazhdomu rossiianinu—imennoi privatizatsionnyi schet," *Delovoi mir*, no. 88 (8 May 1992), 2.

60. Filippov, "Kuda poshel protsess?"

61. *Current Digest of the Soviet Press* 43 (4 December 1991), 7; from *Izvestiia* (30 October 1991), 2.

62. Anatolii Velednitskii, "Priblizhaetsia delezhka. Gosimushchestva," *Delovoi mir*, no. 110 (10 June 1992), 1.

63. Lora Velinkanova, "Anatolii Chubais: 'Do 80 protsentov gosudarstvennoi sobstvennosti—za cheki,' " *Literaturnaia gazeta*, no. 47 (18 November 1992), 10.

64. Viacheslav Pankov, " 'My nikogda ne stavili zadachu sdelat' kazhdogo grazhdanina sobstvennikom,' " *Finansovye izvestiia*, no. 12 (24–30 March 1994), 1.

65. Nikolai Troitskii, "Prezident nedovolen parlamentom. I gotov vlast' upotrebit'," *Megapolis-Express*, no. 44 (4 November 1992), 3.

66. He announced the action in an August 19 television address. The decree was published August 21. See "O vvedenii v deistvie sistemy privatizatsionnykh chekov v Rossiiskoi Federatsii."

67. "Zakliuchenie Vysshego Ekonomicheskogo Soveta pri Prezidiume VS RF," *Delovoi mir*, no. 197 (13 October 1992), 3.

68. Ibid.

69. Anatolii Chubais, "Privatizatsionnye cheki: Ob''iavlena minutnaia gotovnost'," *Ekonomika i zhizn'*, no. 40 (October 1992), 1.

70. "No to Creeping Coup," *Izvestiia* (26 October 1992), 1–2. Available from "NEWS" library, "SPD" file, in Mead Data Central, Inc., LEXIS/NEXIS (database online).

71. See also Lynn D. Nelson and Irina Y. Kuzes, *Property to the People: The Struggle for Radical Economic Reform in Russia* (Armonk, NY: M.E. Sharpe, 1994).

72. Filippov, "Kuda poshel protsess?" Emphasis added.

73. Åslund, *Post-Communist Economic Revolutions*, 70–74. He also discusses the dysfunctionality of soft budget constraints, the value of competition, the need for rational criteria for the allocation of capital, the relationship between pluralist ownership and political democracy, and the poor organization of state administrations in countries such as Russia.

74. Blanchard, et al., *Reform in Eastern Europe*, 37.

75. "Zakon Rossiiskoi Federatsii 'O privatizatsii gosudarstvennykh i munitsipal'nykh predpriiatii' ot 3 iiulia 1991 goda s izmeneniiami i dopolneniiami, priniatymi 5 iiunia 1992 goda" (chap. 11, par. 3), *Delovoi mir*, no. 138 (21 July 1992), 7. If such personal purchases involved the payment of more than five hundred times the minimum monthly salary, the source of the funds had to be documented.

76. Tat'iana Boikova, "Khristos raspiat po trebovaniiu mass—napominaet akademik Leonid Abalkin," *Delovoi mir*, no. 38 (21–27 February 1994), 19. Emphasis added.

77. Petr Filippov, "Korruptsioner—drug mafiozi," *Delovoi mir*, no. 14 (24–30 January 1994), 20.

78. Fikriat Tabeev, "Vazhnoe zveno ekonomicheskoi reformy," *Ekonomika i zhizn'*, no. 30 (July 1993), 14.

79. Fikriat Tabeev, "Rossiiskii Fond federal'nogo imushchestva," *Ekonomika i zhizn'*, no. 26 (June 1992), 9; emphasis added. For additional detail regarding property funds, see Nelson and Kuzes, *Property to the People*, 124–26.

80. Nikolai Zimin, "Deputaty popravliaiut narod," *Delovoi mir*, no. 81 (30 April 1993), 1.

81. Andrei Shleifer and Maxim Boycko, "The Politics of Russian Privatization," in *Post-Communist Reform: Pain and Progress*, eds. Olivier Blanchard, et al. (Cambridge, MA: MIT Press, 1993), 38.

82. Ibid., 39.

83. Ibid., 56.

84. Maxim Boycko, Andrei Shleifer, and Robert W. Vishny, "Privatizing Russia," *Brookings Papers on Economic Activity*, no. 2 (1993), 142–45.

85. Shleifer and Boycko, "The Politics of Russian Privatization," 57–58.

86. House Committee on Small Business, "The Privatization Experience: Strategies and Implications for Small Business Development" (testimony by Anders Åslund; mimeo), 7.

87. Shleifer and Boycko, "The Politics of Russian Privatization," 59.

88. Ibid., 63.

89. Ibid., 64.

90. This estimate was made by Silvana Malle of the Organisation for Economic Co-operation and Development, in November 1994 ("Successes and Failures of Privatization in Russia" panel at the annual meeting of the American Association for the Advancement of Slavic Studies, Philadelphia, PA [17–20 November, 1994]).

91. Shleifer and Boyko, "The Politics of Russian Privatization."

92. Ibid., 68.

93. Åslund follows Shleifer and Boyko ("The Politics of Russian Privatization") in failing to recognize the political inadequacy of this approach. Writing specifically about the Shleifer and Boyko paper cited above, Åslund argues, "The perhaps most sophisticated part of the Russian privatization program has been its politics, how various stakeholders have been considered and coopted. The approach could either be described as pragmatic and shrewd or unprincipled. In any case, it has been deliberate and flexible." See House Committee on Small Business, "The Privatization Experience" (testimony by Åslund), 15.

94. Graham Allison and Robert Blackwill, "America's Stake in the Soviet Future," *Foreign Affairs* 70 (Summer 1991), 77.

95. Ibid., 93–4.

96. Graham T. Allison, preface to *Window of Opportunity: The Grand Bargain for Democracy in the Soviet Union* by Graham T. Allison and Grigorii Yavlinsky (New York: Pantheon Books, 1991), x. See also Graham T. Allison, William L. Ury, and Bruce J. Allyn, eds., *Windows of Opportunity: From Cold War to Peaceful Competition in U.S.-Soviet Relations* (Cambridge, MA: Ballinger Publishing Company, 1989).

97. John J. Fialka, "U.S. Aid to Russia Is Quite a Windfall—For U.S. Consultants," *Wall Street Journal* 223 (24 February 1994), A1.

98. Ibid.

Chapter 3. Structural and Cultural Factors

1. Ronald Inglehart, *Culture Shift in Advanced Industrial Society* (Princeton: Princeton University Press, 1990), 64.

2. Gary S. Becker, *Human Capital: A Theoretical and Empirical Analysis, with Special Reference to Education* (Chicago: University of Chicago Press, 1993), 16.

3. World Bank, *Russian Economic Reform: Crossing the Threshold of Structural Change* (Washington, DC: World Bank, 1992), 5.

4. Stephan Haggard and Robert Kaufman, "The State in the Initiation and Consolidation of Market-Oriented Reform," in *State and Market in Development*, ed. Louis Putterman and Dietrich Rueschemeyer (Boulder: Lynne Rienner, 1992), 229.

5. John Friedmann, *Planning in the Public Domain: From Knowledge to Action* (Princeton: Princeton University Press, 1987), 303–4.

6. Of course, the same principle should be utilized in taking into account regional variations within a country as well as the multinational context of national reforms.

7. Gary S. Becker, *The Economic Approach to Human Behavior* (Chicago: University of Chicago Press, 1976), 6–7.

8. Karl Polanyi, "Aristotle Discovers the Economy," in *Primitive, Archaic, and Modern Economies: Essays by Karl Polanyi*, ed. George Dalton (Boston: Beacon Press, 1968), 86. See also Karl Polanyi, *The Great Transformation* (Boston: Beacon Press, 1944), 249–50.

9. Jack Hirshleifer, "The Expanding Domain of Economics," *The American Economic Review* 75 (December 1985), 53.

10. John Rawls, *A Theory of Justice* (Cambridge: Harvard University Press, 1971), 449.

11. Ibid., 11–17.

12. Amitai Etzioni, "Socio-Economics: A Budding Challenge," in *Socio-Economics: Toward a New Synthesis*, ed. Amitai Etzioni and Paul R. Lawrence (Armonk, NY: M.E. Sharpe, 1991), 6.

13. Herbert Simon, *Administrative Behavior* (Glencoe, IL: Free Press, 1957).

14. Robert H. Frank, "Rethinking Rational Choice," in *Beyond the Marketplace: Rethinking Economy and Society*, ed. Roger Friedland and A.F. Robertson (New York: Aldine de Gruyter, 1990), 54–55.

15. Paul DiMaggio, "Cultural Aspects of Economic Action and Organization," in Friedland and Robertson, eds., *Beyond the Marketplace*, 120–21.

16. Robert L. Heilbroner, *Behind the Veil of Economics: Essays in the Worldly Philosophy* (New York: W.W. Norton, 1988), 17–18.

17. Ibid., 24–29.

18. Ibid., 32.

19. Henry J. Aaron, "Distinguished Lecture on Economics in Government: Public Policy, Values, and Consciousness," *Journal of Economic Perspectives* 8 (Spring 1994), 19.

20. See, for example, Marek Dabrowski, "The First Half-Year of Russian Transformation," in *Changing the Economic System in Russia*, ed. Anders Åslund and Richard Layard (New York: St. Martin's Press, 1993), 8–9.

21. Anders Åslund, "A Critique of Soviet Reform Plans," in *The Post-Soviet Economy: Soviet and Western Perspectives* ed. Anders Åslund (New York: St. Martin's Press, 1992), 172.

22. Anders Åslund, *Post-Communist Economic Revolutions: How Big a Bang?* (Washington, DC: Center for Strategic and International Studies, 1992), 65.

23. Anders Åslund, " 'Esli Rossiia khochet vyrvat'sia ... ,' " *Moskovskie novosti*, no. 33 (15 August 1993), A13. Emphasis added.

24. Aleksei Chichkin, "Dzhefri Saks snova sufliruet Rossii," *Megapolis-Express*, no. 50 (22 December 1993), 9.

25. See, for example, Dabrowski, "The First Half-Year of Russian Transformation"; and Anders Åslund, "The Gradual Nature of Economic Change in Russia," working paper no. 56, Stockholm Institute of East European Economics, Stockholm, Sweden (1992).

26. Egor Gaidar, "Novyi kurs," *Izvestiia*, no. 26 (10 February 1994), 4.

27. See Teodor Shanin, *Russia as a "Developing Society": The Roots of Otherness: Russia's Turn of Century* (New Haven: Yale University Press, 1985), 18–21.

28. Ibid., 26.

29. James H. Billington, *The Icon and the Axe: An Interpretive History of Russian Culture* (New York: Random House, 1966), 370. The last quotation is from Vissarion Belinsky.

30. Philip G. Roeder, "Varieties of Post-Soviet Authoritarian Regimes," *Post-Soviet Affairs* 10 (January–March 1994), 61.

31. Ibid., 98.

32. Zhores Medvedev, "Rossiia v ozhidanii demokratii," *Delovoi mir*, no. 247 (6–12 December 1993), 12.

33. Irina Khakamada, "Biudzhet–94: peresmotr opasen, korrektivy neobkhodimy," *Moskovskie novosti*, no. 19 (8–15 May 1994), B3.

34. Tat'iana Skorobogat'ko, "Biurokratiia bessmertna?" *Moskovskie novosti*, no. 16 (17–24 April 1994), A6.

35. Irina Savvateeva, "O tekh, kto nami pravit," *Izvestiia*, no. 92 (18 May 1994), 2.

36. John Child, "Society and Enterprise between Hierarchy and Market," in *Societal Change between Market and Organization*, ed. John Child, Michel Crozier, Renate Mayntz, et al. (Aldershot: Avebury, 1993), 203–23.

37. Anatolii Kostiukov, "Prezident nashel svoiu partiiu," *Obshchaia gazeta*, no. 10 (11–17 March 1994), 7.

38. See, for example, Andrei Fadin, "Skuchno ne budet," *Obshchaia gazeta*, no. 1 (1–7 January 1994), 7; Gavriil Popov, "Revansh sovetskoi sistemy," *Izvestiia*, no. 93 (19 May 1994), 4; and Sergei Chugaev, "Vybiraia mezhdu reformami i vlast'iu, politiki obychno predpochitaiut vlast'," *Izvestiia*, no. 63 (5 April 1994), 4.

39. See also Egor Gaidar, "Fashizm i biurokratiia," *Segodnia*, no. 110 (15 June 1994), 10.

40. Gaidar, "Novyi kurs." Emphasis added.

41. Arkadii Solarev, "Gaidar priekhal," *Megapolis-Express*, no. 14 (27 April 1994), 18.

42. Vladimir Orlov, "Gosudarstvo idet s molotka," *Moskovskie novosti*, no. 2 (12 January 1992), 14.

43. Lev Timofeev, "Tenevaia privatizatsiia," *Izvestiia*, no. 90 (14 May 1994), 5.

44. Ibid.

45. Ibid.

46. Aleksandr Kastravets, "Mafiia vsesil'na. A gosudarstvo?" *Delovoi mir*, no. 61 (24 March 1994), 8.

47. Yurii Burtin and Grigorii Vodolazov, "Nadezhdy na 'stabilizatsiiu' tshchetny," *Nezavisimaia gazeta*, no. 102 (2 June 1994), 1.

48. David Lipton and Jeffrey D. Sachs, "Prospects for Russia's Economic Reforms," *Brookings Papers on Economic Activity*, no. 2 (1992), 213.

49. Ibid.

50. Gaidar, "Novyi kurs."

51. Ibid., emphasis added.

52. Diligenskii is head of the Center for Comparative Socioeconomic and Sociopolitical Studies (Institute of the World Economy and International Relations of the Russian Academy of Sciences).

53. German Diligenskii, "Rossiiskie al'ternativy," *Mirovaia ekonomika i mezhdunarodnye otnosheniia*, no. 9 (1993), 8.

54. Aleksei Demichev, "Gosudarstvu tozhe nado popotet'," *Moskovskie novosti*, no. 17 (24 April–1 May 1994), A5.

55. Popov, "Revansh sovetskoi sistemy."

56. Roeder suggests that this type of bureaucratic authoritarianism "seems to produce policy dysfunction and institutional stagnation far earlier" than the party-controlled variant. See Philip G. Roeder, *Red Sunset: The Failure of Soviet Politics* (Princeton: Princeton University Press, 1993), 249.

57. "Rossiiskaia mafiia sobiraet dos'e na krupnykh chinovnikov i politikov," *Izvestiia*, no. 15 (26 January 1994), 1. See also Terrorism, Narcotics and International Operations Subcommittee of the Senate Foreign Relations Committee, "Drug Trafficking," 103rd Cong., 2nd sess., 20 April 1994. Available from Federal Information Systems Corporation, Federal News Service. In Mead Data Central, Inc., LEXIS/NEXIS (database online).

58. "Zadumaites', gospoda predprinimateli," *Delovoi mir*, no. 101 (16–24 May 1994), 1.

59. Boris Krotkov, "Duma otkryvaet pokhod protiv korruptsii," *Delovoi mir*, no. 99 (14 May 1994), 1.

60. Permanent Investigations Subcommittee of the Senate Governmental Affairs Committee, "Organized Crime in the Former Soviet Union," 103rd Cong., 2nd sess., 24 May 1994. Available from Federal Information Systems Corporation, Federal News Service. In Mead Data Central, Inc., LEXIS/NEXIS (database online).

61. Stephen Handelman, "The Russian 'Mafiya,' " *Foreign Affairs* 73 (March–April 1994), 88.

62. Ibid., 89.

63. See Mikhail Maliutin, "Mafiia rvetsia k vlasti?" *Novaia ezhednevnaia gazeta*, no. 194 (12 October 1994), 4.

64. See G. Yavlinsky, B. Fedorov, S. Shatalin, N. Petrakov, S. Aleksashenko, A. Vavilov, L. Grigoriev, M. Zadornov, V. Machits, A. Mikhailov, and E. Yasin, *500 Days (Transition to the Market)*, trans. David Kushner (New York: St. Martin's Press, 1991), 126–29.

65. Graham Allison and Grigory Yavlinsky, *Window of Opportunity: The Grand Bargain for Democracy in the Soviet Union*, (New York: Pantheon Books, 1991) 34, 39–66.

66. Lev Aleinik, "Chernyi rynok kak politicheskaia sistema Rossii," *Segodnia*, no. 39 (1 March 1994), 3.

67. Vasilii Lipitskii, "Razvilki nashei nedavnei istorii," *Nezavisimaia gazeta*, no. 151 (12 August 1993), 2. Emphasis added.

68. Aleinik, "Chernyi rynok kak politicheskaia sistema Rossii."

69. Vladimir Ovchinskii, "Korruptsioner—drug mafiozi," *Delovoi mir*, no. 14 (24–30 January 1994), 20.

70. Boris Aleksandrov, " 'My sozdali ne rynok, a monopol'nokriminal'nuiu ekonomiku,' " *Delovoi mir*, no. 33 (16 February 1994), 1.

71. For similar findings from the Russian Independent Institute for Social and Ethnic Studies, see Natal'ia Tikhonova, "Kharakter myshleniia rossiian ostaetsia neekonomicheskim," *Finansovye izvestiia*, no. 43 (27 September 1994), 8.

72. János Kornai, *Contradictions and Dilemmas: Studies on the Socialist Economy and Society* (Cambridge: MIT Press, 1986), 125–26. See also Vladimir Gimpel'son, "Economic Consciousness and Reform of the Employment Sphere," in *Double Shift: Transforming Work in Postsocialist and Postindustrial Societies,* ed. Bertram Silverman, Robert Vogt, and Murray Yanowitch (Armonk, NY: M.E. Sharpe, 1993), 39–52.

73. Tatyana Zaslavskaya, *The Second Socialist Revolution: An Alternative Soviet Strategy,* trans. Susan M. Davies with Jenny Warren (Bloomington: Indiana University Press, 1990), 57. A large number of other works underscore these observations. See, for example, Elizabeth Teague, "Gorbachev's 'Human Factor' Policies," in *Gorbachev's Economic Plans: Study Papers Submitted to the Joint Economic Committee, Congress of the United States,* vol. 2, 100th Cong., 1st sess., 1987, S. Prt. 100–57, 224–39; Timofeev, "Tenevaia privatizatsiia"; and Nikolai Shmelev and Vladimir Popov, *The Turning Point: Revitalizing the Soviet Economy* (New York: Doubleday, 1989), 186–87.

74. Zoia V. Kupriianova, "Trudovaia motivatsiia," *Ekonomicheskie i sotsial'nye peremeny,* no. 6 (October 1993), 36. The sample included 1,981 respondents from throughout Russia.

75. In 1989, 24 percent of respondents believed that "Those who work hard will receive more," but in 1993 only 13 percent agreed with that statement.

76. Liudmila Khakhulina, "Otnoshenie naseleniia k differentsiatsii dokhodov i sotsial'nomu rassloeniiu," *Ekonomicheskie i sotsial'nye peremeny,* no. 4 (August 1993), 8; and Aleksandr Golov, "Formula uspekha ostaetsia prezhnei," *Izvestiia,* no. 129 (13 July 1993), 5.

77. Discussed in Khakhulina, "Otnoshenie naseleniia k differentsiatsii dokhodov i sotsial'nomu rassloeniiu," 9.

78. Yurii Shishkov, "Na puti k rynochnoi ekonomike," *Sotsiologicheskie issledovaniia,* no. 9 (1992), 75.

79. See Lynn D. Nelson and Irina Y. Kuzes, *Property to the People: The Struggle for Radical Economic Reform in Russia* (Armonk, NY: M.E. Sharpe, 1994), 155–74.

80. Victor Turner, *Dramas, Fields and Metaphors* (Ithaca: Cornell University Press, 1974), 14.

81. See, for example, Child, "Society and Enterprise between Hierarchy and Market," 216.

82. Mary K. Farmer and Mark L. Matthews, "Cultural Difference and Subjective Rationality: Where Sociology Connects with the Economics of Technological Choice," in *Rethinking Economics: Markets, Technology and Economic Evolution,* ed. Geoffrey M. Hodgson and Ernesto Screpanti (Aldershot: Edward Elgar, 1991), 106.

83. Some of the basic themes in this large stream of research are highlighted in Hans Haferkamp and Neil J. Smelser, eds., *Social Change and Modernity* (Berkeley: University of California Press, 1992); Mary Douglas, *How Institutions Think* (Syracuse: Syracuse University Press, 1986); Stuart Toddington, *Rationality, Social Action and Moral Judgment* (Edinburgh: Edinburgh University Press, 1993); Robert L. Hamblin, R. Brooke Jacobsen, and Jerry L.L. Miller, *A Mathematical Theory of Social Change* (New York: John Wiley and Sons, 1973); Pierre Bourdieu and James S. Coleman, *Social Theory for a Changing Society* (New

York: Russell Sage Foundation, 1991); and Ulf Hannerz, *Cultural Complexity: Studies in the Social Organization of Meaning* (New York: Columbia University Press, 1992).

84. Gaidar, "Novyi kurs."

85. See Milton Friedman, *Monetarist Economics* (Cambridge, MA: Basil Blackwell, 1991), 150–52.

86. Ibid., 141.

87. Richard E. Ericson, "The Classical Soviet-Type Economy: Nature of the System and Implications for Reform," *Journal of Economic Perspectives* 5 (Fall 1991), 25. Emphasis added.

88. Richard E. Ericson, "Economics," in *After the Soviet Union: From Empire to Nation*, ed. Timothy J. Colton and Robert Legvold (New York: W.W. Norton, 1992), 55–59.

89. Ibid., 61. Sachs makes the same mistake. See Jeffrey Sachs, "Life in the Economic Emergency Room," in *The Political Economy of Policy Reform*, ed. John Williamson (Washington, DC: Institute for International Economics, 1994), 508. But Åslund got this part right. He states, "Private ownership is necessary for the creative destruction, enterpreneurship and innovation that Joseph Schumpeter cherished. In neither practice nor theory, can these properties develop under predominant state ownership." Thus Åslund, unlike Ericson, correctly applies the "creative destruction" idea to the post-restructuring stage of economic development. See Anders Åslund, "Principles of Privatisation for Formerly Socialist Countries," working paper no. 18, Stockholm Institute of [Soviet and] East European Economics, Stockholm, Sweden (January 1991), 4.

90. Joseph A. Schumpeter, *Capitalism, Socialism and Democracy* (New York: Harper Torchbooks, 1950), 83. Emphasis in original.

91. Ibid., 82. Emphasis added.

92. Richard E. Ericson, "Self-Evident Truths: The Challenge of Marketization," *The Harriman Institute Forum* 7 (September–October 1993), 3.

93. János Kornai, *The Road to a Free Economy: Shifting from a Socialist System: The Example of Hungary* (New York: W.W. Norton, 1990), 82.

94. Hamblin, et al., *A Mathematical Theory of Social Change*, 9.

95. Friedmann, *Planning in the Public Domain,* 47.

96. Ibid., 223.

97. Åslund, "Principles of Privatisation for Formerly Socialist Countries," 11.

98. Richard E. Ericson, "Priority, Duality, and Penetration in the Soviet Command Economy." RAND Note reports N–2643-NA, The RAND Corporation, Santa Monica, CA (December 1988), 3.

99. Richard E. Ericson, "Soviet Economic Reforms: The Motivation and Content of *Perestroika*," *Journal of International Affairs* 42 (Spring 1989), 328.

100. Ibid., 331.

101. Richard E. Ericson, "What Is to Be Done?" *The New Republic* 202 (5 March 1990), 38.

102. Ericson, "The Classical Soviet-Type Economy," 26.

103. Ibid.

104. Ericson, "Economics," 78. Emphasis added.

105. Ibid., 82.

106. Åslund, "A Critique of Soviet Reform Plans," 169.

107. See John B. Dunlop, *The Rise of Russia and the Fall of the Soviet Empire* (Princeton: Princeton University Press, 1993), 263ff.

108. Åslund, "A Critique of Soviet Reform Plans," 170.

109. Ibid., 178.

110. Ibid., 177.

111. Ibid., 176.

112. Ibid., 177. Emphasis added.

113. Åslund, "Principles of Privatisation for Formerly Socialist Countries," 22.

114. David Lipton and Jeffrey Sachs, "Creating a Market Economy in Eastern Europe: The Case of Poland," *Brookings Papers on Economic Activity*, no. 1 (1990), 77. Emphasis in original.

115. Åslund, "The Gradual Nature of Economic Change in Russia," 17.

116. Ibid., 8.

117. Anders Åslund, "Prospects for a Successful Change of Economic System in Russia," working paper no. 60, Stockholm Institute of East European Economics, Stockholm, Sweden (November 1992), 21.

118. Ibid., 22.

119. Jeffrey Sachs, "The Economic Transformation of Eastern Europe: The Case of Poland," *Economics of Planning* 25 (1992), 17.

120. Ibid., 21.

121. Anders Åslund, "Adapting to the World Economy: Interests and Obstacles," in *Rethinking Russia's National Interests*, ed. Stephen Sestanovich (Washington, DC: Center for Strategic and International Studies, 1994), 93. Åslund also made this statement, with only cosmetically different wording, in a 1992 version of this article (working paper no. 58, Stockholm Institute of East European Economics, 10).

122. See, for example, Jeffrey Sachs, "Betrayal," *The New Republic* (31 January 1994), 14–18.

123. Jessica Eve Stern, "Moscow Meltdown: Can Russia Survive?" *International Security* 18 (Spring 1994), 40.

124. Ibid., 46.

125. Ibid., 54.

126. Ibid., 64–65.

127. Ibid., 64.

128. Peter Reddaway, "Russia on the Brink?" *New York Review of Books* 40 (28 January 1993), 30. See also Elizabeth Teague, "Regionalizm v Rossii: ekonomicheskii aspekt," in *Federalizm, regionalizm i konstitutsionnaia reforma v Rossii*, ed. Ariel Cohen (Washington, DC: Heritage Foundation, 1993), 33–42.

129. C. Fred Bergsten, "The Rationale for a Rosy View," *The Economist* 328 (11–17 September 1993), 61. Emphasis added.

130. Ibid.

131. Personal communication.

132. Åslund, "The Gradual Nature of Economic Change in Russia," 16.

133. Åslund, "Prospects for a Successful Change of Economic Systems in Russia," 28.

134. Sachs, "Russia's Struggle with Stabilization: Conceptual Issues and Evidence," paper prepared for the Annual Conference on Development Economics, World Bank, Washington, DC (28–29 April 1994), 46.

Chapter 4. Contrasting Economic Priorities
in Russian Reform

1. Robert Heilbroner, *Behind the Veil of Economics* (New York: W.W. Norton, 1988), 196.

2. Mark Masarskii, "Ia skorbliu po pogibshim predpriiatiiam," *Delovoi mir*, no. 235 (22–28 November 1993), 1.

3. Egor Gaidar, "Rossiia i reformy," *Izvestiia*, no. 187 (19 August 1992), 3.

4. John Maynard Keynes, *The Collected Writings of John Maynard Keynes*, vol. 4, *A Tract on Monetary Reform* (New York: Macmillan, 1971), 65. Emphasis in original.

5. Gavriil Popov, Moscow's former mayor and a progressive democratic voice in Russia, was just one of many Russian analysts who argued that Gaidar was following a "Westernized" approach, which, Popov maintained, was being promoted by the West to destroy Russia's military-industrial potential and ensure Western competitive economic advantage. See Gavriil Popov, "Tret'ia model'," *Nezavisimaia gazeta*, no. 37 (25 February 1994), 5.

6. See, for example, Kim Sok Khwan, "Nam udalos' dobit'sia glavnogo . . . ," *Ekonomika i zhizn'*, no. 25 (June 1993), 7.

7. Ibid.

8. Jeffrey Sachs, "Betrayal," *The New Republic* (31 January 1994), 15.

9. David Lipton and Jeffrey D. Sachs, "Prospects for Russia's Economic Reforms," *Brookings Papers on Economic Activity*, no. 2 (1992), 213ff.

10. Anders Åslund, "The Gradual Nature of Economic Change in Russia," in *Changing the Economic System in Russia*, ed. Anders Åslund and Richard Layard (New York: St. Martin's Press, 1993), 19, 22. Emphasis in original. This chapter was taken from a paper that was presented at a June 1992 conference—six months after the initiation of price liberalization in Russia.

11. Anders Åslund, "Ukraine—Going, Going . . ." *New York Times* (10 June 1994), A29.

12. Jeffrey D. Sachs, "Russia's Struggle with Stabilization: Conceptual Issues and Evidence," paper prepared for the Annual Bank Conference on Development Economics, World Bank, Washington, DC (28–29 April 1994), 34.

13. Egor Gaidar, "Novyi kurs," *Izvestiia*, no. 26 (10 February 1994), 4.

14. Sachs, "Russia's Struggle with Stabilization: Conceptual Issues and Evidence," 1.

15. Luiz Carlos Bresser Pereira, José María Maravall, and Adam Przeworski, *Economic Reforms in New Democracies: A Social-Democratic Approach* (New York: Cambridge University Press, 1993), 8.

16. See, for example, Samuel P. Huntington, *The Third Wave: Democratization in the Late Twentieth Century* (Norman: University of Oklahoma Press, 1991), 59–72.

17. Grigorii Yavlinskii, "Inaia reforma," *Nezavisimaia gazeta*, no. 26 (10 February 1994), 4. Emphasis added.

18. Milton Friedman, *Monetarist Economics* (Cambridge, MA: Basil Blackwell, 1991), 22.

19. "Novyi biudzhet: ni vashim, ni nashim," *Novaia ezhednevnaia gazeta*, no.

68 (14 April 1994), 2. The State Duma faction of YABLOKO deputies represent the bloc headed by Yavlinskii.

20. Evgenii Yasin, "Starye diskussii i novye problemy," *Segodnia*, no. 5 (12 January 1994), 9.

21. Sergei Glaz'ev, "Bor'ba s infliatsiei," *Ekonomika i zhizn'*, no. 47 (November 1993), 1; and Sergei Glaz'ev, "Uroki liberalizatsii v Rossii," *Segodnia*, no. 85 (30 November 1993), 9.

22. Yasin, "Starye diskussii i novye problemy."

23. Yavlinskii, "Inaia reforma."

24. Leonid Lopatnikov, "Situatsiia—94," *Delovoi mir*, no. 83 (18–24 April 1994), 11.

25. See, for example, Friedman, *Monetarist Economics*, 50.

26. Arkadii Sosnov, "Reformy konchilis'? Zabud'te," *Moskovskie novosti*, no. 17 (24 April–1 May 1994), B3.

27. Boris Krotkov, "Biudzhet, god 1994: situatsiia arkhislozhnaia," *Delovoi mir*, no. 81 (16 April 1994), 1. See also Grigorii Yavlinskii, Mikhail Zadornov, Sergei Ivanenko, and Aleksei Mikhailov, "Biudzhet–94." *Nezavisimaia Gazeta*, no. 70 (14 April 1994), 4.

28. Ibid.

29. Irina Demchenko, "Partiia v biudzhet," *Moskovskie novosti*, no. 16 (17–24 April 1994), A6. Emphasis added.

30. Ibid.

31. Boris Boiko, "Duma ne reshilas' otvergnut' proekt biudzheta," *Kommersant-daily*, no. 69 (16 April 1994), 2.

32. Yavlinskii, et al., "Biudzhet—94."

33. He writes here about demonopolization, the creation of a competitive environment, privatization with a strong emphasis on defense of property rights, the development of national industry, and the creation of an effective financial system (to support savings, capital investments, and growth).

34. Yavlinskii, "Inaia reforma."

35. *The Current Digest of the Post-Soviet Press* (hereafter, *CDPSP*) 44 (8 July 1992), 10; from *Moskovskie novosti* (24 May 1992), 9–16.

36. Lopatnikov, "Situatsiia—94."

37. Ibid.

38. *CDPSP* 44 (8 July 1992); from *Moskovskie novosti* (24 May 1992), 9–16.

39. Ibid.

40. Glaz'ev, "Bor'ba s infliatsiei."

41. Glaz'ev, "Uroki liberalizatsii v Rossii."

42. International Monetary Fund, World Bank, Organisation for Economic Co-operation and Development and European Bank for Reconstruction and Development, *A Study of the Soviet Economy*, vol. 2 (Paris: OECD, 1991), 16.

43. "O sotsial'no-ekonomicheskom polozhenii Rossii v 1993 godu" (po materialam Goskomstata Rossii), *Ekonomika i zhizn'*, no. 6 (February 1994), 7.

44. Glaz'ev, "Bor'ba s infliatsiei."

45. International Monetary Fund, et al., *A Study of the Soviet Economy*, vol. 2, 16.

46. Yevgeny Spiridonov, "A New Concept of Monopoly Control in Russia," *Business World*, no. 33 (13 September 1993), 5.

47. International Monetary Fund, et al., *A Study of the Soviet Economy*, vol. 2, 30.

48. Yuri Shishkov, "Na puti k rynochnoi ekonomike," *Sotsiologicheskie issledovaniia*, no. 9 (1992), 75.

49. See Sergei Leskov, "'Oboronka' zakhvatila monopoliiu v oblasti kholodil'nikov," *Izvestiia*, no. 251 (30 December 1993), 4; and Igor' Achil'diev, "Oboronka poka zhiva," *Megapolis-Express*, no. 1 (5 January 1994), 10.

50. International Monetary Fund, et al., *A Study of the Soviet Economy*, vol. 2, 16.

51. Glaz'ev, "Bor'ba s infliatsiei."

52. Alan Smith, *Russia and the World Economy: Problems of Integration* (New York: Routledge, 1993), 174.

53. Boris Boiko, "Parlamentskie slushaniia vymiraiut kak dinozavry," *Kommersant-daily*, no. 123 (6 July 1994), 3.

54. Boris Krotkov, "Perevesti krizis v upravliaemyi rezhim," *Delovoi mir*, no. 112 (31 May 1994), 1.

55. Elena Kotel'nikova, "Chast' monopolii budet zakonno vyvedena s rynka," *Kommersant-daily*, no. 34 (25 February 1994), 3.

56. Andrei Borodenkov, "Raiskii klumat dlia slonov," *Moskovskie novosti*, no. 45 (7 November 1993), A10.

57. Ol'ga Osetrova, "Kuda poshel protsess?" *Delovoi mir*, no. 26 (7–13 February 1994), 19.

58. Yurii Yaremenko, "Temp reformirovaniia poterian," *Nezavisimaia gazeta*, no. 251 (30 December 1993), 3.

59. Mancur Olson, "Why Is Economic Performance Even Worse When Communism Is Abolished?" working paper no. 28, Center for Institutional Reform and the Informal Sector, University of Maryland at College Park (1992), 2–3.

60. Glaz'ev, "Bor'ba s infliatsiei."

61. Stanislav Shatalin, "Rynok trebuet upravleniia," *Ekonomika i zhizn'*, no. 5 (February 1994), 1.

62. Yurii Yaremenko, et al., "The Russian Economy: Ways Out of the Crisis," *Studies on Russian Economic Development* (*Problemy prognozirovaniya*) 4 (April 1993), 85.

63. Yaremenko, "Temp reformirovaniia poterian."

64. Yaremenko et al., "The Russian Economy," 85, 87.

65. Sergei Glaz'ev, "Nesostoiavsheesia vystuplenie na rasshirennom Sovmine," *Nezavisimaia gazeta*, no. 154 (16 August 1994), 4.

66. Yavlinskii "Inaia reforma."

67. Åslund, "The Gradual Nature of Economic Change in Russia," 26.

68. Anders Åslund, "Adapting to the World Economy: Interests and Obstacles," in *Rethinking Russia's National Interests*, ed. Stephen Sestanovich (Washington, DC: Center for Strategic and International Studies, 1994), 93.

69. Leonid Abalkin, "Dominiruiushchii faktor: ekonomicheskii krizis i puti ego preodoleniia," *Delovoi mir*, no. 39 (24 July 1993), 10.

70. Lev Makarevich, "Promyshlennaia elita predrekaet mrachnoe budushchee," *Finansovye izvestiia*, no. 39 (24–30 July 1993), 2.

71. See Ministerstvo Rossiiskoi Federatsii po delam grazhdanskoi oborony i chrezvychainym situatsiiam, "Rossiia—eto apokalipsis segodnia," *Nezavisimaia gazeta*, no. 26 (10 February 1994), 1–2 (report summary); Viacheslav Shakhov,

"'Ob''edinenie kapitalov pozvolit strakhovat' investitsii,'" *Finansovye izvestiia*, no. 42 (22–28 September 1994), 4; and Boris Brui, "Poka politiki sporiat, Rossiia vyrozhdaetsia," *Nezavisimaia gazeta*, no. 187 (23 September 1993), 6.

72. Andrei Cherniavskii, "Investitsii i rynok," *Ekonomika i zhizn'*, no. 20 (May 1993), 22.

73. Vladimir Alisov, "Proekt biudzheta 'iavno ne po silam Rossii,'" *Segodnia*, no. 99 (28 May 1994), 3.

74. Stanislav Assekritov, "Iur'ev den' privatizatsii," *Delovoi mir*, no. 65 (28 March–3 April 1994), 21.

75. Boiko, "Parlamentskie slushaniia vymiraiut kak dinozavry."

76. Glaz'ev, "Nesostoiavsheesia vystuplenie na rasshirennom Sovmine."

77. Lev Makarevich, "Inostrannyi kapital ne khochet idti v Rossiiu," *Finansovye izvestiia*, no. 52 (29 October–4 November 1993), 3; and John Lloyd, "Russian Investment 'to Surge,'" *Financial Times*, 2. Available from "NEWS" library, "FINTME" file, in Mead Data Central, Inc., LEXIS/NEXIS (database online).

78. "Utechka kapitalov iz Rossii dostigla 1,000,000 dollarov v mesiats," *Novaia ezhednevnaia gazeta*, no. 15 (26 January 1994), 1.

79. Shahid Yusuf, "China's Macroeconomic Performance and Management During Transition," *Journal of Economic Perspectives* 8 (Spring 1994), 82.

80. Louisa Vinton, ". . . but Investment on the Decline," *RFE/RL Daily Report*, no. 121 (28 June 1994), available from listserv@ubvm.cc.buffalo.edu, Internet; and Vadim Bardin, "Investory reshili vziat' svoiu sud'bu v Rossii v sobstvennye ruki," *Kommersant-daily*, no. 117 (28 June 1994), 3. See also "Luchshe rasschityvat' na sebia," *Delovoi mir*, no. 122 (10 June 1994), 1.

81. Vinton, ". . . but Investment on the Decline."

82. See, for example, Bardin, "Investory reshili vziat' svoiu sud'bu v Rossii v sobstvennye ruki."

83. See, for example, Igor' Karpenko, "Anatolii Chubais preduprezhdaet rossiian . . . ," *Izvestiia*, no. 183 (23 September 1994), 4.

84. Dmitrii Volkov, "Boris Yeltsin prizyvaet zapadnye kompanii v Rossiiu," *Segodnia*, no. 185 (28 September 1994), 2.

85. "Luchshe rasschityvat' na sebia."

86. Vinton, ". . . but Investment on the Decline."

87. Henry M. Quinlan, "Chto za utechkoi kapitala?" *Delovoi mir*, no. 28 (10 February 1994), 7.

88. "Country Risk Rankings 1993," *Euromoney*, no. 299 (March 1994), 178–80.

89. "Emerging-Market Indicators," *The Economist* 330 (19 February 1994), 124.

90. Lynn D. Nelson and Irina Y. Kuzes, *Property to the People: The Struggle for Radical Economic Reform in Russia* (Armonk, NY: M.E. Sharpe, 1994), 111–14.

91. Lidiia Belokonnaia, "No Faith in the Future," *Business World Weekly*, no. 2 (27 January 1992), 3; and *Current Digest of the Soviet Press* 43 (11 September 1991), 23; from *Izvestiia* (7 August 1991), 3.

92. Vladimir Tikhonov, "Vlast' i rynok," *Vek* (*Delovoi mir* supplement), no. 11 (22–29 October 1992), 6.

93. Lynn D. Nelson, Liliia V. Babaeva, and Rufat O. Babaev, "Perspectives on Entrepreneurship and Privatization in Russia: Policy and Public Opinion," *Slavic Review* 51 (Summer 1992), 278.

94. "O predpriiatiiakh i predprinimatel'skoi deiatel'nosti," *Ekonomika i zhizn'*, no. 4 (January 1991), 16–17.

95. Valentina Sal'nikova, "Pul's malogo biznesa Rossii," *Delovoi mir*, no. 134 (15 July 1992), 5.

96. Leonid Shinkarev, "Chastnoe delo millionov," *Izvestiia*, no. 6 (14 January 1993), 5.

97. Ol'ga Osterova, "Podderzhit li gosudarstvo predprinimatelia," *Torgovo-promyshlennye vedomosti*, no. 5 (November 1992). See also N. Palkina, "Podderzhka malykh predpriiatii v Rossii," *Ekonomika i zhizn'*, no. 39 (September 1992), 16.

98. Shinkarev, "Chastnoe delo millionov."

99. Vil' Dorofeev, "Znaki vozrozhdeniia," *Nezavisimaia gazeta*, no. 171 (9 September 1993), 5.

100. Masarskii, "Ia skorbliu po pogibshim predpriiatiiam."

101. See Elena Kotel'nikova, "Chubais reshil ukrepit' svoi pozitsii 'sverkhu' i 'snizu,' " *Kommersant-daily*, no. 169 (4 September 1993), 3.

102. Tikhonov, "Vlast' i rynok."

103. Fedor Rusinov and Mikhail Ioffe, "Rossiiskoe predprinimatel'stvo," *Delovoi mir*, no. 6 (14 January 1993), 12.

104. Tikhonov, "Vlast' i rynok."

105. "Realizm v politike" (round-table discussion), *Nezavisimaia gazeta*, no. 124 (5 July 1994), 5.

106. Irina Khakamada, "Liberaly ob''ediniaiutsia," *Rossiiskie vesti*, no. 122 (29 June 1993), 2.

107. See Mikhail Glukhovsky, "Yeltsin's Council Means Business," *Delovie lyudi*, no. 26 (September 1992), 20–21.

108. Larisa Il'ina, "Ivan Kivelidi: 'Biznes pridet k vlasti ne ran'she 2000 goda,' " *Delovoi mir*, no. 124 (3 July 1993), 9.

109. Ibid. See also Mikhail Leont'ev, "Ivan Kivelidi: Otnoshenie gosudarstva k predprinimateliam ostaetsia po-prezhnemu naplevatel'skim," *Segodnia*, no. 86 (2 December 1993), 9.

110. Igor' Skliarov, "Malyi biznes: namereniia i vozmozhnosti," *Ekonomika i zhizn'*, no. 25 (June 1994), 1.

111. Leonid Lopatnikov, "Chinovnikam—milliardy, predprinimateliam—obeshchaniia," *Delovoi mir*, no. 2 (10–16 January 1994), 2. See also Leonid Lopatnikov, "A tsifry? Ikh prosto vycherknuli ... ," *Delovoi mir*, no. 89 (25 April–1 May 1994), 11; and Igor' Skliarov, "Malyi biznes: kakova vlast', takova ego podderzhka," *Ekonomika i zhizn'*, no. 41 (October 1994), 1.

112. Alla Aloian, "Malyi biznes: problemy i prioritety," *Delovoi mir*, no. 133 (25 June 1994), 5.

113. Lopatnikov, "A tsifry? Ikh prosto vycherknuli. . . ."

114. Lopatnikov, "Chinovnikam—milliardy, predprinimateliam—obeshchaniia."

115. Aloian, "Malyi biznes: problemy i prioritety."

116. Skliarov, "Malyi biznes: kakova vlast', takova ego podderzhka."

117. Lopatnikov, "Chinovnikam—milliardy, predprinimateliam—obeshchaniia."

118. Yurii Chirkov, "Malye shansy dlia malogo biznesa," *Delovoi mir*, no. 127 (18 June 1994), 4.

119. Aleksandr Kastravets, "Mafiia vsesil'na. A gosudarstvo?" *Delovoi mir*, no. 61 (24 March 1994), 8.

120. Elizaveta Mikhailova, "Sozidatelem byt' vse trudnee," *Delovoi mir*, no. 98 (13 May 1994), 2.

121. Mark Goriachev, "Den'gi reshaiut vse," *Izvestiia*, no. 166 (2 September 1993), 4.

122. Chirkov, "Malye shansy dlia malogo biznesa."

123. Seifali Akhundov, "Chinovniki nastupaiut," *Obshchaia gazeta*, no. 22 (3–9 June 1994), 3.

124. Ibid.

125. "Malyi biznes khochet vyiti iz podpol'ia. Kto protiv?" *Tsentr plius*, no. 18 (1993), 3.

126. "Stolichnyi biznes derzhitsia na 'tenevikakh,' " *Nezavisimaia gazeta*, no. 111 (17 June 1993), 4.

127. Egor Gaidar, "Na karte—budushchee ne tol'ko Rossii," *Delovoi mir*, no. 161 (26 August 1993), 11. Emphasis added.

128. Vadim Medvedev, "Proidena li nizhniaia tochka ekonomicheskogo krizisa?" *Nezavisimaia gazeta*, no. 136 (22 July 1993), 4. See also Vil' Dorofeev, "Znaki vozrozhdeniia"; and Aleksandr Ioffe, "K nam—milosti prosim," *Ekonomika i zhizn'*, no. 4 (February 1994), 8; and Prokopii Drachev, "Malyi rossiiskii biznes i bol'shoi zapadnyi kapital," *Delovoi mir*, no. 95 (2–8 May 1994), 12.

129. Mikhailova, "Sozidatelem byt' vse trudnee."

130. Yavlinskii, "Inaia reforma."

131. Ioffe, "K nam—milosti prosim."

132. "Novyi biudzhet: ni vashim, ni nashim," 1.

133. Lipton and Sachs, "Prospects for Russia's Economic Reforms," 229, 213.

134. Åslund, "The Gradual Nature of Economic Change in Russia," 21.

135. Masarskii, "Ia skorbliu po pogibshim predpriiatiiam." Emphasis added.

136. Ann Devroy and Margaret Shapiro, "Yeltsin Gets $1.6 Billion in U.S. Aid; Summit Ends with Pledges of Partnership," *Washington Post* (5 April 1993), A1. Available from "NEWS" library, "WPOST" file, in Mead Data Central, Inc., LEXIS/NEXIS (database online). See also Elena Druzhinina, "Peterburgskii 'sammit' Evrobanka zavershen," *Delovoi mir*, no. 84 (20 April 1994), 1.

137. Daniel Williams, "Rich Nations Approve Aid to Russia," *The Washington Post* (16 April 1993), A1. Available from Mead Data Central, Inc., LEXIS/NEXIS (database online).

138. Jeffrey Sachs, "Betrayal," 14.

139. Thomas W. Lippman, "House Leaders Criticize Aid-to-Russia Program; New Coordinator Sought," *Washington Post* (12 June 1994), A27. Available from Mead Data Central, Inc., LEXIS/NEXIS (database online).

140. Foreign Operations, Export Financing and Related Programs Subcommittee of the House Appropriations Committee, "The Former Soviet Union and Eastern Europe," 103rd Cong., 2nd sess., 10 May 1994. Available from Federal Information Systems Corporation, Federal News Service. In Mead Data Central, Inc., LEXIS/NEXIS (database online).

141. See, for example, Sergei Viktorov, "Vlasti reshili, chto nuzhny melkim predprinimateliam," *Kommersant-daily*, no. 87 (14 May 1994), 3.

142. Leonid Kuznetsov, "Aleksandr Volovik: 'Biznes—eto kogda vygodno vsem,' " *Delovoi mir*, no. 60 (23 March 1994), 6.

143. "Krizis v Rossii budet preodolen v ... godu," *Novaia ezhednevnaia gazeta*, no. 57 (2 December 1993), 3.

144. Kuznetsov, "Aleksandr Volovik."

145. Andrei Yurevich, "Uchenye popolniaiut riady maloobespechennykh i bezrabotnykh," *Megapolis-Express*, no. 29 (28 July 1993), 14.

146. Organisation for Economic Co-operation and Development (OECD), *Science, Technology and Innovation Policies: Federation of Russia*, vol. 1, *Evaluation Report* (Paris: OECD, 1994), 11.

147. Leskov, " 'Oboronka' zakhvatila monopoliiu v oblasti kholodil'nikov"; and Achil'diev, "Oboronka poka zhiva."

148. OECD, *Science, Technology and Innovation Policies: Federation of Russia*, vol. 1: *Evaluation Report*, 32.

149. Sasun Karapetian, "Strukturnaia reforma cherez prizmu potrebitel'skoi korziny," *Delovoi mir*, no. 126 (7 July 1993), 12.

150. See Moisei Gel'man, "Polubeznadzornaia konversiia," *Delovoi mir*, no. 113 (30 May–5 June 1994), 8; Aleksei Shulunov, "K chemu vedet biudzhetnaia strategiia pravitel'stva," *Nezavisimaia gazeta*, no. 106 (8 June 1994), 1–2; and G. Kuznetsova, V. Ermakov, and Y. Volkov, "Oboronka' v proryve?" *Ekonomika i zhizn'*, no. 3 (January 1994), 18.

151. Dmitri Moskvin and Feliks Binshtok, "Gaidar's Secret Plan: Once the Dear Country Will Awaken Poor," *Rabochaya tribuna* (3 February 1993), 1–2. Available from "NEWS" library, "SPD" file, in Mead Data Central, Inc., LEXIS/NEXIS (database online).

152. OECD, *Science, Technology and Innovation Policies: Federation of Russia*, vol. 1: *Evaluation Report*, 54–55. This estimate includes both definitive and temporary emigration.

153. Igor' Krylov, "Rossiiskaia nauka glazami evropeiskikh spetsialistov," *Delovoi mir*, no. 189 (30 September 1993), 4.

154. Ibid.

155. OECD, *Science, Technology and Innovation Policies: Federation of Russia*, vol. 1: *Evaluation Report*, 49–50.

156. Boiko, "Parlamentskie slushaniia vymiraiut kak dinozavry."

157. Sergei Glaz'ev, "Deindustrializatsiia Rossii uzhe stala real'nost'iu," *Nezavisimaia gazeta*, no. 41 (3 March 1994), 4.

158. OECD, *Science, Technology and Innovation Policies: Federation of Russia*, vol. 1: *Evaluation Report*, 11.

159. Glaz'ev, "Uroki liberalizatsii v Rossii."

160. The OECD report *Science, Technology and Innovation Policies* translates this as "Russian Foundation for Fundamental Science" (p. 29).

161. Stanislav Simanovskii, "Utechka umov: fatal'naia neizbezhnost' ili ... ," *Delovoi mir*, no. 151 (18–24 July 1994), 25.

162. Andrei Vaganov, " 'My bezdarno teriaem nauchnye shkoly,'" *Nezavisimaia gazeta*, no. 165 (1 September 1993), 6.

163. OECD, *Science, Technology and Innovation Policies: Federation of Russia*, vol. 1: *Evaluation Report*, 17.

164. Evgenii Semenov, "Nauka vozroditsia vmeste s gosudarstvom," *Delovoi mir*, no. 103 (3 June 1993), 11.

165. Kim Smirnov, "Bez velikoi nauki net velikoi Rossii," *Evrika* (supple-

ment to *Novaia ezhednevnaia gazeta*), no. 9 (15 June 1994), 3.

166. OECD, *Science, Technology and Innovation Policies: Federation of Russia*, vol. 1: *Evaluation Report*, 56.

167. "Novyi biudzhet: ni vashim, ni nashim."

168. Khakamada, "Liberaly ob''ediniaiutsia."

169. Yaremenko, et al., "The Russian Economy: Ways Out of the Crisis," 87.

170. David Lipton and Jeffrey Sachs, "Creating a Market Economy in Eastern Europe: The Case of Poland," *Brookings Papers on Economic Activity*, no. 1 (1990), 78.

171. Ibid., 89.

172. John McMillan and Barry Naughton, "How to Reform a Planned Economy: Lessons from China," *Oxford Review of Economic Policy* 8 (Spring 1992), 131. See also Peter Murrell, "Can Neoclassical Economics Underpin the Reform of Centrally Planned Economies?" *Journal of Economic Perspectives* 5 (Fall 1991), 59–76.

173. McMillan and Naughton, "How to Reform a Planned Economy."

174. Ibid., 132.

175. Jeffrey D. Sachs and Wing Thye Woo, "Structural Factors in the Economic Reforms of China, Eastern Europe and the Former Soviet Union," paper prepared for presentation at the Economic Policy Panel meeting in Brussels, Belgium (22–23 October 1993), 3.

176. Roman Frydman, Andrzej Rapaczynski, and John S. Earle, *The Privatization Process in Central Europe* (New York: Central European University Press, 1993), 151; OECD, *Industry in Poland: Structural Adjustment Issues and Policy Options* (Paris: OECD, 1992), 17; and Anna Sabbat-Swidlicka, "Poland: The End of the Solidarity Era," *RFE/RL Research Report* 3 (7 January 1994), 83.

177. Lipton and Sachs, "Creating a Market Economy in Eastern Europe," 76.

178. Andrew Berg, "Does Macroeconomic Reform Cause Structural Adjustment? Lessons from Poland," *Journal of Comparative Economics* 18 (June 1994), 398; and Andrew Berg and Jeffrey Sachs, "Structural Adjustment and International Trade in Eastern Europe: The Case of Poland," *Economic Policy* 14 (April 1992), 117–73. See also Jeffrey Sachs, "The Economic Transformation of Eastern Europe: The Case of Poland," *Economics of Planning* 25 (1992), 5–19.

179. Berg, "Does Macroeconomic Reform Cause Structural Adjustment?" 396–400.

180. "Poland Survey," *The Economist* 331 (16 April 1994), after p. 60 (insert p. 8).

181. See Keith Crane, "Taking Stock of the 'Big Bang,' " in *Stabilization and Privatization in Poland: an Economic Evaluation of the Shock Therapy Program*, ed. Kazimierz Z. Poznanski (Boston: Kluwer Academic Publishers, 1993), 81–82.

182. Jeffrey Sachs, "Life in the Economic Emergency Room," in *The Political Economy of Policy Reform*, ed. John Williamson (Washington, DC: Institute for International Economics, 1994), 509.

183. Aleksei Pushkov, "Chudesa i paradoksy pol'skikh reform," *Moskovskie novosti*, no. 15 (10–17 April 1994), A13. The study found that another 20 percent opposed the reforms and the majority (60 percent) were either uncertain or "politically passive."

184. Ibid.

185. Aleksandr Kuranov, "K prezidentstvu s konstitutsiei napereves," *Nezavisimaia gazeta*, no. 108 (10 June 1994), 4.

186. Louisa Vinton, "Walesa Threatens to Dissolve Parliament," *RFE/RL Daily Report*, no. 73 (18 April 1994).

187. Kazimierz Z. Poznanski, "Poland's Transition to Capitalism: Shock and Therapy," in Poznanski, ed., *Stabilization and Privatization in Poland*, 16.

188. Jeffrey Sachs, "The Reformers' Tragedy," *New York Times* (23 January 1994), E17.

189. Gary H. Jefferson and Thomas G. Rawski, "Enterprise Reform in Chinese Industry," *Journal of Economic Perspectives* 8 (Spring 1994), 66.

190. Barry Naughton, "What Is Distinctive about China's Economic Transition? State Enterprise Reform and Overall System Transformation," *Journal of Comparative Economics* 18 (June 1994), 475, 470.

191. Thomas S. Kuhn, *The Structure of Scientific Revolutions* (Chicago: University of Chicago Press, 1962), 149.

192. Sachs, "Betrayal," 18.

193. Naughton, "What Is Distinctive about China's Economic Transition?" 472.

194. McMillan and Naughton, "How to Reform a Planned Economy," 131.

195. Åslund, "The Gradual Nature of Economic Change in Russia," 34.

196. Anders Åslund, "Prospects for a Successful Change of Economic System in Russia," working paper no. 60, Stockholm Institute for East European Economics, Stockholm, Sweden (November 1992), 15.

197. Lipton and Sachs, "Prospects for Russia's Economic Reforms," 215.

198. Josef C. Brada, "The Transformation from Communism to Capitalism: How Far? How Fast?" *Post-Soviet Affairs* 9 (1993), 101.

199. Sachs and Woo, "Structural Factors in the Economic Reforms of China, Eastern Europe and the Former Soviet Union," 4, 6.

200. Ibid., 4.

201. Ibid., 11.

202. Ibid., 12–13.

203. Ibid., 18.

204. Naughton, "What Is Distinctive about China's Economic Transition?" 476.

205. Sachs and Woo, "Structural Factors in the Economic Reforms of China, Eastern Europe and the Former Soviet Union," 21.

206. See, for example, Vladislav Borodulin, "Shokhina ne podveli tol'ko agrarii," *Kommersant-daily*, no. 178 (21 September 1994), 5; Irina Denisova, "Vperedi-period povyshennoi nervnosti," *Obshchaia gazeta*, no. 10 (11–17 March 1994), 8; and Aleksei Novikov, "Amerika Rossii podarila parokhod," *Novaia ezhednevnaia gazeta*, no. 8 (15 January 1994), 2.

207. See, for example, Anders Åslund, "A Critique of Soviet Reform Plans," in *The Post-Soviet Economy: Soviet and Western Perspectives* ed., Anders Åslund (New York: St. Martin's Press, 1992), 178.

208. Wing Thye Woo, "The Art of Reforming Centrally Planned Economies: Comparing China, Poland, and Russia," *Journal of Comparative Economics* 18 (June 1994), 279.

209. See, for example, Yusuf, "China's Macroeconomic Performance and Management During Transition," 71.

210. Ibid.

211. The Window of Opportunity proposal.
212. Woo, "The Art of Reforming Centrally Planned Economies," 281.
213. Ibid.

Chapter 5. Coordination Issues in Russia's Privatization Program

1. Andrei Shleifer and Maxim Boycko, "The Politics of Russian Privatization," in *Post-Communist Reform: Pain and Progress*, ed. Olivier Blanchard, et al. (Cambridge: MIT Press, 1993), 80.

2. I. Elistratov, "Prezidentu Rossii dan 'zelenyi svet' na provedenie radikal'nykh reform," *Izvestiia*, no. 262 (2 November 1991), 1.

3. *Current Digest of the Soviet Press*, vol. 44 (12 February 1992), 8; from *Izvestiia* (14 January 1992), 1.

4. Petr Filippov, "Kuda poshel protsess?" *Delovoi mir*, no. 26 (7–13 February 1994), 19.

5. The Federal Property Fund was to be under the authority of the Russian Supreme Soviet.

6. The Federal Property Fund's responsibility for an enterprise's activity was to be in direct proportion to the percentage of a firm's voting shares that had not been distributed, up to 20 percent (see "Polozhenie o Rossiiskom Fonde federal'nogo imushchestva," *Reforma*, no. 52 [December 1993], 1). Elsewhere, we elaborate in more detail about the functions of property management committees, property funds, and privatization commissions. See Lynn D. Nelson and Irina Y. Kuzes, *Property to the People: The Struggle for Radical Economic Reform in Russia* (Armonk, NY: M.E. Sharpe, 1994), 121–25.

7. The legal basis for the Russian privatization program was articulated in the law on privatization of State and Municipal Enterprises that was passed by the RSFSR Supreme Soviet on July 3, 1991. See "O privatizatsii gosudarstvennykh i munitsipal'nykh predpriiatii v RSFSR," *Zakony RSFSR o privatizatsii gosudarstvennykh i munitsipal'nykh predpriiatii, zhil'ia* (Moscow: Sovetskaia Rossiia, 1991), 3–36. The original legislation was amended June 5, 1992. See "'O privatizatsii gosudarstvennykh i munitsipal'nykh predpriiatii' ot 3 iiulia 1991 goda s izmeneniiami i dopolneniiami, priniatymi 5 iiunia 1992 goda," *Delovoi mir*, no. 138 (21 July 1992), 6–7.

8. See Nelson and Kuzes, *Property to the People*, 121–54.

9. Gennadii Ponomarev, "Grimasy zakonodatel'stva, ili moskovskaia privatizatsiia," *Chelovek i zakon*, no. 9 (1993), 25.

10. Anatolii Rubinov, "Prodaetsia ne vse . . . ," *Literaturnaia gazeta*, nos. 18–19 (11 May 1994), 10.

11. Lora Velikanova, "Larisa Piiasheva: 'Vaucher—eto eshche ne sobstvennost',' " *Literaturnaia gazeta*, no. 20 (18 May 1994), 10.

12. Petr Filippov, "Chto meshaet 'otovarit' ' privatizatsionnyi chek," *Ekonomika i zhizn'*, no. 37 (September 1993), 10.

13. "Osnovnye napravleniia ekonomicheskoi politiki Rossiiskoi Federatsii," *Kommersant*, no. 9 (24 February–2 March 1992), 22.

14. "Repurchases," in the Fund's terminology, of a member country's soft currency in exchange for hard currency.

15. "Ekonomicheskaia strategiia pravitel'stva Rossii" (part 3), *Biznes, banki, birzha*, no. 14 (1992), 1.

16. Seven percent were undecided.

17. Forty-four percent were satisfied with the then-current pace, and 8 percent were undecided.

18. Filippov, "Kuda poshel protsess?"

19. See, for example, Shleifer and Boycko, "The Politics of Russian Privatization," 78–79.

20. Igor' Karpenko, "Programma privatizatsii 1993 goda: sub'ekty federatsii trebuiut vnesti v nee ser'eznye izmeneniia," *Izvestiia*, no. 93 (20 May 1993), 4.

21. "O gosudarstvennykh garantiiakh prava grazhdan Rossii na uchastie v privatizatsii," *Ekonomika i zhizn'*, no. 20 (May 1993), 15.

22. See Mikhail Berger, "Chem grozit pokushenie na vaucher," *Izvestiia*, no. 135 (21 July 1993), 2; and Ol'ga Berezhnaia, "Deputaty namereny vernut' gosimushchestvo ministerstvam," *Moskovskie novosti*, no. 30 (25 July 1993), 1.

23. Igor' Karpenko, "Parlament pytaetsia otniat' u naroda pravo vladet' svoei sobstvennost'iu," *Izvestiia*, no. 136 (22 July 1993), 1.

24. Mazaev emphasized these points when we interviewed him during the early summer. These ideas are also prominent in a *Nezavisimaia gazeta* interview with Mazaev that was published in July (Ivan Rodin, "Sobstvennost' vozvrashchena sovetam," *Nezavisimaia gazeta*, no. 136 [22 July 1993], 1).

25. Igor' Karpenko, "Protsess privatizatsii vosstanovlen," *Izvestiia*, no. 140 (28 July 1993), 2.

26. Mikhail Berger, "Raznoglasiia v pravitel'stve po povodu ekonomicheskoi politiki," *Izvestiia*, no. 168 (4 September 1993), 1.

27. Nikolai Podlipskii, "Privatizatsiia v Rossii mozhet poiti vostochnoevropeiskim putem," *Kommersant-daily*, no. 169 (4 September 1993), 3.

28. Irina Matveeva, "Mer osudil vauchernuiu privatizatsiiu," *Kommersant-daily*, no. 171 (8 September 1993), 2.

29. Ivan Zasurskii, "Boris El'tsin gotov pereiti ot privatizatsii po Chubaisu k privatizatsii po Lobovu," *Nezavisimaia gazeta*, no. 170 (8 September 1993), 1.

30. Ibid.

31. Boris Krotkov, "B matche s Lobovym lidiruet Chubais," *Delovoi mir*, no. 174 (14 September 1993), 1.

32. Steve Liesman, "U.S. Officials Urge Progress on Reform," *The Moscow Times*, no. 297 (15 September 1993), 11.

33. Ibid. Emphasis added.

34. Daniel Williams, "Problems in Russia Imperiling Aid Again," *Washington Post* (16 September 1993), A25.

Chapter 6. An Assessment of the Voucher Privatization Program

1. Aleksandr Radygin, "Delo Chubaisa zavershit tol'ko vtorichnyi rynok," *Moskovskie novosti*, no. 22 (29 May–5 June 1994), B1.

2. Leonid Mikhailov, "Ot bednogo sotsializma—k bednomu kapitalizmu," *Nezavisimaia gazeta*, no. 233 (3 December 1992), 2.

3. A Yeltsin decree of June 28, 1994, specified that, in enterprises that had been converted to joint stock companies but had not distributed the agreed-upon number shares to personnel in the enterprise by June 30, the shares could be claimed for vouchers until July 31. (See "Poslednie shagi vauchera," *Delovoi mir*, no. 137 [30 June 1994], 1.) On July 20, Yeltsin further decreed that for three months, beginning September 1, citizens who still had their vouchers could use them to purchase shares of enterprises located *only* in the territory where each voucher had been issued. (See "O dopolnitel'nykh merakh po zashchite interesov grazhdan na etape perekhoda ot chekovoi k denezhnoi privatizatsii," *Ekonomika i zhizn'*, no. 30 [July 1994], 8.)

4. See Mikhail Lantsman, "Prezident zashchitil rynok privatizatsionnykh chekov," *Segodnia*, no. 136 (21 July 1994), 2.

5. See Boris Boiko, "Gosduma podygrala GKI," *Kommersant-daily*, no. 125 (8 July 1994), 2; "Goskomstat RF o khode privatizatsii," *Segodnia*, no. 191 (6 October 1994), 2; Lev Makarevich, "Nereshitel'nost' v reformakh dorogo obkhoditsia ekonomike," *Finansovye izvestiia*, no. 47 (11 October 1994), 2; and Igor' Skliarov, "Malyi biznes: kakova vlast', takova ego podderzhka," *Ekonomika i zhizn'*, no. 41 (October 1994), 1.

6. Boiko, "Gosduma podygrala GKI."

7. It was also consistent with the patterns of share distribution in the enterprises included in our 1993 study. Of the 390 production enterprises in our study that had undertaken privatization by June 1993, 164 had already distributed shares among either enterprise personnel or shareholders outside the enterprise or to a combination of these two categories of owners. We analyzed the percentage of shares in these enterprises that had been turned over to enterprise workers, the percentage distributed through voucher auction, and the percentage retained by the state. (The sale of shares to outsiders for money was also an option, but it was an insignificant factor among the enterprises in our study.) Personnel in these 164 firms owned at least 50 percent of the total number of shares in 95 percent of the enterprises (n = 156). In 85 of those enterprises, personnel owned 100 percent of the shares (54 percent of enterprises where personnel were majority shareholders). Among these enterprises, personnel accounted for an average of 80 percent of the enterprise shares. The state was the majority shareholder in only 4 enterprises (2.4 percent). In only 33 enterprises (20 percent) had *any* shares been distributed through voucher auctions, but in only 5 cases did the percentage of voucher-auctioned shares that were held outside the enterprise match or exceed the number of shares held by workers. Interestingly, the average number of personnel employed at these 5 enterprises was 287, while the average number of workers among worker-controlled enterprises was 1,248. Although the government had decided in 1992 that large production enterprises were to be prime candidates for "people's" privatization, a year later it was clear that this expectation was not being realized.

The property fund that has jurisdiction over the auctioning of an enterprise's shares has the option of deciding that a certain percentage of shares will be sold for money rather than being auctioned for vouchers. These proceeds are typically used to cover the cost of carrying out the voucher auction and to help the property fund meet its operating expenses. Yeltsin's July 6, 1993 decree On Additional

Measures to Secure Rights of Russian Citizens Participating in Privatization emphasized that "not less than 80 percent of the total number of shares to be sold of every enterprise, or of the total value of the enterprise as an object of privatization to be sold through auction or competition, must be purchased with privatization checks [vouchers]." At least 29 percent of the shares of privatizing joint stock companies were to be offered through voucher auctions. (See "O dopolnitel'nykh merakh po zashchite prava grazhdan Rossii na uchastie v privatizatsii," *Ekonomika i zhizn'*, no. 31 [July 1993], 4.)

8. Boris Krotkov, "Anatolii Chubais o perspektivakh privatizatsii—94," *Delovoi mir*, no. 267 (31 December 1993), 1.

9. Eight percent were uncertain.

10. Sergei Mikhailov, "O nekotorykh itogakh privatizatsii v 1993 godu," *Ekonomika i zhizn'*, no. 14 (April 1993), 15.

11. Lev Makarevich, "Vauchery golosuiut za chetvertyi variant privatizatsii," *Finansovye izvestiia*, no. 14 (4–10 February 1993), 3.

12. Andrei Borodenkov, " 'Uralmash' poshel c molotka," *Moskovskie novosti*, no. 30 (25 July 93), 13.

13. Ibid.

14. Ibid.; and "Kakha Bendukidze, predsedatel' pravleniia AO 'Bioprotsess,' " *Delovoi mir*, no. 264 (24 December 1993–2 January 1994), 1.

15. "Kakha Bendukidze, predsedatel' pravleniia AO 'Bioprotsess.' "

16. See Oleg Bogomolov, "Razdaetsia nicheinoe bogatstvo," *Nezavisimaia gazeta*, no. 13 (23 January 1993), 4.

17. See, for example, World Bank, *Russian Economic Reform: Crossing the Threshold of Structural Change* (Washington, DC: International Bank for Reconstruction and Development / World Bank, 1992), 88–89.

18. See "Programma uglubleniia reform," *Izvestiia*, no. 224 (9 October, 1992), 2.

19. Aleksandr Borisov, ". . . plius sploshnaia vaucherizatsiia vsei strany," *Megapolis-Express*, no. 35 (2 September 1992), 3.

20. Vladimir Kucherenko, "Massovaia privatizatsiia: led eshche ne tronulsia, no uzhe tresnul," *Megapolis-Express*, no. 34 (26 August 1992), 3.

21. " 'Obshchestvennoe mnenie' informiruet . . . ," *Delovoi mir*, no. 140 (5 July 1994), 1; and "Privatizatsiia v obshchestvennom mnenii," *Izvestiia*, no. 124 (2 July 1994), 2. See also Andrei Kobich, "Bol'she vsekh vaucherov ukral 'Tekhnicheskii progress,' " *Kommersant-daily*, no. 113 (22 June 1994), 14; Irina Demina, "Chekovye fondy—golovnaia bol' rossiiskikh vlastei," *Moskovskie novosti*, no. 26 (26 June–3 July 1994), B7; and Vsevolod Orlov, "Anatolii Chubais: 'Esli udaetsia podkupit' absoliutno vsekh, znachit, idet protsess, kotoryi vsem nuzhen,' " *Novaia ezhednevnaia gazeta*, no. 54 (25 March 1994), 1.

22. See, for example, Viktor Smirnov and Viktor Ivanov, "Provintsial'nye chekovye fondy ispytyvaiut krizis," *Kommersant-daily*, no. 7 (19 January 1994), 2; and Ol'ga Proskurnina, "Rossiia—eto samaia bol'shaia v mire offshornaia zona," *Novaia ezhednevnaia gazeta*, no. 124 (6 July 1994), 2.

23. "Gosudarstvennaia programma privatizatsii gosudarstvennykh i munitsipal'nykh predpriiatii v Rossiiskoi Federatsii na 1992 god," *Ekonomika i zhizn'*, no. 29 (July 1992), 15.

24. Dmitrii Vasil'ev, "1 oktiabria—nachalo privatizatsii v Rossii. Dlia kogo? Chto nuzhno sdelat' k etomu sroku?" *Izvestiia*, no. 214 (25 September 1992), 2.

25. Dmitrii Vasil'ev, "Privatizatsiia: voprosy i otvety," *Izvestiia*, no. 224 (9 October 1992), 2.

26. In some categories, enterprises needed to apply for permission to privatize.

27. Vladimir Zhuravlev, "Proshchal'noe slovo vauchera," *Delovoi mir*, no. 140 (5 July 1994), 1; and Aleksandr Frenkel', "Promyshlennost' Rossii v mae," *Delovoi mir*, no. 99 (14 May 1994), 4.

28. Enterprises have been reassessed since January 1992, but Yeltsin's July 6, 1993 decree On Additional Measures to Secure Rights of Russian Citizens Participating in Privatization (see n. 7) guaranteed that enterprise reassessment after January 1992 would not affect the prices of enterprise shares in voucher privatization.

29. Vasilii Seliunin, "Tret'ia popytka," *Izvestiia*, no. 211 (22 September 1992), 1, 3.

30. "Gosudarstvennaia programma privatizatsii gosudarstvennykh i munitsipal'nykh predpriiatii v Rossiiskoi Federatsii na 1992 god," 15–18.

31. Anatolii Chubais, "Remarks Delivered by Vice-Premier Anatolii Chubais at the International Institute for Applied Systems Analysis, July 9, 1993" (mimeo).

32. Elena Kotel'nikova, "Viktor Chernomyrdin sdelal stavku na Goskomimushchestvo," *Kommersant-daily*, no. 185 (28 September 1993), 2.

33. House Committee on Small Business, "The Privatization Experience: Strategies and Implications for Small Business Development," 103rd Cong., 2nd sess., 14 April 1994 (testimony by Anders Åslund; mimeo), 1.

34. Ibid., 17.

35. Stanislav Assekritov, "Iur'ev den' privatizatsii," *Delovoi mir*, no. 65 (28 March–3 April 1994), 21. Emphasis in original.

36. Lora Velikanova, "Larisa Piiasheva: 'Vaucher—eto eshche ne sobstvennost',' 170," *Literaturnaia gazeta*, no. 20 (18 May 1994), 10.

37. "Kontseptsiia poslechekovoi privatizatsii," *Ekonomika a zhizn'*, no. 17 (April 1994), 16.

38. See, for example, Elena Kotel'nikova, "Goskomimushchestvo ozhidaet sotszakaz," *Kommersant-daily*, no. 67 (14 April 1994), 3; and Elena Rubleva, "Vozrozhdeniiu komandnoi ekonomiki prepiatstvuet privatizatsiia," *Finansovye izvestiia*, no. 4 (3–9 February 1994), 1–2.

39. Irina Demchenko, "Chubais obygral Chubaisa," *Moskovskie novosti*, no. 28 (10–17 July 1994), 7. See also Roman Artem'ev, "Moment istiny Viktora Chernomyrdina," *Kommersant-daily*, no. 127 (12 July 1994), 8; Boiko, "Gosduma podygrala GKI"; and Aleksandr Bekker, "Duma upuskaet svoi shans," *Segodnia*, no. 132 (15 July 1994), 2.

40. Keith Bush, "Privatization Squabble Intensifies," *RFE/RL Daily Report*, no. 102 (31 May 1994). Available from listserv@ubvm.cc.buffalo.educ, Internet.

41. This schedule was not followed, as it turned out.

42. Boiko, "Gosduma podygrala GKI."

43. Chubais, "Remarks Delivered by Vice-Premier Anatoly Chubais," 6. Emphasis added.

44. "Gotov proekt ukaza o privatizatsii," *Segodnia*, no. 134 (19 July 1994), 1. See also Elena Kolokol'tseva, "Privatizatsiia kak povod dlia prezidentskogo ukaza," *Segodnia*, no. 134 (19 July 1994), 2.

45. See Elena Afanas'eva, "Gonka za Chubaisom: Duma propuskaet khod," *Novaia ezhednevnaia gazeta*, no. 136 (22 July 1994), 2; and Aleksandr Bekker,

"Programma Chubaisa poshla po rukam," *Segodnia*, no. 131 (14 July 1994), 1.

46. See, for example, Thomas de Waal, "New Firing Further Isolates Premier," *Moscow Times* (international weekly edition) 1 (13 November 1994), 36.

47. Igor' Karpenko, "12 000 predpriiatii v Rossii stali chastnymi. Ezhednevno na auktsiony postupaet 1 000 000 chekov," *Izvestiia*, no. 109 (10 June 1994), 1.

48. Anatoly Chubais and Maria Vishnevskaya, "Main Issues of Privatisation in Russia," working paper no. 48, Stockholm Institute of East European Economics, Stockholm, Sweden (June 1992), 11.

49. John Lloyd, "Moscow Woos Foreign Investors," *Financial Times* (28 June 1994), 4. Available from "NEWS" library, "FINTME" file, in Mead Data Central, Inc., LEXIS/NEXIS (database online). See also Vadim Bardin, "Investory reshili vziat' svoiu sud'bu v Rossii v sobstvennye ruki," *Kommersant-daily*, no. 117 (28 June 1994), 3.

50. Aleksandr Radygin, "Delo Chubaisa zavershit tol'ko vtorichnyi rynok," *Moskovskie novosti*, no. 22 (29 May–5 June 1994), B1.

51. Evgenii Yasin, "D'iavol—v detaliakh," *Literaturnaia gazeta*, no. 22 (1 June 1994), 1.

52. Boris Fedorov, "Konets vaucheram. Nachalo privatizatsii," *Izvestiia*, no. 123 (1 July 1994), 2.

53. Egor Gaidar, "Fashizm i biurokratiia," *Segodnia*, no. 110 (15 June 1994), 10.

54. Merilee S. Grindle and John W. Thomas, *Public Choices and Policy Change: The Political Economy of Reform in Developing Countries* (Baltimore: Johns Hopkins University Press, 1991), 121.

55. Stephan Haggard and Robert R. Kaufman, "Introduction," *The Politics of Economic Adjustment: International Constraints, Distributive Conflicts, and the State*, ed. Haggard and Kaufman (Princeton: Princeton University Press, 1992), 19–20. See also John Waterbury, "The Heart of the Matter? Public Enterprise and the Adjustment Process," in *The Politics of Economic Adjustment*, ed. Haggard and Kaufman, 190–92.

56. Waterbury, "The Heart of the Matter?" 190–92.

Chapter 7. In the Balance

1. Boris Yeltsin, *The Struggle for Russia*, trans. Catherine A. Fitzpatrick (New York: Times Books, 1994), 288.

2. Viktor Chernomyrdin, "No Exits on the Road to Market: Despite Setbacks, Russia Will Not Abandon Its Commitment to Economic Reform," *Financial Times* (16 May 1994), 15. Available from "NEWS" library, "FINTME" file, in Mead Data Central, Inc., LEXIS/NEXIS (database online).

3. Václav Klaus, "My voshli v period reabilitatsii," *Delovoi mir*, no. 83 (18–24 April 1994), 1.

4. Ibid.

5. See Lynn D. Nelson and Irina Y. Kuzes, *Property to the People: The Struggle for Radical Economic Reform in Russia* (Armonk, NY: M.E. Sharpe, 1994).

6. Liudmila Khakhulina, "Tri goda ekonomicheskikh reform: izmeneniia v otsenkakh i mneniiakh naseleniia," *Ekonomicheskie i sotsial'nye peremeny*, no. 1 (1993), 20. The study included 3,002 employed respondents.

7. *Megapolis-Express*, no. 7 (13 February 1992), 15. The survey included 1,960 respondents.

8. Tat'iana Boikova, "Draka poka ne zakazana," *Megapolis-Express*, no. 7 (13 February 1992), 21.

9. Aleksandr Sidiachko, "Pravitel'stvo y nas khoroshee," *Megapolis-Express*, no. 25 (17 June 1992), 19.

10. Vladimir Boikov, "Vlast' priznaiut, no uzhe ne doveriaiut," *Megapolis-Express*, no. 30 (29 July 1992), 7. The survey included 1,200 respondents in thirty regions of Russia and was conducted by the Institute for Complex Social Studies from June 1 until June 5.

11. See, for example, Boris Grushin, "Kogda Rossiiskie lidery mnenii liubiat svoego prezidenta?" *Nezavisimaia gazeta*, no. 8 (16 January 1993), 1–2.

12. Vladimir Shokarev, "Reiting Federal'nogo Sobraniia prevysil reiting pravitel'stva," *Segodnia*, no. 4 (11 January 1994), 2.

13. VTsIOM carried out a survey among 1,603 respondents in several cities on September 24–28, 1993—just after Yeltsin shut down the Russian parliament. Forty-four percent said then that they trusted Yeltsin and the executive branch more than Rutskoi, Khasbulatov, and the legislative branch ("Kolichestvo Rossiian, ravnodushnykh k rospusku parlamenta, vozroslo v tri raza," *Segodnia*, no. 60 [2 October 1993], 3). Even at that time, 32 percent supported neither side in the standoff, but Yeltsin's standing declined decisively after the events of October 3 and 4.

A nationwide survey by the Institute of Sociology in November found that only 19 percent of respondents had supported his decision to storm the Russian White House, and 58 percent judged that action to have been "a national shame in which both branches of power are to be blamed" (Viktor Kuvaldin, "Poslednee preduprezhdenie," *Nezavisimaia gazeta*, no. 251 [30 December 1993], 2; see Vladimir Boikov, "Rossiiane—o kliuchevykh problemakh zhizni obshchestva, o nadezhdakh na 1994-i god," *Delovoi mir*, no. 2 [10–16 January 1994], 14).

14. Kuvaldin, "Poslednee preduprezhdenie"; and Boikov, "Rossiiane—o kliuchevykh problemakh."

15. What is striking about public opinion on this issue in our research cities is the robustness of opposition to the country's dissolution—opposition that is pronounced across segments of the population that diverge both ideologically and sociodemographically. Even the youngest adults, age 18 to 25, opposed the breakup of the USSR by a wide margin. Fifty-nine percent called it "the wrong decision," compared to only 26 percent who believed that it was the correct thing to do. (Fifteen percent were uncertain.) Most respondents with graduate degrees opposed the action (62 percent opposed and one-third favored it), and in Moscow, which is generally regarded as the most reform-oriented Russian city, 68 percent disagreed with the decision to fragment the Union.

16. Data are from primary sources in each city.

17. Igor' Ognev, "Novyi Smolenskii gubernator nameren sokratit' chislo chinovnikov," *Izvestiia*, no. 87 (12 May 1993), 2.

18. *Biulleten' Tsentral'noi izbiratel'noi komissii Rossiiskoi Federatsii*, no. 1 (1994), 37, 63.

19. Tat'iana Boikova, "Gaidar prizval pravitel'stvo k otkazu ot kompromissov," *Megapolis-Express*, no. 50 (22 December 1993), 16. See also Egor Gaidar, "Novyi kurs," *Izvestiia*, no. 26 (10 February 1994), 1, 4.

20. *Biulleten' Tsentral'noi izbiratel'noi komissii Rossiiskoi Federatsii*, no. 1 (1994), 35, 57. Russia's Choice was just slightly behind the Agrarian party, with 11.9 percent of the vote.

21. See, for example, Lidiia Malash, "Mafiia v Ekaterinburge," *Megapolis-Express*, no. 32 (18 August 1993), 12; and Otdel prestupnosti, "Predprinimatelei obvinili v grabezhe i vymogatel'stve," *Kommersant-daily*, no. 61 (6 April 1994), 14.

22. *Biulleten' Tsentral'noi izbiratel'noi komissii Rossiiskoi Federatsii*, no. 1 (1994), 37, 62.

23. The Movement for Democratic Reforms had 9 percent support, and the Communist Party of the Russian Federation, 8 percent.

24. Serge Schmemann, "As Russian Voting Nears, Pessimism Seems to Rise," *New York Times* (international edition), (11 December 1993), 5.

25. Leonid Sedov, "Politicheskii analiz. Nakanune i posle vyborov," *Ekonomicheskie i sotsial'nye peremeny*, no. 2 (March–April 1994), 29.

26. Vladimir Shokarev and Aleksei Levinson, "Elektorat Zhirinovskogo," *Ekonomicheskie i sotsial'nye peremeny*, no. 2 (March–April 1994), 31.

27. Ibid., 32. See also Yurii Levada, "Ne brosat'sia ot illiuzii k panike," *Izvestiia*, no. 240 (15 December 1993), 4. Several analysts have suggested that Yeltsin's advisers were instrumental in creating the "Zhirinovsky phenomenon," and that their strategy of playing with this kind of fire backfired.

28. The study included 2,018 respondents. See Leonid Sedov, "Mezhdu putchem i vyborami," *Ekonomicheskie i sotsial'nye peremeny*, no. 1 (January 1994), 14.

29. There is evidence that the turnout in April was also lower than reported, although the magnitude of discrepancy between the actual and the reported percentages is not known. See A. Sobianin, E. Gel'man, and O. Kaiunov, "Politicheskii klimat v Rossii v 1991–1993 gg," *Mirovaia ekonomika i mezhdunarodnye otnosheniia*, no. 9 (1993), 20–32.

30. Vera Tolz, "Falsification of Results of December Vote Announced," *RFE/RL Daily Report*, no. 87 (6 May 1994). Available from listserv@ubvm.cc.buffalo.edu, Internet. The review board was set up by Yeltsin. See also Valerii Vyzhutovich, "Tsentrizbirkom prevrashchaetsia v politicheskoe vedomstvo," *Izvestiia*, no. 83 (4 May 1994), 4; Anatolii Kostiukov, "Provokatsia po neostorozhnosti," *Obshchaia gazeta*, no. 19 (13–19 May 1994), 8; and Otdel politiki, "Kommentarii," *Kommersant-daily*, no. 95 (26 May 1994), 3.

31. Sedov, "Politicheskii analiz."

32. Fifty percent disagreed, and 30 percent were uncertain.

33. Sedov, "Mezhdu putchem i vyborami," 15.

34. Jeffrey Sachs, "Kak pokonchit' s infliatsiei," *Izvestiia*, no. 202 (22 October 1993), 4.

35. Maxim Boycko, Andrei Shleifer, and Robert W. Vishny, "Privatizing Russia," *Brookings Papers on Economic Activity*, no. 2 (1993), 139, 178.

36. See also Liudmila Khakhulina and Boris Golovachev, "Chetyre goda ekonomicheskikh reform: izmeneniia v otsenkakh i mneniiakh naseleniia," *Ekonomicheskie i sotsial'nye peremeny*, no. 3 (May–June 1994), 14.

37. Consistent with these results, a study by the Institute of Complex Social Studies in November 1993 found that only 19 percent of respondents were even "partly satisfied" with the way privatization had been carried out. See Boikov,

"Rossiiane—o kliuchevykh problemakh," 14. And a national survey of 1,965 workers in November and December by the Russian Center for Public Opinion Research (VTsIOM) found that only 20 percent expected the privatization of the enterprises where they worked to benefit them personally, and only a quarter thought that privatization would be beneficial for their enterprises overall. Most directors did not expect privatization to help them individually (37 percent expected a positive result) or their enterprises (40 percent). See Liudmila Khakhulina, "Vospriiatie naseleniem sotsial'no-ekonomicheskoi situatsii v strane," *Ekonomicheskie i sotsial'nye peremeny*, no. 2 (March–April 1994), 37. These judgments do not merely reflect weariness with the hardships of economic reform; they show dissatisfaction with its course.

38. VTsIOM's periodic survey of confidence in leaders found in January 1994 that economist Grigorii Yavlinskii received a marginally higher confidence rating than Yeltsin (Igor' Nikitin, "Yavlinskomu po-prezhnemu doveriaet bol'shinstvo," *Moskovskie novosti*, no. 7 [13–20 February 1994], A6), and *Nezavisimaia gazeta*'s monthly ranking of "the most influential" Russian politicians, based on votes of a standing panel of fifty leading figures in several fields, placed Yeltsin behind Prime Minister Viktor Chernomyrdin in February. This ranking held until May, when Yeltsin returned to first place after the signing of the Civic Accord agreement. By September, Yeltsin still led Chernomyrdin, but not by much (8.73 to 8.54). (See Aleksandr Kinsburskii, "100 vedushchikh politikov Rossii v fevrale," *Nezavisimaia gazeta*, no. 41 [3 March 1994], 1; Vladimir Shokarev, "Naselenie vse men'she doveriaet politicheskim lideram," *Segodnia*, no 69 [14 April 1994], 3; Aleksandr Kinsburskii, "100 vedushchikh politikov Rossii v mae," *Nezavisimaia gazeta*, no. 101 [31 May 1994], 5; and Aleksandr Kinsburskii, "100 vedushchikh politikov Rossii v sentiabre," *Nezavisimaia gazeta*, no. 189 [4 October 1994], 1.)

39. Yavlinskii took second place, with 8 percent of the "vote." Several other candidates garnered significant support, but nearly half of the respondents were unwilling to choose any candidate. When respondents were asked, "Should Yeltsin run for president in the next elections?" 53 percent answered that he should not. Only 29 percent believed that he should be a candidate (Yurii Levada, "Kto na starte?" *Moskovskie novosti*, no. 31 [24–31 July 1994], 6).

40. Julia Wishnevsky, "Democratic Opposition in Russia: Is There an Alternative to the Russian President Boris Yeltsin?" paper presented at the annual meeting of the American Association for the Advancement of Slavic Studies, Philadelphia, PA (17–20 November 1994). Also see " 'Obshchestvennoe mnenie' informiruet . . . ," *Delovoi mir*, no. 106 (24 May 1994), 1; and Vladimir Shokarev, "Esli vibirat' prezidenta zavtra, to im stanet El'tsin," *Segodnia*, no. 97 (24 May 1994), 3.

41. In August 1994, only 1 percent of the six thousand respondents in a study of sixty cities/regions throughout Russia stated that their attitude about Yeltsin's activity was "very positive." Another 8 percent reported their attitude as "positive," and an additional 10 percent answered "somewhat positive." In contrast, 13 percent were "very negative," 26 percent were "negative," and 18 percent were "somewhat negative" (Nugzar Betaneli, "Vse ne tak stabil'no, kak dumaiut vlasti," *Obshaia gazeta*, no. 40 [7–13 October 1994], 8). Sixteen percent were "indifferent," and 8 percent responded "difficult to say."

42. Louisa Vinton, "CIS Statistics Show Severe GDP Decline," *RFE/RL Daily Report*, no. 146 (3 August 1994).

43. "Emerging-Market Indicators," *The Economist* 332 (23 July 1994), 104.

44. Ibid.

45. Tat′iana Zaslavskaia, "Etot vrednyi 'chelovecheskii faktor,' " *Moskovskie novosti*, no. 1 (2–9 January 1993), A8. Emphasis added.

46. Yeltsin, *The Struggle for Russia*, 158–59.

47. Ibid., 165.

48. For a recent illustration, see Gaidar, "Novyi kurs."

49. *The Struggle for Russia*, written and produced by Sherry Jones, directed by Foster Wiley, 89 min. (Boston: WGBH Educational Foundation, 1994), videocassette. See also, for example, Anders Åslund, "A Critique of Soviet Reform Plans," in *The Post-Soviet Economy: Soviet and Western Perspectives* ed., Anders Åslund (New York: St. Martin's Press, 1992); and Jeffrey D. Sachs, "Russia's Struggle with Stabilization: Conceptual Issues and Evidence," paper presented at the Annual Bank Conference on Development Economics. World Bank, Washington, DC, 28–29 April 1994.

50. Andrei Kozyrev, "The Lagging Partnership," *Foreign Affairs* 73 (May/June 1994), 60, 62. An aspect of this reformulation of national priorities that was prominent in Kozyrev's article was Russia's increasingly urgent moves to repair neglected economic and political ties with other former Union republics of its "near abroad."

51. Ibid., 61.

52. David Lipton, "Reform Endangered," *Foreign Policy*, no. 90 (Spring 1993), 57.

53. Richard Layard, foreword to Jeffrey Sachs, *Poland's Jump to the Market Economy* (Cambridge: MIT Press, 1993), ix.

54. Grigorii Yavlinskii, "Inaia reforma," *Nezavisimaia gazeta*, no. 26 (10 February 1994), 4.

55. See Julia Wishnevsky, "Problems of Russian Regional Leadership," *RFE/RL Research Report* 3 (13 May 1994), 6–13.

56. *The Current Digest of the Soviet Press* 43 (20 March 1991), 1; from *Komsomolskaia pravda* (22 February 1991), 1.

57. See Nelson and Kuzes, *Property to the People*.

58. Philip Hanson, "The Center versus the Periphery in Russian Economic Policy," *RFE/RL Research Report* 3 (29 April 1994), 28.

59. Quoted in Julia Wishnevsky, "Democratic Opposition in Russia."

60. Ibid.

61. Steven Erlanger, "Russian Premier Assails Reformers in Cabinet for 'Poorly Thought-Out Experiments,' " *New York Times* (international edition), (19 December 1993), 18.

62. Ibid.

63. Ibid.

64. Elaine Sciolino, "U.S. Is Abandoning 'Shock Therapy' for the Russians," *New York Times* (21 December 1993), A1.

65. Thomas L. Friedman, "Good Works and Prayers: Can Russia Help Itself? American Visitors Ask," *New York Times*, (16 January 1994), 1.

66. Ann Devroy, "Yeltsin Says Reforms to Proceed," *Washington Post*, no. 40 (14 January 1994), 1. Clinton was reportedly warned on January 13, however, of Gaidar's imminent resignation (see Daniel Williams, "U.S. Reassessing Russian Stance on Reform," *Washington Post*, no. 47 [21 January 1994], A29).

67. John M. Goshko, "Talbott Offers Reassurance on Democracy in Russia," *Washington Post*, no. 51 (25 January 1994), A15.

68. Andrei Sveshnikov, "Inostrannye sovetniki pravitel'stva khlopnuli dver'iu," *Finansovye izvestiia*, no. 3 (27 January–2 February 1994), 1; and Anna Politkovskaia, "Professor Anders Åslund nazyvaet imena lobbistov," *Megapolis-Express*, no. 5 (2 February 1994), 7.

69. Fred Hiatt, "Yeltsin Names Cabinet Short on Reformers: Strongest Free-Market Supporter Quits," *Washington Post*, no. 47 (21 January 1994), 1, 31; and Steven Erlanger, "Leading Reformer Resigns as Yeltsin Picks New Cabinet," *New York Times*, (21 January 1994), A1.

70. House Foreign Affairs Committee, "U.S. Policy Toward the Former Soviet Union," 103rd Cong., 2nd sess., 25 January 1994. Available from Federal Information Systems Corporation, Federal News Service. In Mead Data Central, Inc., LEXIS/NEXIS (database online).

71. Aleksei Portanskii, "MVF schitaet, chto tol'ko zhestkaia finansovaia politika uluchshit zhizn' rossiian," *Izvestiia*, no. 32 (18 February 1994), 3.

72. Natal'ia Kalashnikova, "Gerashchenko pokazal zapadnym ministram pradedushku Gaidara," *Kommersant-daily*, no. 36 (1 March 1994), 4. The G-7 includes the United States, Japan, Germany, France, Great Britain, Canada, and Italy.

73. See Liudmila Telen', "Parizhskii klub daet 'dobro,' " *Moskovskie novosti*, no. 13 (27 March–3 April 1994), 12A; Yurii Ershov, " 'Bol'shaia semerka' obeshchaet, no trebuet," *Delovoi mir*, no. 43 (1 March 1994), 1; and " 'Semerka' obeshchaet Rossii pomoshch', no nastaivaet na energichnykh reformakh," *Finansovye izvestiia*, no. 9 (3–9 March 1994), 1.

74. "Group of 7 Optimistic on Low-Inflation Growth This Year," *New York Times*, (25 April 1994), D2. Russia's plan was to reduce the budget deficit to no more than 7.5 percent and to reduce inflation to a monthly rate of 7 percent by the end of the year.

75. Chernomyrdin, "No Exits on the Road to Market."

76. Ibid.

77. Leonid Lopatnikov, "Situatsiia—94," *Delovoi mir*, no. 83 (18–24 April 1994), 11.

78. Anders Åslund, "Russia's Success Story," *Foreign Affairs* 73 (September/October 1994), 63.

79. Lopatnikov, "Situatsiia—94."

80. Oleg Moroz, "Aleksandr Livshits: 'Nizkaia infliatsiia tozhe opasna,' " *Literaturnaia gazeta*, no. 28 (13 July 1994), 10; Grigorii Tsitriniak, " 'Mne detiam svoim v glaza smotret'. . . ," *Literaturnaia gazeta* (5 October 1994), 11; and Gleb Cherkasov, "Sergei Glaz'ev nazval privatizatsiiu 'raznovidnost'iu kaznokradstva,' " *Segodnia*, no. 185 (25 September 1994), 2.

81. Sergei Glaz'ev, "Nesostoiavsheesia vystuplenie na rasshirennom Sovmine," *Nezavisimaia gazeta*, no. 154 (16 August 1994), 4.

82. Tat'iana Romanenkova and Aleksei Vorob'ev, "Prem'er byl izlishne optimistichen," *Nezavisimaia gazeta*, no. 133 (16 July 1994), 1–2; and Irina Demina, "Doklad odobrili?" *Moskovskie novosti*, no. 29 (17–24 July 1994), 6.

83. Romanenkova and Vorob'ev, "Prem'er byl izlishne optimistichen," 1; and Demina, "Doklad odobrili?"

84. Romanenkova and Vorob'ev, "Prem'er byl izlishne optimistichen," 2.

85. Glaz'ev, "Nesostoiavsheesia vystuplenie na rasshirennom Sovmine," 1, 4; Vladimir Gurevich, "Legkie resheniia—samye opasnye" (interview with Evgenii Yasin), *Moskovskie novosti*, no. 28 (10–17 July 1994), 27; and Moroz, "Aleksandr Livshits: 'Nizkaia infliatsiia tozhe opasna.' "

86. See Tsitriniak, " 'Mne detiam svoim v glaza smotret'' . . . "; and Grigorii Yavlinskii, Mikhail Zadornov, Sergei Ivanenko and Aleskei Mikhailov, "Biudzhet–94," *Nezavisimaia gazeta*, no. 70 (14 April 1994), 4.

87. John Lloyd, "IMF/World Bank in Madrid: Russia Fails to Achieve Its Mission; Moscow Faces the Unknown as Opposition Grows to Its Loan Requirements," *Financial Times* (4 October 1994), 5. Available from "NEWS" library, "FINTME" file, in Mead Data Central, Inc., LEXIS/NEXIS (database online).

88. Paul Lewis, "Rich and Poor Nations Split on Aid Plan," *New York Times* (3 October 1994), D1. Available from "NEWS" library, "NYT" file, in Mead Data Central, Inc., LEXIS/NEXIS (database online).

89. Politica Weekly Press Summary: Electronic Mail Version," (22–28 October 1994), 1–2; from *Segodnia* (28 October 1994). Available from (dwestman@ccs.carleton.ca, Internet.

90. Wishnevsky, "Democratic Opposition in Russia."

91. Quoted in Yergin and Gustafson, "Let's Get Down to Business, Comrade," *Financial Times*, (9 July 1994), 1. Available from "NEWS" library, "FINTME" file in Mead Data Central, Inc., LEXIS/NEXIS (database online). Yasin was appointed to the post of economics minister later, on November 8.

Appendix A

1. The population estimates for these cities are for 1990 and are taken from *Demograficheskii ezhegodnik SSSR: 1990* (Moscow: Gosudarstvennyi komitet SSSR po statistike, 1990).

2. We were unable to secure the lists we needed from the property management committee in Ekaterinburg to be certain of the total number of privatized and privatizing production enterprises there.

3. There are several different definitions of the terms "privatized" and "privatizing". We considered enterprises to have begun privatization if they had been transformed into joint stock companies.

4. Among these 171 respondents, we reinterviewed 38 in 1993. A large proportion of the privatization decision makers at work in 1993 had not held their positions a year earlier.

5. Lynn D. Nelson and Irina Y. Kuzes, *Property to the People: The Struggle for Radical Economic Reform in Russia* (Armonk, NY: M.E. Sharpe, 1994), 202.

6. Nelson and Kuzes, *Property to the People*, 202–3; and Lynn D. Nelson and Neil W. Henry, "Simultaneous Control and Crosstabular Presentation with Polytomous Variables: The Case of Religion Predictors," *Journal for the Scientific Study of Religion* 29 (1990), 255–63.

Index

About the Authors

Dr. Lynn D. Nelson teaches sociology at Virginia Commonwealth University, where his research specialty is Russian politics and society. He held a Fulbright lectureship in the Soviet Union in 1990, and for several years he has studied reform in Russia, concentrating his research in Moscow, Ekaterinburg, Voronezh, and Smolensk. In 1987 he was a visiting fellow at Harvard University's Russian Research Center.

Irina Y. Kuzes was trained at the Institute of Urban Planning in Moscow, where she conducted research on problems of urban land use. This background gave her a unique orientation to privatization issues, which have been the focus of her work since 1991. She is a correspondent for the journal *Znanie–sila* and has also published articles in *Literaturnaia gazeta* and *Moscow News*.

Nelson and Kuzes are also the authors of *Property to the People: The Struggle for Radical Economic Reform in Russia* (1994).